Heritage
and
Urban Renewal

INTACH

HERITAGE AND URBAN RENEWAL

ISBN: 978-81-7305-469-3

Published by:
INTACH
The Indian National Trust for Art and Cultural Heritage
71, Lodhi Estate, New Delhi - 110003

First Hardback Edition: **2014**

Distributed by:
Aryan Books International
Pooja Apartments, 4B, Ansari Road, New Delhi-110 002 (India)
Tel.: 23287589, 23255799; Fax: 91-11-23270385
E-mail: aryanbooks@gmail.com
www.aryanbooks.com

Editor: Rajeshwari Tandon
Design and Production: Silverline Communications

CONTENTS

Acknowledgement

Shri S. K. Misra - Founder Member and Chairman, INTACH

It is the ground reality today that there is immense pressure on urban land. Urban density is in fact increasing beyond manageable limits. And compounded by a burgeoning population. The greatest challenge confronting conservationists is how to protect urban heritage, the historic landmarks of the city and the graceful ambience, its green cover and water bodies, all of which are being overrun by unbridled water resources in the urban landscape have been bull dozed out of existence. The older generation often cannot recognize places that fill their childhood memories. The future generation is likely to grow up in a cemented environment.

Awareness for the need to conserve urban heritage has however grown dramatically. Only the solutions will continue to remain elusive unless a holistic approach to urban conservation and development is adopted. They are to be found only in town planning – restructuring city, and incorporating these elements in the redevelopment of the city to meet contemporary needs. In effect it means preservation of not only iconic landmarks of history but also the social, cultural and economic fabric that must define contemporary urban renewal.

I believe this seminar on Heritage and Urban Development is one of the most important international meetings to be held by INTACH. Till date urban renewal has not figured in our national policies. The subject is of imminent significance to all countries across the world. We have in our midst international experts who have been addressing these issues in their own countries, and have been specially invited to share their experience with our conservationists, town planners and government officials at this Seminar.

I have great expectations that the deliberations over the next two days will enable us to arrive at some Indian solutions to urban renewal that is much needed in all our cities, big and small. The recommendations of this Seminar will be brought to the attention of the Government authorities concerned, and hopefully will make an impact on our future policies.

Heritage Conservation and the Process versus Passion Conundrum

A. G. Krishna Menon - Convenor for INTACH Delhi Chapter

After over two decades of passionate advocacy by several interest groups around the country, it has now become politically correct to espouse the cause of heritage conservation in the management of cities in India. Unfortunately, it has not changed ground realities, because city planners and administrators continue to pursue business-as-usual. Success of advocacy may in fact have provoked a reaction: devious strategies are developed to circumvent heritage issues when they appear on the radar of the zealous proponents of urban projects (often the government).

These issues were foregrounded with the initiation of the Jawaharlal Nehru National Urban Renewal Mission (JNNURM) in 2005. The government had woken to the anomaly of the country's growing economic stature and it's failing cities to formulate a bold, innovative and time-bound Mission to renew 63 major cities. Besides infusing massive amounts of funds to improve urban infrastructure, it also mandated structural reforms in urban governance. The Mission produced 'tool-kits' to guide civic authorities to access project funding and undertake the mandated reforms.

Soon after the Mission was launched, INTACH highlighted the potential damage that mega-infrastructure projects funded by JNNURM could inflict on historic precincts. Their concerns also drew attention to the consequences of removing social safety nets like rent control to make urban renewal projects economically viable. In sum, INTACH argued that the Mission's success could lead to the loss of valuable tangible and intangible cultural resources that existed in historic cities.

INTACH partnered the government to discuss these issues at a national conclave in Mysore in May 2006. As a follow-up INTACH was asked to produce a 'heritage tool-kit' to guide the process of formulating heritage-sensitive City Development Plans, on the basis of which project funding would be released.

The heritage tool-kit has been in circulation for almost four years but it appears that the results have not been satisfactory. The diagnosis points to the failure of the *process* followed by municipal authorities who clearly did not adhere to the directives given in the tool-kits. This disconnect between intentions and reality has led the government to give a contract to UNESCO to formulate yet another tool-kit to guide Detailed Project Reports and 'mainstream' heritage conservation in the formulation of JNNURM projects. As a regular interlocutor on heritage conservation issues, I am beginning to wonder whether the new tool-kit will yield the desired results and whether we should not consider other strategies to achieve conservation objectives.

The success of any *process* will depend on the mindset of urban planners and city managers who are expected to follow them. It determines their willingness to accommodate the imperatives of heritage conservation in Mission funded urban renewal projects. Given the socio-economic history of our country, their mindset could be described as being deeply imbued with *development* ideology: they are not sympathetic to heritage conservation, which is considered the antithesis of development. Even well-defined and structured processes recommended by tool-kits will not mitigate the influence of this classic ideological dichotomy. To map its consequences consider three foundational questions which define conservation practice.

First, *why* conserve? In the conservation classroom this question is compellingly explained but in public discourse or planning practice it continues to be contested. While everyone will agree that iconic historic monuments like the Qutab Minar and Humayun's Tomb in Delhi should be preserved, not many understand the rationale to conserve dilapidated historic precincts like Shahjahanabad and Nizamuddin *basti*. This is where JNNURM projects could inflict the greatest damage. Indian planners reflexively prefer to adopt the modernist approach to urban renewal, best exemplified by Chinese city planners who have ruthlessly destroyed their historic cities in order to modernize them. For example, in the once historic city of Suzhou, only isolated historic gardens, a few pagodas and a small stretch of the traditional network of canals have been preserved as tourist attraction in a sea of modern development. The mindset of the Indian urban planner and city manager operates on a similar lines, thus subverting any process based on classroom answers to the question, 'why conserve'.

Next the question, *what* to conserve? Can historic cities like Shahjahanabad and Nizamuddin become the objects of conservation in the present system of managing cities? It cannot happen, I have argued elsewhere, because of a deep flaw in the *imagination* of the Indian urban planner: they cannot imagine, let alone consider protecting, an 'Indian' city with its organic network of roads and mixed land uses. Consequently, they are unable to value the hybrid urbanism which exists in historic cities – what Frederic Jameson calls 'messy urbanism'- as a heritage resource, thus making it vulnerable to modernist urban renewal. But we know that it contains the tangible and intangible heritage of Indian society, its so called 'living heritage'. They prefer to modernize historic cities in the image of models like Suzhou, thus blunting any tool-kit designed to compensate for such limitations in their imagination.

Finally, *how* to conserve? This brings us back to the issue of 'processes'. Urban planning in India is rooted in colonial imperatives. Heritage conservation too, has acquired its attributes: the process is Eurocentric and top down. New processes, like the JNNURM tool-kits, tend to reinforce these attributes even as they aspire to accomplish the opposite. Consequently, the reform objectives of JNNURM will not succeed in the routine. The tool-kits will remain ineffective, and it's well-meaning 'processes', subverted. The *process* is not the key to the problem of heritage conservation.

Recently I gained an insight into the systemic failures in implementing heritage conservation projects while writing the history of INTACH on the occasion of its 25th anniversary. Talking to people associated with its beginning, I heard a litany of complaints bemoaning the loss of 'passion' in dealing with heritage projects today. Of course, INTACH as an institution needed to professionalize its activities over the years, but it struck me that it did not have to discard its 'passion'. I realized that the conundrum between passion and process is endemic to the conservation movement in India: it was not a divisive problem but its defining characteristic. We need to pursue both passion and process to succeed in our conservation endeavours.

Contemporary advocates for conservation need to take their cues from earlier activists who succeeded by pressing their claims *against* the system. Today, to make conservation work, conservation professionals also need to work *against* the prevalent processes of urban renewal. In many of my own conservation projects I have found that it can pay surprising dividends.

Session 1

Presentation by Indian Experts

The Framework for the Planning and Management of Urban Renewal Schemes in India

Prof. Edgar F. Ribeiro - Consulting Urban & Regional Planner

A. The Emerging Context for Urban Renewal in India

1. In the West, the term 'Urban Renewal' primarily implies actions by city governments to infuse activities in their rundown core areas often abandoned in favour of planned peri-urban neighbourhoods. Even so, infusing housing and activities in tandem in such blighted areas has never been easy, especially if existing footprints have to be respected by a new gentry and culture. In the cities of the East, on the other hand, 'Renewal' largely implies an organized decongesting of activities and people from the core so that a compatible mix of uses is retained and supported by improved services and facilities. This task, notably in India is a lot more difficult as it also lacks the use of war damaged neighbourhoods as in many European cities for programmed renewal actions.

2. Generally city governments of India are short of resources for urban renewal and need support of state and federal governments for such critical interventions. More importantly and in sharp contrast to the West, the larger Indian cities are gaining population at the expense of rural India and smaller towns. In the process invariably the core areas or

the inner city with their heterogeneous mix of activities are favoured locations of new entrants as they offer more opportunities for survival through marginal or sporadic employment.

3. Thus, urban renewal in India, though part of urban development plans for several decades, has rarely taken off as it involves projects or schemes with a fair amount of rehabilitation or resettlement incorporated as part of implementable renewal. Typical inner city renewal projects like Town Planning Schemes (TPS) under state planning instruments have long approval and developmental gestations and have been successful only in parts. Likewise, the erstwhile Environmental Improvement of Urban Slums Scheme (EIUS) and which graduated from Central to State Plan funds support has helped in upgrading small pockets of identified slums but without inbuilt maintenance mechanisms. By and large, inner city interventions continue as being 'firefighting' in approach and action and in crisis situations. A common problem oft quoted is the lack of access to land which largely is riddled with mutated private ownerships and built space, worsened by rent control that *interalia* thwarts most forms of repair and maintenance.

4. In this scenario, for decades, peri-urban growth in India has been given greater weightage than urban renewal by urban planners, developers and managers. However, access to land for urban expansion is becoming more expensive and difficult to access, largely due to changes in the Land Acquisition Act leading to negotiated prices and which are unaffordable even for Government for large and long-term projects. Therefore the inner cities are being revisited for higher density mixed compatible uses growth.

5. Lately, this strategy coupled with channelised and programmed peri-urban expansion received a boost through the large plan-funds programme regulated by the Central Government called the Jawaharlal Nehru National Urban Renewal Mission (JNNURM). Through this mission a large sum of central funds, matched by States and City Governments

has been made available to the larger urban centres of India for

a) infrastructure upgrading,
b) housing for all income groups, and
c) environmental and heritage conservation.

This is through 20 year perspective Development Plans and inbuilt 5-year development programme platforms for projects or schemes. More importantly the initiative and responsibility is to be by the Municipalities and Panchayats and not by the States of the Union. Thus, urban renewal has been intrinsically equated to down-top Municipal actions through Municipal Corporations with Mayors and made up of Wards with elected Councillors, accountable to an electorate through participatory development. This form of development is embedded in the neighbourhoods that make up the electoral Wards and which constitute the Municipalities and Panchayats of the Revenue Districts of the States of India, without jurisdictional overlaps.

B. Urban Renewal and Urban Expansion

1. In 2001, less than 300 million persons (about 3 in 10 of the total) were under Municipal governance in India (in about 5000 urban local bodies comprising of Municipal Corporations, Municipal Councils and Town Panchayats). By 2051, it is expected that over 800 million persons (about half of the total population of the nation) would be under Municipal governance in around 7000 ULBs. This population would be living in neighbourhoods of higher densities. The rest would be regulated by around one hundred thousand Panchayats, in a scenario of an urban-rural continuum emerging in settlements primarily through a national network of inter-settlement road and rail connectors that are gradually defining regional swathes of primary sector lands; within states and their Districts.

2. In this fast changing pattern, most Municipal Corporations and several Municipal Councils have spread out into census defined Urban Agglomerations (UA's) of contiguous Municipalities and Panchayats.

The fact however is that in most cases the core or the inner city is embedded in the primary municipal area - invariably a Municipal Corporation. Thus, though most metropolitan UAs comprising of contiguous Municipalities and Panchayats are being gelled as Metropolitan Planning Committee Areas (MPC's) under the 74th Constitutional Amendment Act, it is only the main Municipal Corporation area of such UAs that get recognized for the urban renewal funds under the central JNNURM Scheme.

3. In this coalescing of urban renewal funds within LSG boundaries, most major UAs have emerged through three distinct outward urban spreads in either radial or linear form or in combination of both depending on land formations and their imposed transport corridors. Thus we invariably have:

a) The Inner City comprising of high density contiguous lands prior to Development Plan (Master Plan) interventions;
b) The Extended City, the result of planned interventions through regulated densities; and
c) The Peri-Urban City as the reception centres of new growth or of activities to be displaced from the inner city to the urban periphery.

4. Very generally, the Municipal Corporations deal with the inner city and the extended city whereas (very generally) the other contiguous Municipalities and Panchayats deal with the peri-urban city. By and large, development actions for the constituencies in Corporation areas have been in house with support from Improvement Trusts or equivalents and laterly (after 1950) from State regulated Development Authorities through Development Plans or Master Plans. However, the Constitution of India, requires that planned development actions be primarily by the Municipalities and Panchayats on basis of the umbrella MPC plan. Thus Municipal Corporations are required to develop, regulate and maintain the inner city through urban renewal policies, plans and programmes as also the extended city – in part or full, primarily through de-densification and as now comprising the intermediate city. All State (and even Central) parastatal and sectoral

projects have thus to work within the basic LSG priorities.

5. Urban renewal actions are now gelling in metropolitian and large cities of India for their inner cities through projects aimed at infrastructure and area level upgrading or restructuring or redevelopment with weightage given to existing settlement footprints and compatible mixed uses. The missing link has been participation or stakeholder planned development through the statutory electoral Wards that make up the Municipalities and Panchayats of India each with an accountable elected councilor or Panch. Thus sustainable development through Local Area Plans (LAP's) for Wards of the inner city of the Municipal Coporation and large Municipal Councils is a crucial platform for urban renewal through projects, schemes or layouts.

C. Key Elements of Urban Renewal in Large Municipalities.

1. In this emerging era of an urban – rural continuum and changing technologies, several inner city activities function better in the metropolitan fringe. The most critical of these is the distributive trade and which from a 19th century rail based activity has today transited to a road-cum rail based one at the urban periphery and where inter and intra settlement distribution and road-rail (and even air) transfers are facilitated at interchange nodes. Containerization has facilitated the process and most materials and even perishables (their storage and distribution) are vacating critical inner city spaces and where more compatible alternative uses in lieu are possible. Railway national track conversion to uniform broad gauge is also facilitating the process and where stabling, commodity transfers; rake formation and maintenance terminals are facilitated at the periphery near inter-settlement truck terminals, wholesale markets, storage and even interstate bus terminals and depots.

2. Restructuring of the inner city is thus incrementally taking place, punctuating the fact that urban renewal has longer gestation periods for implementation than peri-urban development. Primarily, urban renewal

has to rely on a variety of intra-settlement (primarily inner city) modes of transportation minus the animal drawn vehicles, with priority given to walk trips and non-motorized point-to point transport. Motorized two and three wheelers can thereby be better regulated and the motor car captured at convenient inner city points with idle parking facilities. Now below ground city rail nodes can also offer such transfer facilities. Bus routes can also be restructured so as to facilitate the inner city mixed use ambience and assisted by non-polluting means of transportation of people and goods. In fact, heterogeneous traffic of a wide compatible variety for moving goods and people suited to inner city mixed uses and footprints of meandering streets and alleys add to the ambience of the Municipal regulated inner city.

3. With the above two major actions catered to, urban renewal in the context of JNNURM requires weightage to -

a) heritage
b) inclusive housing
c) infrastructure upgrading and
d) participatory governance through Local Area Plans (LAPs) for all electoral wards of the Municipality that incorporates five-year programme plans. The reference point has perforce to shift to the Ward Committee composed of the Ward electoral constituency under the elected and therefore accountable Councilor and who collectively with other Councilors comprises the umbrella Municipality.

a. **Heritage** - This constitutes the most neglected area of urban renewal given the fact that the bulk of the built heritage and their defined urban spaces are in the inner city. Holistically, heritage comprises of sites, remains, ruins, buildings, and landscapes of archaeological, historical, architectural, cultural and ecological significance and which require to be statutorily mapped on the Muncipal Development Plans and their ward level LAP's . The principal heritage actors are the Archaeological Survey of India (for protecting listed national monuments and areas), the State Departments of Archaeology (for protecting listed regional monuments and areas), the National and State Departments of Environment for protecting / conserving ecologically sensitive areas and landscapes, and National and State Departments of Tourism and their parastatals for promoting heritage tourism. None of these have their project areas or buildings mapped on Development Plans which now offer participatory statutory support for preservation / conservation as part of a development process. Also, laws from the State list dealing with Urban and Regional Planning and also with Municipal and Panchayat Development, encourage the listing of areas and buildings for conservation in addition to the protection support to selected archaeological areas and buildings with their 'no or limited development' boundaries (generally 300 meters). If statutory mapping action is now taken on this aspect as in Mumbai and other main cities of Maharashtra and also as in Hyderabad, urban renewal would receive a big boost. At present a lot of inner city heritage is being systematically destroyed for commercial gain in the absence of this coordinated mapped statutory support, especially in terms of heritage spaces round monuments. Listing on LAPs of Wards is of particular importance as collective support of the ward electorate is possible in favour of heritage. It has to be underlined that conservation permits new uses for old buildings and that FAR / FSI if adversely affected can be utilized elsewhere through Transfer of Development Rights (TDR's).

b. **Inclusive Housing** - The inner cities of India as in several Asian and African nations have the largest range of income percentiles than any other built-up zones of settlements. They are therefore required to cater to decreasing percentages of pavement/door step dwellers and to acceptable percentages of in-situ sanitized and upgraded dwelling units and also to increasing percentages of in-situ reconstruction including some new units on cleared inner city lands. A constant upgrading or strengthening of existing building stock is also necessary. Primarily it has to be borne in mind that several household units or small compatible manufacture units and services function well in the inner city through informal work and living within the same household or near by it. Thus new units that segregate work from housing, are not always successful and are often unsuited to mixed–use living. Quite clearly, incremental upgrading upto four storeyed walkups and workable in terms of access to fire services, ambulances and emergencies in general are priorities for development control norms carefully crafted separately for each urban renewal LAPs. In fact, several LAPs would be for heritage Wards and all Wards - heritage or otherwise, have to give priority to point-to-point transport like cycle-rickshaws and hand carts that connect inner city work-cum living spaces to the larger zonal, city and regional fabric. The maximum damage to inner built form is through space purchased for work by persons living outside the inner city. Such groups are largely car owning and find traditionally built spaces unsuited to business efficiency. Thus, unauthorized use in the inner city stands out, most of it in R.C.C and precipitated by Development Control rules based on general set-backs and road widening.

c. **Infrastructure Upgrading** - Apart from transportation restructuring and implementable traffic and idle parking regulations, the inner city needs upgrading of water and sewerage systems, of drainage channels and of power supply and its usage. Modernizing toilets and kitchens is inevitable, but the individual house systems get intricate as joint family households change over to several single households and more space gets added as households expand in situ. Replacing worn out inner-city service networks, appropriately separating water from sewerage lines, providing power through underground cables and widening and covering drainage channels, all cost money and time. It requires beneficiary support for metered and full recovery of user charges and enhanced levels of house tax and scavenging and other levels of cess. The inner city also needs pay and use ablution facilites near railway and bus nodes, health centres and tourism areas. Solid waste management has also to be properly regulated especially for wet wastes as disproportionately generated due to traditional and upgraded eateries, guest houses and organized street vending that add flavour to the inner city.

d. **Participatory governance** - As already indicated, this is best organized through Electoral Wards each under an accountable Councilor. All Central and State Government sectoral departments and parastatals, all Local Government support bodies, and other Trusts and Institutions are to be subject to the LAP with its 20 year ward level perspective plan. 5 yearly programme plan and annual budgets – all mapped and debated at time of change by the Ward Constituency. Mapped transparency is to be the key for urban renewal with several wards working in unison yet through competition for not only the above mentioned issues but also for several other aspects like hoarding control, street furniture and lighting, noise and other pollution control. They are also to act as neighbourhood watchdogs for unauthorized use, bearing in mind that each electoral ward is an all-inclusive economic group of several neighbourhoods or area sabhas.

4. Conclusion

Inner city land is a scarce commodity with each parcel capable of multiple uses. As ownerships are intricate, urban renewal needs a mapped platform for incremental development and with conservation / preservation as intrinsic components. Access to small portions of land has to be through TDRs (as in Mumbai) that primarily enables conservation of heritage buildings and sites and encourages in-situ upgradation of below poverty line (BPL) sites with some guarded reconstruction. Also, incremental upgrading through Municipal Town Planning Schemes (TPS) as in Ahmedabad helps through collective upgradation by a few contiguous plot owners through an organized layout with some lung spaces. Government owned land and of land added to government stock through the Urban Land Ceiling Act, evacuee properties etc, can be used for infusing inner city social facilities in terms of education, health welfare and protection. Some FAR / FSI incentives can also be given to enable road widening and the like. There are no other reliable sources of access to land in the inner city, particularly as the Land Acquisition Act has now become expensive and increasingly subject to negotiated prices. In the process urban renewal in the Indian context has perforce to be incremental through detailed Development Plans and projects / schemes with beneficiary participation.

Session 2

Presentations by Foreign Experts

Managing Change in Historic Urban Environments: Australia

Dr. Anita Smith - Charles La Trobe Research Fellow, La Trobe University; Member, Australian Delegation to the UNESCO World Heritage Committee; ICOMOS[1]

Introduction

Australia, like most places across the globe is experiencing a rapidly increasing urban population associated with increased housing numbers and density. And this requires additional retail, commercial, transport and other infrastructure to retain the cities as 'liveable'.

This is impacting on our historic urban environments. Some of these impacts are positive – there has been major revitalisation of the 19th century inner urban areas since the late 1970s – but most of the impacts are negative, putting the values, fabric and landscape of our historic areas under threat and, I would argue, reducing the long term sustainability of our cities.

Change in historic urban environments is inevitable and is to be embraced – turning our cities into urban museums, frozen in some artificial construct of their past is neither an option nor appropriate. The

[1] *I am most grateful to the Australia-India Council (www.dfat.gov.au/aic) for providing me with a grant to attend the INTACH Urban Renewal Seminar.*

key to the long term 'liveability' of our cities is to manage change through processes that provide us with such conservation solutions that are sustainable, that respect the values of historic heritage and support the kinds of societies that we wish to pass on to our future generations.

Over the past years our understanding of cultural heritage and our policies and practice for conserving historic environments have become increasingly sophisticated and are embedded in our legislation and urban planning processes. However, alongside this, pressures from development have also greatly increased, especially in the past decade. In Australia we are now losing the ground we have worked so hard to gain. Heritage values are increasingly being marginalised in favour of development.

This offers an opportunity for critical reflection on our practice and in particular the methods and processes by which we articulate and communicate the values of historic urban environments and translate these values into sound management planning. It provides an opportunity to re-look at conservation philosophy and in particular how we assess heritage values and what we understand by managing of those values.

It seems to me that in Australia our success in having heritage place management recognised in policy at all levels of government – national, state and local - has made us somewhat complacent. Underpinning this complacency has been the assumption of a shared, common understanding of heritage values and their worth rather than constant and rigorous evaluation of our practice in light of changing community understandings of and attitudes to heritage values.

Background: Heritage Protection in Australia

Since the 1970s, Australia has taken a leading role in the development of conservation theory and practice at an international level. For a country that has, on a global scale, very recent urban fabric this may seem odd but it was precisely because our claims to have 'historic heritage' were not recognised at an international level until very recently, along with the rapidity at which it was disappearing in the late 20th century that architects and historians in the 1970s felt compelled to argue for the recognition of our late 18th and 19th century places and in doing so brought heritage conservation issues into the public domain and eventually into planning legislation.

Best known of the outcomes of this first generation of Australian heritage practitioners is the 'Australia ICOMOS Charter for the Conservation of Places of Cultural Significance', better known as the 'Burra Charter'[2], Burra being the historic mining town where Australia ICOMOS took the decision to develop a set of guidelines to manage changes to historic environments which led in 1979 to the writing of the Charter. The success of the 'Burra Charter' in providing a framework for managing the values of heritage places is evident in its having now been translated into French, Spanish and Indonesian. It also provided the framework for the 'Principles for the Conservation of Heritage Sites in China' and has been adopted as a set of principles and guidelines by all government heritage agencies in Australia. It is available both as a text document and in an illustrated version.

Essentially the 'Burra Charter' is a process that begins with assessment of the heritage values that a place may have – aesthetic, historic, scientific, architectural, social, spiritual, etcetera; the identification of threats to those values; and all individuals, groups, communities, organisations, companies that can be considered stakeholders in the site and need to be consulted in the development of a management plan for the site. Following this, the aims for the site or 'conservation

---

[2] *Australia ICOMOS 1999. Charter for the Conservation of Places of Cultural Significance www.icomos.org/australia*

policy' are clarified through consultations with the stakeholders and a decision making process established to follow through on this policy and protect or manage the heritage values of the site into the future. It is called—a management plan. The management is governed by the values of the site and their expression in the fabric and/or use of the site.

Since the late 1970s the 'Burra Charter' has remained our major professional guiding document and recognised as best practice by Government Heritage agencies and professional organisations. However during the past 30 years there have been substantial changes at the local and international level, in the way the heritage values are perceived and in our processes for conserving those values. To accommodate these innovations the 'Burra Charter' has been revised several times, most recently in 1999, to accommodate new and changing approaches especially to recognise cultural landscapes as a specific type of site and community social values and intangible spiritual values.

In Australia heritage conservation takes place through national, state and local government agencies, each with a distinct heritage legislation and mandate. Indigenous, Aboriginal heritage places are protected under specific state legislations, distinct from that protecting historic heritage.

Australia's national heritage legislation[3] protects places considered to be of national heritage significance and included in our National Heritage List and places on Commonwealth land. These include natural, indigenous and non-indigenous historic heritage places. Places on the National Heritage List include our World Heritage sites, seventeen in all, of which two are historic heritage places. Places on the National Heritage List that are not on Commonwealth land are protected under this national legislation however their day to day management is the responsibility of the relevant State Government.

---

[3] *Environment Australia (http://www.environment.gov.au/heritage/about/index.html)*

Australia has 6 states and 2 territories. Each of the states has its own heritage legislation. Under this legislation, places assessed to have heritage values of significance at a state level are protected through their inclusion in a Historic or an Aboriginal or a natural Heritage Register depending on the kinds of values the place may signify. For example in the State of Victoria, there is the Victorian Heritage Register for historic places of significance to the state and the Victorian Aboriginal Heritage Register of places of significance to Aboriginal people[4].

Each State Government also has its own local planning legislation. It is through this legislation that the majority of historic heritage places are protected. Places considered to have local heritage values are recognised and protected in the local government planning schemes. In Victoria, each local government area or council has its own planning scheme to guide urban and regional planning. The planning scheme consists of a number of zonings and overlays and their provisions that the local government authority must consider when assessing a planning application. These are mandated in the legislation and include, at least in Victoria, a Heritage Overlay[5].

Properties are included on the Heritage Overlay when a panel of experts – a planning panel – accepts the recommendation of a local area heritage study, commissioned specifically to identify places for inclusion in the Heritage Overlay. The places may be individual structures, complexes or precincts identified under this quite rigorous assessment process to have local heritage significance that is, whether they have historic, aesthetic, scientific or social value for the local community. Through the Heritage Overlay, a local government planner assessing a

---

4 *Victorian Heritage Register http://www.heritage.vic.gov.au/Home.aspx ; Victorian Aboriginal Heritage Register http://www.aboriginalaffairs.vic.gov.au*

5 *Victoria's Heritage Overlay is described at: http://www.heritage.vic.gov.au//Local-government/Heritage-overlays.aspx*

planning application for their area will be alerted about the need to consider the heritage values of the place in their assessment of the planning permit application, and where relevant to their statutory or legislative requirements to protect this heritage if it is also included on the State Heritage Register or National Heritage List.

These three tiers of protection for heritage – national, state and local government – create a complex but by all appearances quite stringent system for the protection of historic heritage places. Does this work in practice?

Places included on the National Heritage List are allotted the greatest level of protection, being considered to reach a threshold of importance to the nation as a whole. These places are least likely to be subject to impacts from development. To a lesser extent this is also true of places included on the State Heritage Registers although development applications for these places have been increasing, especially for those in the city centres and inner historic urban areas. Places of recognised heritage values that are most likely to be impacted by development are those included in the Heritage Overlay, being considered to be of significance only to the local community.

Protecting Heritage Values: Melbourne's Central Business District

My own city, Melbourne, has the most extensive collection of 19th and early 20th century buildings and the most extensive controls for protection of historic urban fabric of any Australian city. The city is located on Port Phillip Bay and today consists of the Central Business District and large port area which is ringed by industrial areas and the 19th and early 20th century inner suburbs. Beyond this are the extensive post-war suburbs that reflect the massive post-war migration to Australia that created our multicultural society. Beyond this are the outer suburbs that have continued the urban sprawl since the 1980s, making Melbourne one of the largest cities in the world on spatial extent, but with a current – albeit rapidly growing - population of around 4 million. The suburban pattern of Melbourne and the other major Australian cities was until very recently, individual — ¼ acre blocks and freestanding houses. This is rapidly changing. Over the last decade, planning authorities have recognised that the ever increasing suburban footprint is unsustainable and there is a need to increase residential stock in the city and in inner 19th century suburbs through construction of new apartment blocks, conversion of existing buildings to residences and infill of open spaces including dual occupancy of residential blocks. Along with developments in infrastructure, especially for motor vehicle transport, it is this need for city and inner urban housing and associated amenities, placing pressure on the historic urban environment of the city. This can be a plus point in revitalising historic buildings, especially warehouses and industrial buildings no longer used for their original function, but this has also resulted in some very poor planning decisions.

The plan of central Melbourne's Central Business District is a rectangular grid laid out by the colonial surveyor Hoddle in 1837 on the northern edge of the Yarra River. By the end of the 19th century Melbourne contained many fine, very grand buildings, a consequence of the great wealth brought to the then British colony by the gold rushes in Victoria from the 1850s to the 1880s. Some of this 19th century fabric remains including Parliament House, the Treasury Building and Flinders Street Station, while much has disappeared – sometimes being replaced by excellent examples of more recent architecture especially high rises such as the ICI building, Melbourne's first glass curtain building, while others remain in a modified form. This has created the familiar architectural patchwork of today's modern cities and the interesting, colourful variety of the city streets continues to evolve within the framework of the planning scheme.

When an application for development of a place included on the Heritage Overlay is received by the planning department in the City of Melbourne, their assessment of the application and the granting or otherwise of a planning permit will weigh heritage values against the developer's arguments in favour of the proposal. This will include economic, environmental and social arguments for the development and the measures for mitigation of impact on heritage values through the development process.

The arguments in favour of development are increasingly couched in terms of 'sustainability'. Decisions made by planners in regard to a development application for a site with recognised heritage values can be contested through a legal process – by those in favour or those opposed to the development. This means that although we recognise that a place has heritage values, the nature and extent of change that may be allowed to take place at the site before the heritage values are diminished or lost may be contested. This has left the door open for some very poor decisions to be made, including the removal of some important heritage icons or their values being substantially compromised or lost through retention of only the facade, an approach that was common in the 1980s but has thankfully gone out of favour.

We have learnt from our mistakes and modified our approaches to conservation. Rather than to tear down the structures, or simply leave a facade, in general the planning and heritage agencies will aim to retain the fabric of the place, in many cases seeking to incorporate the proposed new use into the existing structure and in doing so, creating a new set of values for the place.

Until recently this approach has appeared to serve us well, and many of the diverse heritage assets of the city have been retained. There were compromises to enable the city to grow and change but overall the outcomes have been very carefully negotiated in a thorough assessment process and dialogue between the heritage agencies, the planners and the developers.

Towards a More Robust Approach to Protecting Heritage Values

More recently, despite our very comprehensive heritage and planning legislation and a strong history of heritage conservation, the conservation or management of heritage values in Australia's historic urban areas appears to be at an impasse. Heritage values are increasingly being marginalised in the planning process. Although the general public are aware of and appreciate heritage, the conservation of heritage values appears to be increasingly seen as expendable by the general public and government when weighed against the need for housing, infrastructure, roads and other transport systems that is being generated by our rapidly increasing urban populations. This year, this has been compounded by the fast tracking of development projects to provide employment opportunities to offset job losses occurring as a consequence of the global financial crisis. These projects will not be required to go through the usual planning approvals process where the heritage values may be fully considered. Many are located in the historic urban areas of the inner suburbs. Of these, the high-density-high-rise housing projects potentially pose the greatest threat as they push the boundaries of current height controls, altering streetscapes and site lines and setting a precedent for future increases in density, bulk and height of buildings.

There are many reasons why the conservation of historic heritage appears to be losing ground, not the least of which is the pressure on governments from developers who see the retention of historic urban fabric as limiting their opportunities and their financial returns. In particular, both in Australia and elsewhere there has been an increasing desire on the part of developers and architects to construct signature architectural monuments, inevitably skyscrapers, in a form so innovative and distinctive that will be globally recognisable and an icon for the city. This can be a great thing, producing some truly marvellous buildings that in future may become heritage in their own right.

But the questions surrounding the potential impact to heritage values of the existing, surrounding environment through the construction of these icons– a source of intense discussion at the previous four World Heritage Committee meetings - point to the larger underlying general issue that we, at least in Australia, are facing. In short, the arguments posed by architects and developers in favour of the destruction, removal or alteration of the fabric of our heritage places and urban environments are on the whole far more sophisticated than those put forward by heritage managers in favour of retention of the fabric of a place or modification of the proposed structure to retain the values of the surrounding historic environment. Not only are they more sophisticated but they are increasingly, and correctly, couched within the framework of social, cultural and environmental 'values' while all too often those in favour of conservation continue to argue in terms of conservation of existing 'fabric'. Simply retaining the fabric of a place does not necessarily retain its heritage values and developers, or at least their advisers, have recognised this and use it very successfully in their arguments in favour of change. Most places have multiple heritage values and not all are expressed in fabric. Historic, social and spiritual values may be about the use of the place, its associations with past or recent events and community attachments to place.

The continuing emphasis on fabric in the conservation of a place is limiting both our ability to protect what is meaningful and important about a place and to engage in arguments in relation to developments that will generate successful outcomes for managing change in our historic urban areas so as to retain heritage values. This however is not simply a matter of heritage practitioners becoming more skilful in articulating the values of places and how change will impact those values – adversely or positively. The inadequacies or narrowness of the ways in which we have articulated the heritage values of urban environment have in turn become enshrined in the legislation and policy that is aimed at protection of these places.

In this regard there are several key limitations in the current legislation. Firstly, 'threat' continues to be primarily understood in terms of impacts to fabric rather than to heritage values which may lie in past, current use or associations with place may equally be impacted by proposed changes to the place. Secondly, the legal framework for our planning and heritage legislation operates primarily at the level of cadastral units - individual buildings or complexes - with the result that cultural or urban landscapes, streetscapes, views and sight lines are poorly recognised in the legislation and very difficult to protect. Thirdly, our processes for protection continue to be largely reactive. Many places on our State Heritage Registers and Heritage Overlays were included twenty or more years ago and at that time their values were assessed primarily in terms of architectural uniqueness or representivity. Since that time the statement of values for these places has not been reviewed in light of the advances we have made in understanding the complexity of heritage values and how these are expressed. This means that from a statutory perspective we are limited in arguing the impacts that a development proposal may have.

Although in Australia we have been lucky enough to have comprehensive heritage legislation, this needs to be more responsive to changing attitudes to heritage, to multiple heritage values and to the ways in which communities express their attachments both to individual buildings and to the landscapes in which they exist. We recognise that places need to be able to change to accommodate different uses, to be economically sustainable. We cannot afford, nor do we want to turn places of heritage value into unusable museums. We want them to continue to live but to achieve this and to maintain their heritage values we need to do much more thinking about how the heritage values are expressed not only in the fabric of the place but within the physical, social and spiritual life of our historic urban areas. Importantly we need to better understand the role of setting and view field in heritage management and to articulate robust arguments around heritage values in response to the assessment of development proposals.

The Plan for an Integral Revitalization of the Historical City Centre of Vitoria-Gasteiz

Mr. Francisco Azconegui - Expert in Heritage Restoration and Urban Renewal; Director of The Centre for Artisan Trades in Vitoria-Basque Country, Spain

1. Introduction

Vitoria-Gasteiz is the capital of the Basque Country, which is an autonomous community or region in the North of Spain. The city of Vitoria-Gasteiz offers its 230,000 inhabitants a great quality of life, it is an example of sustainable development and its per capita income is above the Spanish average.

1.1 Origin of the City and its Historical Centre

- First settlements on the Hill of Gasteiz in the 8th and 9th centuries.
- Fortification in the second half of the 11th century and creation of the three streets: Santa Maria, Escuelas (Schools) and Fray Zacarias.
- Official founding of the city in 1181, by King Sancho VI the Wise of Navarre.
- 12th and 13th centuries. Urban growth towards the West with three new streets: Correria (referring to the leatherworkers), Zapateria (shoemakers) and Herreria (blacksmiths). Urban growth towards the East with another three new streets: Cuchilleria (blade makers), Pintoreria (painters) and Nueva Dentro.

1.2 Implementation of a great project by King Alfonso VIII: building the Santa Maria Cathedral, this has partly inspired author Ken Follet in his book "World without End".

1.3 Socioeconomic growth of the City in the 15th and 16th centuries. Great economic activity due to Vitoria being an important crossroads. Remarkable monuments were built (palaces, towers, churches), making it a veritable Heritage City.

1.4 Vitoria is limited to the historical quarter until the end of the 18th century, when a great project by the architect Olaguibel allows the city to grow through what has been named as the Ensanche (widening).

1.5 Great value of the Heritage of the Historical Centre: architectural, urban and monumental treasures.

2. Evolution of the Medieval Centre

The Historical Centre (Casco Historico) has a population of around 8,000. The growth of the city – since the second half of the 20th century (in 1950 Vitoria had only 52, 000 inhabitants) – and the gradual decrease in residents and activity, have caused problems which are recurring issues also in other European Historical Centres:

- general decay of buildings and homes
- ageing population
- abandonment
- basic infrastructures badly conserved
- insufficient urban equipment

These problems mean that the Historical Centre is the most degraded area of the city from a physical, social and economic point of view.

Historically, and up until now, this area is:

- prone to marginalization
- where people and groups are at risk of social exclusion ternd to settle
- losing its ancient trade activities
- economically excluded
- looking deteriorated, conflictive and marginalized
- Under the threat of becoming a ghetto within a city with an otherwise high quality of life.

3. Plan for an Integral Revitalization of the Historical Centre

3.1 Since the legal management tool was created (a municipal company, called Agencia Municipal de Renovacion Urbana y Vivienda S.A – Municipal Agency for Urban Renovation and Housing, PLC), the most outstanding of the interventions that have been carried out in the Medieval Centre have centred around the restoration of buildings and homes, and the creation of basic infrastructures; these have been called "first generation policies"

3.2 The Plan for an Integral Revitalization of the Historical Centre requires facing the challenge of putting this area back at the heart of the city's activity, by implementing "second generation policies" which:

- Provide solutions towards improving the quality of life of the residents in this area, putting the levels of housing on a par with those of the rest of the city.
- Establish the Historical Centre as a socio-economic and cultural axis, to serve and be enjoyed by the citizens of the whole city.
- Facilitate people coming together and living together, encouraging the growth of social networks.
- Bring value to the Historical Centre as the number one patrimonial

resource of Vitoria-Gasteiz and the Basque Country, in order to increase the city's appeal (also to tourists) and competitiveness.

3.3 Basis of the Plan:

The Plan for an Integral Revitalization of the Historical Centre is based on the following potentials and tools for action:

3.3.1 The firm determination of the Local Governing Council, who have committed 10.6 million Euros annually in real investments; the efforts made to obtain a wide degree of consensus between the different local Political groups, at the Level of Province, of the Autonomous Community and of the National Government.

3.3.2 The commitment of the European Union, by guaranteeing a funding of 7.5 million Euros between 2008 and 2014.

3.4 Actions being Carried Out:

They correspond to the following lines of intervention:

3.4.1 Urban and housing interventions: redesigning various streets, building homes, eliminating aerial cabling and obsolete systems; development of a Plan for improving access to the Historical Centre and eliminatingarchitectural barriers in Public buildings.

3.4.2 Plan for economic reactivation: relocating economic activities (trade, entertainment, services) to formerly empty buildings; installing a centre for business and advanced digital services, and re-training the hospitality sector.

3.4.3 Plan for social improvement and community involvement: creating a venue for sociocultural and sporting activities, called "El Campillo'; creating a special centre to address the interest and needs of the neighbor, in this way bringing our Agency into the heart of the Historical Centre.

3.4.4 Heritage and sociocultural activities: restoring outstanding monuments (Escoriaza Esquivel and others), and dedicating them to social uses; creating a Center for Heritage Studies; drawing up a Master Plan for the 11th century Medieval Wall, with the aim of creating a unique urban landscape and public walkway of great social and tourist appeal.

3.5 The Centre for Artisan Trades of the Historical City:

This is a fundamental element in the strategy of the Plan for an Integral Revitalization of the Historical Centre, and is framed within the development of essential Municipal priorities:

- Implementing programmes and actions that promote and improve employment possibilities, as a reaction to the rapid increase in unemployment caused by the present crisis.
- Carrying out interventions in the Historical City with the aim of promoting and revitalizing its development, bringing back the Artisan trades that used to liven up its main streets.

The Centre for Artisan Trades is strategic due to its nature – aimed not only at conventional training in certain trades, but also generating entrepreneurial professionals — and strategic as well due to it's effects, since it will be a driving force in dynamizing the local economic activity and will become a tool towards social integration in the Historical Centre.

Courses include Architectural Painting, Carpentry, Fine Woodwork, Design and Creation of Furniture, as well as all subjects related to Metalwork. This Centre has been operational since June 2009 with remarkable success.

22@Barcelona Project: Tradition & Innovation

Ms. Aurea Gallen - Director of the Department of Urban Planning Studies City Council of Barcelona, Spain

City Council of Barcelona

Barcelona is a city without any possibility of expansion due to its strictly defined geographic limits: the Serra of Collserola mountain, the Besos and Llobregat rivers and the Mediterranean Sea. As a consequence its renovation has to be based on internal transformations. Over the last 25 years the urban development of Barcelona has been the result of a very intense work on the existing fabrics, which has adopted several modalities along the process.

City Council of Barcelona

From the urban policy carried out in the 80s which focused on high quality public space actions as a way of regenerating the city, to the strategy of recycling industrial urban fabrics which has been carried out since the beginning of the present decade.

The recycling of urban fabrics involves the gradual renovation of areas that are no longer able to accommodate the activities they used to. The transformation process is structured on the basis of existing fabrics and buildings.

The plan called 22@Barcelona, approved in 2001, opened the door to this new line of action in Barcelona's urban development. The Plan, which is currently in process, structures the transformation of the old industrial sector of the Poblenou which for a century and a half contained the greatest concentration of factories in Catalonia. The Plan was a strategic challenge to maintain the productive capacity of the city and encourage the introduction of economic activities compatible with residential development and the efficient use of space. It aims to steer a progressive transformation of more than 200 ha of the existing city. This process is to be developed over the course of many years, supported by Barcelona's network of streets, the supporting infrastructure and services that run through these streets.

So the 22@Barcelona Plan responds to a two-fold objective: urban refurbishment and economic revitalization.

As An Urban Refurbishment Project

It completes the process of regeneration of the Poblenou, a very central District with a strong industrial tradition that goes back to the 19th century. For many years this sector had been excluded from the dynamics of the city due to its industrial character and its bad accessibility conditions. Over the last 30 years the District was progressively being run down due to the decrease in the industrial activity. The works in infrastructures carried out in the city for the Olympic Games in 1992, like the building of the ring roads, the elimination of railway lines which were an obstacle to further

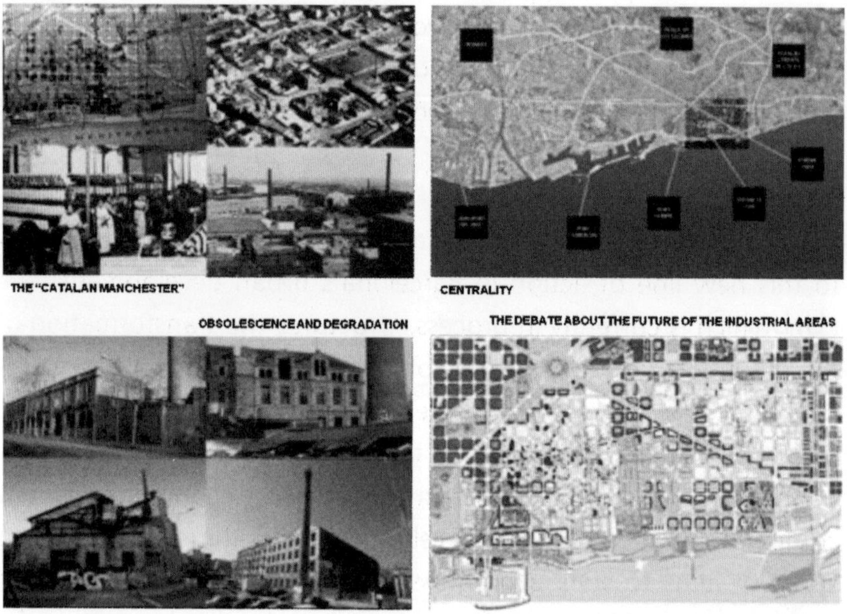

development and the opening up of the seafront, set the conditions for the transformation of the Eastern part of the city, specifically for the Poblenou's.

The Existing Fabric as a Support of the Transformation

The 22@ Barcelona Project opened a new way of building the city through a long-term transformation process, taking place over approximately 15 years, that adapts to both the area's pre-existing elements and its new needs. Proposals are based on pre-existing physical conditions, maintaining streets and historic features and elements as a support for new developments. The final image is the result of a balanced mix of existing and replacement elements

Urban Density

The project opts for a dense and compact city which encourages synergies between the various urban agents and promotes a more rational use of land. For this reason it overcomes the characteristic low density of traditional industrial areas increasing building levels in the sector from a net index of 2m_c/m_l to 3m_c/m_l. This increase in the index in private developments along with the change of use is an incentive for real-estate developers but is also linked to certain obligations: payment of urbanization fees, presence of new activities (@ activities) or cessions of land free of compensation to the community – a third of private land will be made public - to create new green areas, facilities and social housing.

Urban Diversity

Understood, on the one hand, as co-existence of uses, opposed to a model of territorial specialization, the project opts for a mixture that promotes social cohesion and more balanced and sustainable urban and economic development. Production activities therefore coexist with

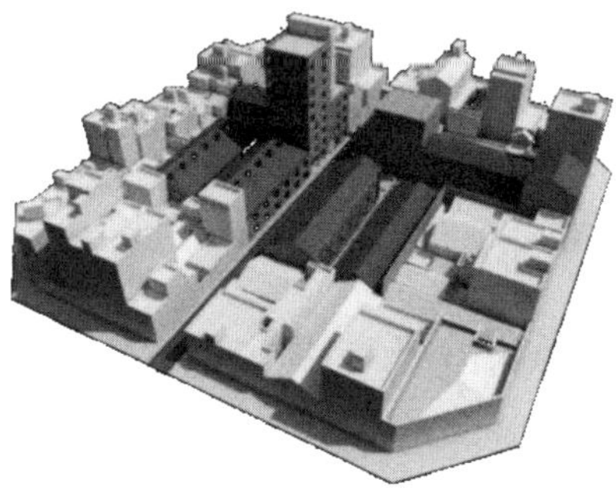

centres of research, continuing education, technology transfer, housing and commerce, in a high-quality setting that makes density compatible with a balanced range of open spaces and facilities.

On the other hand, diversity refers to the morphological complexity of the territory. Prior to transformation, the former industrial sector of Poblenou was characterized by a mix within the Cerdà gride of buildings of different sizes, uses and styles, forming a diversity of irregular fabrics. The 22@ Project searches to maintain this morphological complexity by integrating the new developments into the existing fabrics.

Flexibility

Unlike traditional urbanization plans, the general regulation does not define a detailed and precise organization of the area. The 22@ Project establishes the guidelines for the transformation process implementing flexible regulatory mechanisms to adapt urban evolution to the specific situation of each place, an appropriate timescale to avoid disruptions and the user needs of the resulting spaces. It regulates means of development that adjust to the circumstances of new complexity and progressive urban development. It establishes a range of initiatives of very varied scope, including direct actions on existing plots, private sector plans for single street blocks and large-scale public plans for more than one block, involving complex management processes and plot redistribution.

Key Points in the Urban Regeneration Project

Some elements are considered basic for structuring the renewal of the sector, like the following:

Promoting the presence of knowledge-intense activities

The 22@ Project encourages non-pollutant, nuisance-free productive activities and the implantation of the most innovative sectors, which receive the designation "@ activities" and are characterized by being intensive in their use of information and communication technologies and dense in highly qualified jobs. In order to promote the implantation of these kind of activities able to revitalize the economy, the 22@Barcelona project grants an increased building level to transforming plans that include a percentage of no less than 20% of @ activities in their functional programmes. This strategy encourages developers to reach agreements with innovative companies and build spaces that are specially designed to meet their needs. The presence of innovative activities alongside traditional local

activities, create a rich and varied productive fabric that serves to increase the competitiveness of the business world.

Advanced infrastructures

The 22@ Project, jointly with the Special Infrastructure Plan, aims to address the deficient existing network of infrastructures by redeveloping 35 kms of streets to implant highly competitive services. More dynamic activities call for a high level of services to enable them to develop with optimum efficiency. It provides the sector with a modern power supply grid, centralized climate control and pneumatic waste collection systems. It also includes a new mobility plan that aims to ensure that over 70% of people going to 22@ sector do so using public transport, on foot or by bicycle. The Special Infrastructure Plan represents an investment of 180 million euros, for the most part generated by the transformation process of property development.

Public facilities

The project allocates 10% of transformed land for public facilities.

Some of these facilities, the ones called 7@, will be associated with the productive system (training, research and information of new technologies). Through this new concept of facilities, the 22@ district encourages synergies between productive activities and universities or other research centres. Other facilities are for local use, helping to mitigate the neighbourhood's deficit of communal facilities.

Housing

The Plan is committed to the combination of productive and residential spaces so that residents can live near their work, as well as promote local commerce and ensure use of public space at all times of the day. In this respect the project recovered more than 4,600 traditional dwellings that were built in this area before it was stipulated as an exclusively industrial use for all the city's production land. The new 22@ code, which combines urban uses, recognizes the existence of these dwellings and provides an incentive to their rehabilitation. Furthermore, it facilitates the construction

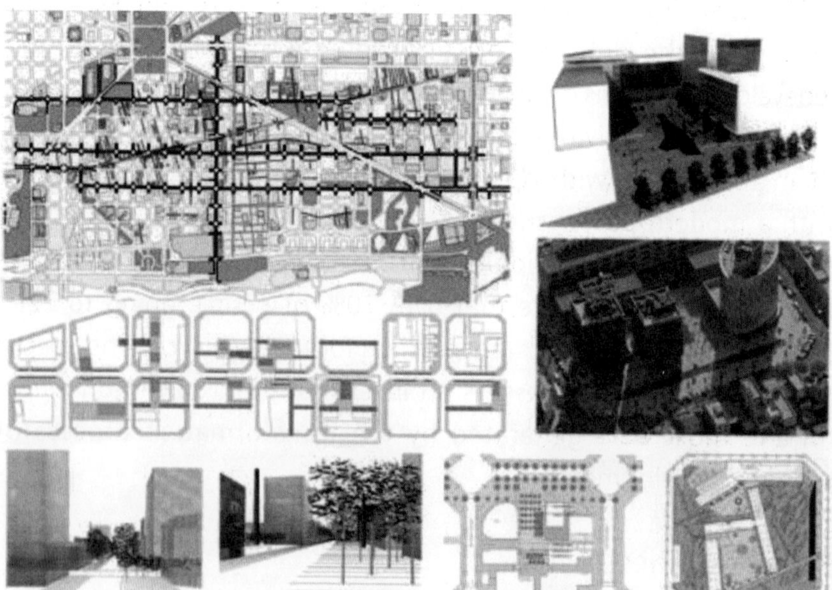

of 4,000 social housing units which will serve to promote social diversity in Poblenou.

Public space

The Plan recognizes public space as the support of urban life, as the place where citizens can establish relations with others above all. For that reason public spaces have a decisive role in renovating the city areas. The 22@ Project assigns 10% of former private industrial land for the creation of over 114,000 m_ of new green areas and

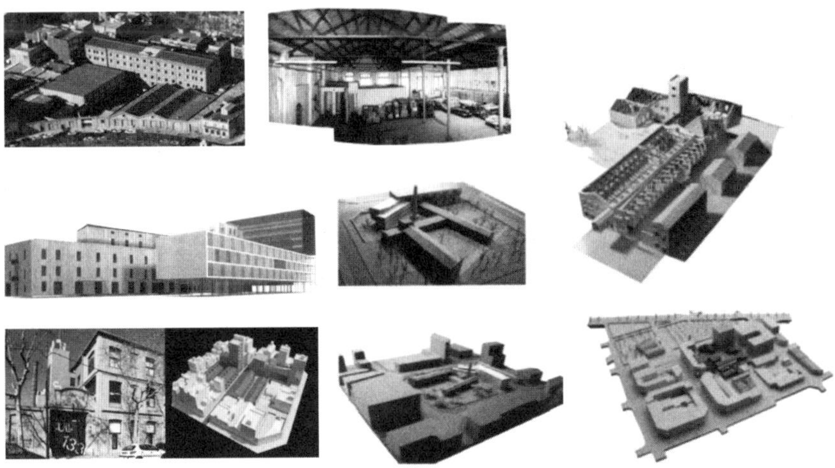

establishes high standards of quality in its streets and public spaces. These open spaces are supported for the existing plot division, recovering passages or highlighting interesting architectural elements, such as chimneys or old industrial warehouses. New civic streets are also created to complement the traditional thoroughfares running through the area.

Industrial heritage

Heritage is one of the most tangible signs of a community's identity, a key element when analysing cultural, economic and urbanistic development in our cities.

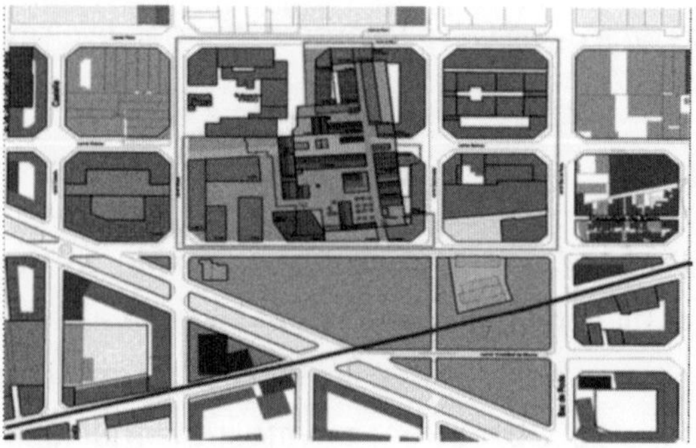

In order to encourage the process of recovering these symbols of Poblenou's industrial history, the 'Poblenou Industrial Protection Plan' has been developed, including in the heritage list a total of 114 elements which will help to guarantee the preservation of this historical and cultural legacy.

The 22@ Project highlights the spatial variety that characterizes Poblenou and promotes a diverse urban model in which new buildings and public spaces combine with historic layouts and features of the neighbourhood's industrial past to create a highly cultural environment that blends tradition and innovation.

Finally, as a project of economic revitalization, it is also a unique opportunity to reinstate Poblenou as the economic heart of the city. 22@Barcelona Project is a spur to the competitiveness of the productive fabric in the form of a series of projects, seen as driving forces of the territory's economic development. This series of initiatives create clusters in different areas in which Barcelona can take on a leading role, by concentration in the territory of companies, public bodies and benchmark science and technology centres that are considered strategic, including media, information and communication technologies (ICT), medical technologies and energy, among others. Since it began, the 22@Barcelona Project

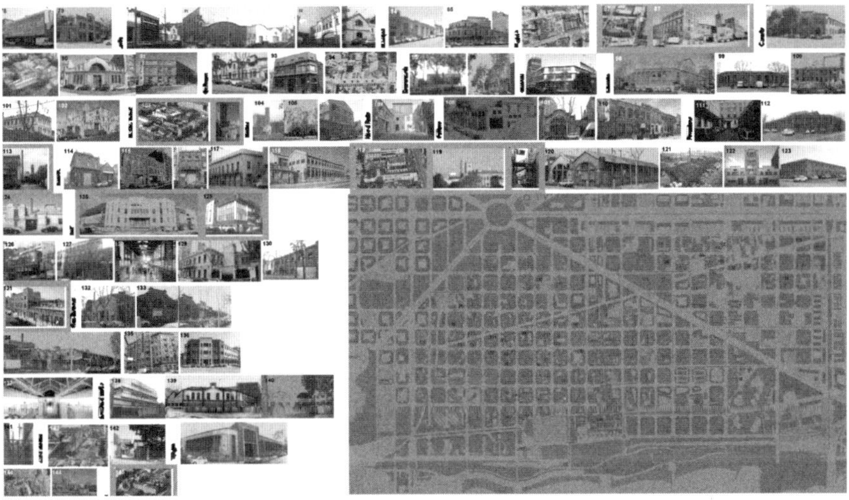

has attracted 1,063 new companies and institutions, of which more than a half belong to one of the above mentioned four strategic sectors.

Urban Renewal and Built Heritage Conservation: The Singapore's Experience

Mr. Ler Seng Ann - Group Director (Conservation & Development Services), Conservation & Urban Design Group, Urban Redevelopment Authority, Singapore

Introduction

Singapore is a small city-state of about 700 sq km with no hinterland compared to other cities. It has a multi-racial population of about 4.8 million. It faces constraints both on land and sea space, making planning a tricky business.

Despite this, Singapore is highly rated as a liveable city in Asia in the recent 2009 Mercer's Worldwide Quality of Living Survey[1]. Besides its efficient infrastructure, it is also recognized as a modern city with an impressive skyline of old and new buildings.

Urban Renewal

Historically, Singapore was a British colony, a part of Malaysia and then an independent country. During those years, the city centre grew and literally became an urban slum. The introduction of motor transportation resulted in acute congestion on the narrow roads which had originally been planned in the 1820s for horse-drawn carts.

---

1 based on report carried in Singapore's Straits Times on 29 April 2009

When the city centre became too packed, families started to move to the outskirts. Soon squatter settlements sprang up in these areas, leading to the setting up of the Singapore Improvement Trust (SIT) by the British colonial government in 1927 to arrest the problem of urbanization and improve the general physical environment of the city. Only piecemeal improvements were made as the SIT did not have the power to draw up comprehensive plans or control development.

After the Second World War ended, more efforts were made to solve the housing problem. The Housing Committee was set up in 1947. By then, the population had swelled to 1 million. The number of housing units already built were not enough to meet the increased demand of the expanding population, let alone improve the living conditions of the thousands living in the city's slums.

At that time, 25 per cent of the population was squeezed into 1 per cent of Singapore's total land area. Some old shophouses each housed as many as 100 people at any one time. They lived in cramped cubicles and even the corridors became living spaces and sanitation was very poor. The slums were both a health and fire hazard.

Urban renewal was, therefore, very urgent in the late 1960s. The emphasis then was to clear the 800,000 slums and squatters, improve living conditions of the people by providing affordable new homes like public housing to the booming population and construct new infrastructures at a rapid pace. The primary concern was to revitalize and transform the city into a modern, efficient centre for finance, business and tourism.

The Singapore government and the private sector worked as a team to help with the social and economic development. The government provided the expertise, sites, infrastructure, social programmes including public housing programme and a favourable investment climate. The private sector with its financial mobility and managerial skills carried out the economic projects especially commercial buildings.

Legislations like the Recovery of Possession of Controlled Premises (Special Provisions) Bill of 1969 and the Land Acquisition Act introduced also helped to facilitate the revitalization and renewal efforts.

The Urban Renewal Department, the predecessor of the Urban Redevelopment Authority (URA), was set up in 1966 within the Housing & Development Board, to oversee the Urban Renewal Programme and the release of land under the government Sales of Sites Programme. This resulted in the transformation of Singapore's central area from one ringed with slums and squatters to a modern financial and business hub.

Built Heritage Conservation

So, how do we deal with the conservation of built heritage in this kind of environment? The pragmatic way is to do it selectively and as an integral part of Singapore's city planning. We took a 'win-win' approach by allowing redevelopment while conserving the key historic buildings at the same time.

We see built heritage as more than stone and mortar. We see it as a dynamic record of our ancestral lifestyle, cultures and traditions, passed lovingly from generation to generation. It shapes our values, inspires our aspirations and bestows upon us our unique identity. The old buildings add variety to our streetscape and city skyline. Being physical links to our past, they contribute towards giving Singaporeans a greater sense of history and belonging.

We were very fortunate for the following reasons:

1. Our planners and policy makers had the foresight to consciously avoid or delay encroachment of new developments in the historic areas, thus enabling the retention of large tracts of these prime areas for conservation.

2. The reclamation at Marina South (the current Marina Bay – the extension of the existing city centre) and other areas made available land for new intensive development to meet future growth, thus releasing the pressure to redevelop these historic areas.

Our early efforts focussed on the rehabilitation and the reuse of selected State-owned buildings and protection of some large significant institutional and religious buildings like the Armenian Church, the oldest church in Singapore built in 1835. The Sri Mariamman Temple and the Sultan Mosque, both more than 100 years old, are also some of the earliest buildings protected since the 1970s.

Four Periods of Conservation Efforts

Singapore is a relatively young nation, having gained independence only in 1965. Initially, the new government focused on the immediate issues of overcrowding in the urban centres, severe traffic congestions and environmental blight. In 1970, five years after independence, the first of the four periods of conservation efforts in Singapore started.

Incubation Period (1970 -1983)

This period marked Singapore's first major conservation milestone. Thirty State-owned shophouses on Murray Street and Cuppage Terrace, in the heart of the old city were identified for restoration. It was undertaken by the URA and although in its infancy, this rehabilitative act awakened the conservation consciousness of Singaporeans who owned old buildings. Around this time (1971), the Preservation of Monuments Board was also formed and subsequently 18 national monuments, mostly religious and civic buildings, were gazetted between 1973 and 1979.

Formative Period (1983 -1988)

As urban renewal and the public housing programme started to become successful, the conservation of more buildings was looked at in a comprehensive manner. This direction was set in the Central Area Structure Plan formulated in 1985 which marked out the old parts of Singapore where Sir Stamford Raffles founded Singapore. These included designated places for the Chinese in Chinatown and the Malays in Kampong Glam. The Indians came later and congregated around what we today call Little India.

URA protected these 3 whole areas of architectural and historical heritage, known as Historic Districts after the government was confident that there was sufficient land to meet our future needs based on the land use, infrastructure and development strategies proposed for the Central Area of Singapore.

Full scale studies were also taken to identify other areas for conservation. In 1986, URA announced the conservation of some 3200 buildings in 7 areas, namely, Chinatown, Kampong Glam, Little India, Boat Quay, Clarke Quay, Cairnhill and Emerald Hill.

Building on its early successes with Murray Street and Cuppage Terrace, URA embarked on its first shophouse conservation project in 1987 covering some 220 units of old dilapidated shophouses in the Tanjong Pagar area within the Chinatown Historic District. Thirty two of these were beautifully restored initially by the URA. They demonstrated how old buildings could be restored and retained as an economically viable undertaking. Following this, the remaining 188 shophouses were progressively released by URA for sale to start Singapore's first large-scale private participation in conservation.

Consolidation Period (1989 – 1992)

In 1989, 17 years after the first conservation efforts were started, URA was formally appointed as the national conservation authority. With this formal appointment, URA began to consolidate Singapore's programme for conservation in the face of rapid urban redevelopment on the island.

In the same year, the Conservation Plan, first exhibited in 1986 was finalized and adopted. This was followed by the gazetting (legally conferring conservation status) of the seven areas announced in 1986. Five other areas: Blair Plain, Beach Road, River Valley, Jalan Besar and Geylang comprising some 1,200 buildings were also added to the conservation area list. The Preservation of Monument Board also added another ten more national monuments to its list of protected buildings.

In 1991, conservation efforts in Singapore took an important big step when URA launched the "Conservation Initiated by Private Owners' Scheme". This scheme allows private individual owners to volunteer their buildings, which were of architectural and historical significance, for conservation in return for development incentives.

Refinement Period (1992 onwards)

By 1992, most of the key areas identified in the Conservation Plan were gazetted and so old buildings located there were safeguarded against demolition for redevelopment. With these major precincts protected, URA then turned its attention to refining and raising the standards of conservation works while continuing with its efforts to selectively identify another 2,500 buildings for conservation.

To demonstrate the use of proper approaches and practices in restoration works, the URA showcased two restoration projects in Little India and Kampong Glam where proper restoration techniques adhering to URA's conservation guidelines were used. This was supported by making available to the industry, documentation and technical publications where techniques employed were shared liberally. Several television documentaries were also produced. Dialogue sessions with professionals and owners were also held regularly alongside exhibitions and talks for the public.

In 1995, the URA launched the inaugural annual Architectural Heritage Award to recognise the best restoration/conservation projects. This period also saw many privately restored conservation projects winning international awards for their works.

The Conservation Plan

Conservation in Singapore is very much guided by the Conservation Plan. This was first made public in 1986. This is a comprehensive plan in terms of the geographical coverage, range of architectural styles and building types selected. To date, more than 6,900 buildings have been gazetted for conservation.

The selection process considers each building's architectural and historical significance, rarity in terms of building type and whether it enhances the visual character of the area in which they are located. Fifty five buildings, with national historical significance, have also been gazetted as national monuments by the Preservation of Monuments Board.

Broadly speaking, conservation buildings in Singapore are usually found within one of the following four groupings:

a **Historic Districts** (Boat Quay, Chinatown, Kampong Glam and Little India)

These are buildings located in the four earliest historic districts of Singapore. The buildings here are mainly two and three storey shophouses built contiguously in different architectural styles and designs. Seen as a whole, they reflect the evolution of shophouse development in Singapore. The shophouses are largely intact complete with the original texture and fabric. As they depict the lifestyles of the community in Singapore through time, the entire building is conserved. Commercial or residential uses are both permitted in these shophouses.

b **Historic Residential Districts** (Blair Plain, Cairnhill and Emerald Hill)

These three areas were the earliest residential enclaves of the rich in Singapore. Here the buildings selected for conservation were mainly terrace houses built with ornate and decorative facades. To allow for more design flexibility and greater use of the building for modern living, the rear portion of these conservation buildings can be extended and topped up to the eave of the main roof. Adjustment to the floor levels to insert an additional storey is also permitted within the new rear extension.

c **Secondary Settlements** (Beach Road, Geylang, Jalan Besar, Joo Chiat and River Valley)

The five secondary settlements are areas that extended from the earliest historic districts. Conservation in the secondary settlements is on a streetscape basis because the older heritage buildings are usually adjacent to new developments. Owners of conserved buildings may choose to conserve the entire building or have a new rear extension built up to the maximum height allowable for that particular area. Hence, the main building fronting the road is retained, keeping the scale of the streetscape, while the rear portion of the building can be demolished and developed into a new building altogether.

d **Bungalows**

The conservation of bungalows is done on a highly selective

basis. The selected bungalows represent the best of the old bungalow housing stock in Singapore and are therefore excellent examples of their architectural style. The conservation guidelines for these bungalows are essentially the same as those for shophouses as in the fundamental principles of conservation and a respect for the typology of the bungalow. In general, the main building envelope - the roofs and facades, is to be retained and restored, while the retention of the outhouse is optional. Subdivision of the rest of the site for additional bungalow plots is permitted.

Pragmatic Approach to Conservation

The biggest resistance to conservation by owners is usually the loss of economic potential of the historic building and land parcel it occupies once it is conferred conservation status. In land-scarce Singapore, this is a major concern. To overcome this and work towards a win-win solution, URA adopts, wherever possible, a pragmatic approach to arrive at a creative solution to balance the need for development against the need to safeguard built heritage with minimal economic loss to the owner.

Taking the conservation of bungalows as an example, while it is desirable by many conservationists to preserve all the existing settings around the bungalow and curtail new developments around it, this translates into a large economic loss for the owner. The pragmatic approach in action does not restrict owners but allows them to subdivide the rest of the site for additional bungalow plots if so desired. For conservation bungalows located on land where condominium or apartment development is permitted, the owner can proceed to redevelop the rest of the site, keeping only the conserved bungalow as a clubhouse or for residential use.

Another example is easily found in the secondary settlements where many new developments have sprouted out among heritage buildings. Here the conservation objective is to keep the streetscape rather than the entire building form. Taking a pragmatic approach, URA only requires owners to conserve the main building fronting the road. They can choose to demolish and redevelop the back portion into a new extension if desired. This allows the owner to realise the economic potential permissible under the development plan, and at the same time, retain the essential flavour of the conservation building from the street.

Implementation Strategy

Singapore has been successful in implementing the Conservation Plan over the years. This success can be attributed to URA's five-pronged approach, which is refined and updated year after year to ensure its effectiveness.

Start with Pilot Projects

To demonstrate the government's commitment to conservation and its economic viability, Singapore uses State-owned buildings as pilot projects. The successful completion of these pilot projects not only injected a greater sense of confidence among owners, developers and professionals for conservation projects but also demonstrated the proper approach, method and technique for the restoration of these old buildings. They also serve as benchmarks and encourage the private sector to work towards quality restoration.

Involve the Public Sector through Sale of Sites

Singapore understands the importance of involving the private sector in its conservation programme. It wants them to be the major player instead of the government. With the exception of the pilot projects, the majority of the State-owned conservation buildings are released back to the private sector for restoration through the Sale of Site Programme. This gives developers and entrepreneurs the opportunity to participate especially if they do not own any conserved building.

Since the mid-1980s, more than 900 conservation buildings have been released for restoration through the Sale of Sites Programme.

Encouraging Private Conservation

About 80% of the conserved buildings in Singapore are privately-owned. The government recognizes the importance of providing effective assistance to help them restore these buildings. To date, it has provided the following:

a During the early days, as many old properties had tenants protected under the Rent Control Act, the government set up the Tenant's Compensation Board to help property owners resettle tenants and recover their rent control property for restoration. It acted as an arbitrator between the owners and tenants and also to facilitate the resettlement of affected tenants. The Board was dissolved with the abolition of rent control on 1 April 2001.

b Technical guidelines and standards are readily available to assist owners, developers and professionals to facilitate submission of plans and the restoration works on conserved buildings.

c Waivers of development charge (a levy on development with enhanced land value), carpark provision and carpark deficiency charges are given as incentives to encourage private owners towards restoring their conserved buildings.

d Agencies build necessary infrastructure and utility services, and improve the general environment to complement private conservation initiatives.

Actively Promoting Conservation

As the authority responsible for conservation in Singapore, URA actively promotes public awareness of conservation through the media, publications, exhibitions, and talks. A prestigious award scheme - the annual Architectural Heritage Awards was started in 1995 to recognize and honour owners, professionals and contractors of well-restored conservation projects. This in turn spurs the industry towards greater quality restoration of built heritage. Eighty four projects have been recognized under this award over the past 14 years. They comprised national monuments, shophouses, bungalows and 'old and new' integrated developments.

Open Consultative Approach

Finally, URA believes that things can always be improved. Hence, it adopts an open consultative position towards conservation in Singapore. Its conservation officers not only liaise closely with private owners and professionals to work on conservation projects, they also interact regularly with relevant interest groups from the industry and the public to obtain feedback.

An example is the joint reviews of conservation guidelines held with private architects from the Singapore Institute of Architects. Another example is the setting up of the Conservation Advisory Panel, comprising professionals and members of the public. This Panel was formed in 2002 to give inputs on built heritage proposals put up by URA, and to propose other buildings for study for possible conservation, as well as to assist in promoting greater public education and understanding of gazetted built heritage.

This five-pronged approach taken by the URA has seen almost 60% of the 6,900 gazetted conservation buildings successfully restored and rehabilitated to date.

Conclusion

In 2006, after years of putting pragmatic conservation in practice, Singapore's Conservation Programme was internationally recognized when it received the Urban Land Institute Global Excellence Award.

The citation: "Singapore's model conservation programme preserves its rich heritage of vernacular buildings and colourful neighbourhoods in this rapidly modernizing country. Thanks to a collaborative approach among government organizations, the public and developers, the island republic's Urban Redevelopment Authority has achieved a balance between free-market economics and cultural conservation", is indeed an encouragement to us and all those who took the conservation journey with us. It was the result of the strong partnerships that we have formed with developers, architects, engineers, and government agencies.

Conservation will remain a challenging task. It has not been easy, but we have managed to stay on course and we are continuing with this journey. For instance, in planning for new growth areas in the draft Master Plan 2008, we have actively considered old buildings worthy of conservation for legal protection. We also looked at how these buildings could be integrated with new developments and the overall vision for the area.

We have also moved forward to consider buildings of our more recent past and heritage structures. These could be a modern high rise building, an elegant tower, a historic bridge or a beautiful pavilion. There are still many places and landmarks that we can identify with and feel for in Singapore – places where we can spend quality time with our family and friends. Together with professional colleagues within and outside URA, concerned members of public and with the support from the private sector and the encouragement from the Urban Land Institute, we will continue our journey to make Singapore.

A Great Global City to Live-Work-Play in

An Overview of Background, Practice and Direction of Preservation of Heritage in Urban Environment in Sri Lanka

Mr. Prasanna Gunawardena - Chartered Architect & Town Planner
Presidential Advisor Chairman, Urban Settlement Development Authority

Mr. Ranjith Alahakoon - Chartered Architect Senior Lecturer, Faculty of Architecture University of Moratuwa

Heritage, is alerted as having "several different senses", including Natural, and Cultural Heritage and Tradition - "that which is inherited from the past, maintained in the present and bestowed for the future generations" with facets and forms having the stamp of peculiarity of their periods, that have survived in towns and cities through different periods of development, commonly perceived as urban heritage.

Such peculiarities are generally in respect of the predominant styles of architecture of that period, of the buildings and their settings, either adding value by their outstandingly resplendent glory or depreciating the quality of an experience by their state of decay. They are of consequence for urban renewal to depict an event, a tradition or merely to provide a particular experience – an experience of antiquity. Therein also lay the dilemmas and challenges of Urban Renewal.

There is a vast repository of techniques applied world-wide, in carrying out urban renewal by incorporating physical attributes of urban heritage, with information accessed with relative ease. Networking among specialists and enthusiasts are routine. Organizations and groups dedicated to the "cause", spreading awareness of opportunities in resources of urban heritage including Built Heritage, as resources for urban renewal are multiplying with increased networking.

Sri Lanka is home to the Great Heritage of the Sinhalese, the story of which begins even before arrival of Buddhism over 2500 years ago with the establishment of the 'Great Dinasty" of Sinhala kings and their seats of power – including the Historic City of Anurdhapura with urban facets including a social zoning, palaces and hermitages, moats and fortressing, parks and even a "Nagara Guttika" – a Mayor. The embracement of Buddhism by the Sinhala nation, king and his people accepting the Great Sermon at the Mahamewuna Gardens in Anurdhapura by Mahinda Thera, son of Emperor Dharmashoka marks the beginning of the moulding of the Sinhala Civilization in the religious and cultural traditions of Buddhism though not excluding those of Hindu religious traditions and the Yaksha and Naga beliefs which has endured to date as the pre-dominating factor of the Sri Lankan nation.

The Antiquities Ordinance of Sri Lanka, with limited scope for interpretation outside the letter of the Law, is recognized as having served effectively in the preservation of Archeological Sites, Historic Structures, and Cultural Artifacts, of what is directly perceived as National Heritage. However, due to the rigidity of the Ordinance, giving little or no room for interpreting its provisions, arise the dilemmas of application of methodologies and even selecting preserved antiquities for conservation or restoration.

The Ordinance which was once deemed a "nuisance" in urban renewal particularly in respect of preservation of Sri Lanka's Colonial Heritage of almost 500 years, is now seen to have effectively given protection to antiquities of Urban Heritage and achieved a fair degree of acceptance in adhering to its provisions in the handling of assets of Urban Heritage.

With 7 World Heritage Sites, Sri Lanka, a relatively small island nation, is conspicuous in the listing carried out by the World Heritage Committee of UNESCO. However, World Heritage apart, the country is home to a large number of National Heritage artifacts, in the physical environment. Some of these have been protected and guarded by tradition more than addict and others by the wilderness of thick jungle cover, multiple layers of earth cover, enormous sand dunes – or other natural phenomena for over 2500 years of Sinhala Civilization.

Thus, monumental cities, sacred precincts, pleasure parks all endowed with moonstones, ponds, pillars, figures ranging in size from miniature to grand in rock sculptures, frescoes and wall painting as well as engineering feats of channels and reservoirs and irrigation works of the Sinhala Civilization, remained engulfed in obscurity or rack and ruin, abandoned over centuries of decline of the Great Dynasty and aggression and plunder by alien cultures.

Yet, the grandeur of the past had been kept alive through the records of the Mahawansa (Great Dynasty)— a script almost as old as the Sinhala culture - and other historic chronicles, literary works, centuries old customs, folklore and pageantry, giving strength to the people to periodically rise in great rebellions and wars, stalling the onslaughts of dissemination of the colonizers culture and values, to strengthen declining dynasties, preserve indigenous culture, pursue inherited values, create new assets in new seats of power and sacred precincts with creative arts, and the blossoming of literary works and epics of heroism, some equal to those of the Great Dynasty.

Concurrently, under colonial rule, new cities were built in new styles alien to local culture and tradition. Also, networks of infrastructure, at times monumental in tasks, were constructed to serve the economic interests of the colonizers and spread of alien culture and lifestyles establishing the Colonial Heritage of Sri Lanka.

Evidence of the Cultural Heritage of the Sinhalese, protected in the hearts and minds of the people had aroused intellectual curiosity amongst scholarly circles, creating the seeds of a movement, which over time and space has uncovered much of the hidden and suppressed truths of the history of evolution of the Sinhala Civilization. The process continues with the discovery of new evidence accumulating in strength and widening its scope - through institutional build up, laws and enactments and post independence practices of nation building.

An example is the movement that has been developing during the past few decades, now gathering recognition to rectify myths and conniving distortions by historians in the service of colonial interests and alien culture in suppressing the truth about the battle heritage of the 16th century Seethawaka kingdom. Well crafted twists to undermine the status of "divinity" enjoyed by the warrior kings Mayadunne and Rajasingha, the latter responsible for inflicting upon the colonizing Portuguese the single most devastating destruction a colonizing power ever faced is being exposed through new evidence, disclosures and discourse amongst specialists of eminence.

Also, with the local population throughout generations taking pride in the location of Seetha-lena, a revered cave precinct in which Seetha was afforded initial hospitality in Lanka - Seethawaka like other similar scattered all over the island signifies the historic influence and the pride amongst the people of a great inheritance of the Island wherein the epic Ramayana unfolds. As a nation, the current generation of Sri Lankans are experiencing with awe, the shift from myth to hypothesis the reality of unraveling if not unearthing mighty Ravana's "Lankapura", secrets of his "Dandumonara" and of other precincts epochal events of the Ramayana in Sri Lanka - with modern technology establishing facts of a 5000 year old Sri Lankan Civilization.

Though the preservation of Anuradhapura, the ancient seat of the early dynasties of the Sinhalese, and intermittently invaded by Dravidian rulers for over 1000 years, officially commenced with the enactment of the Anuradhapura Preservation Ordinance in 1942, the Anuradhapura Preservation Plan was prepared by the Department of Town and Country Planning, (now National Physical Planning Department - NPPD) to implement the provisions of the Ordinance in the immediate aftermath of national independence in 1948. The Plan, including the New Town of Anuradhapura - the first to be planned and executed in Sri Lanka by Sri Lankans as separate from the Sacred City- was the beginning of a methodology and practice which has now spread through out Sri Lanka, encompassing large number of sacred areas which includes in addition to those of Buddhists also precincts sacred to Hindus, Christians and Islamic.

This by now an entrenched practice of Planning and Development of Sacred Areas, continues to be carried out with state funding by a core team of specialists at the NPPD, in a maze of coordination that includes combining with powers and functions of the subsequent Urban Development Authority Act, involvements of the "Cultural Triangle"[1] though not without conflict with increasing aspirations of local authorities to own the processes. The practice, often being carried out within the urban matrix, impacts on urban renewal prioritized as obligation to revive and restore a long marginalized heritage. Such

---

[1] *The area formed by linking Sri Lanka's and Asia's richest, largest, and most dramatic archaeological heritage sites in the ancient capitals of Anuradhapura, Polonnaruva, and Kandy, with Sigiriya in the center.*

priority is institutionalized in the couplinbg of Urban Development and Sacred Area Development having cabinet status as a single Ministry—that of Urban Development and Sacred Area Development.

Dagobas, temples, *kovils*, churches, mosques as associated structures are repaired and preserved, incongruous activities removed from surroundings, facilities for congregations provided with constructions in matching styles. Such preserved heritage in urban matrix has stimulated revival of century old traditions including festivals and pageants providing congregations the involvement and enjoyment in experiencing their Heritage, and enhancing the wide range of offers to tourists that already exist in the country.

Whilst State funds have ensured some colonial architectural monuments - particularly in Colombo and Galle - to be preserved and utilized; tourism, providing utility value is seen to be the engine of opportunity for the preservation and restoration of architectural monuments of the Colonial Heritage.

Forts and fortresses of the colonial powers have been restored - some smaller ones as museums and more awaiting intervention. The monumentally preserved Galle Fort of the colonial Dutch - a World Heritage Site, where conflicts abound in enlivening the ambience for tourism, is a learning experience in the resolution of these conflicts and practices of conservation. The conflicts, particularly in interventions of the interiors of town houses, in conversion to villas and/or meet standards of luxury for high returns in tourism are compounded by increasing interest of the Municipality in owning the processes of decision making.

In as much as some State Architecture such as Jeoffry Bava creation of the monumental Parliament incorporating facets from Cultural Heritage of different periods of the country's long history to iconize modern Sri Lankan Architecture, his works along with those of a generation of post independence architects and specialists in other creative arts provide stimulating direction for Urban Renewal to be inspired and impacted by Heritage.

Thus with the whole island having in every nook and corner at least some artifact of pre-colonial antiquity, it is the understandable aspiration of rebuilding a nation to prioritize restoration of aspects of heritage that had been neglected, suppressed and or destroyed for centuries whilst economic advantages and advantages of utility drive the conservation of the undisputed colonial Heritage.

Resource-Based Approach to Urban Development in India

Ms. Nicole Bolomey - Programme Specialist for Culture, UNESCO, New Delhi office

1. International Development in the Field of Historic Cities

"...Living historic cities, require a policy of city planning and management that takes conservation as a key point of departure. In this process, the historic city's authenticity and integrity, which are determined by various factors, must not be compromised.

A central concern of physical and functional interventions is to enhance quality of life and production efficiency by improving living, working and recreational conditions and adapting uses without compromising existing values derived from the character and significance of the historic urban fabric and form. This means not only improving technical standards, but also a rehabilitation and contemporary development of the historic environment based upon a proper inventory and assessment of its values, as well as the addition of high-quality cultural expressions." [1]

---

[1] *UNESCO 2005 Declaration on the Conservation of Historic Urban Landscapes*

UNESCO has in recent years worked intensely on the issue of Historic Urban Landscapes and the beneficial relationship between urban development and the conservation of the historic aspects of the cities. This work, based on the 1976 UNESCO *Recommendation concerning the Safeguarding and Contemporary Role of Historic Areas* has culminated in the 2005 *Vienna Memorandum for the Conservation of Historic Urban Landscapes* and the related *Declaration on the Conservation of Historic Urban Landscapes* issued by the World Heritage Committee at its 29th session in 2005. These two documents give the principles and base definitions for urban development in cities with historic values.

The 2005 Vienna Memorandum introduces the term 'historic urban landscape' and explains how the historic urban landscape is embedded with current and past social expressions and developments that are place-based. The historic urban landscape acquires its exceptional and universal significance from a gradual evolutionary, as well as planned territorial development over a relevant period of time through processes of urbanization, incorporating environmental and topographic conditions and expressing economic and socio-cultural values pertaining to societies.[2]

2. Cities of India

Born out of the deep-rooted cultural and spiritual traditions, the historic urban landscapes in India have over the centuries evolved into spaces of timeless appeal. Despite having undergone numerous physical, social and cultural transformations, these historic areas still manage to conjure up the inherent historic values of the place through the unmatched beauty of its traditional architecture and urban morphology coupled with the vibrancy of the markets, *ghats* and other open spaces

---

[2] *UNESCO WHC VIENNA MEMORANDUM on "World Heritage and Contemporary Architecture – managing the Historic Urban Landscape"*

abounding with activities of the people. It is these areas with their multilayered history which have over time become the symbols of the city's image and the places where in the 'culture' of the city resides.

Today, approximately 28 per cent of India's one billion population lives in urban areas. The increasing demand on basic services like water, energy, drainage, housing and mobility are major concerns for the development of the cities, trying to cover both the well articulated demands of the small but increasing affluent urban population, as well as the needs of the large and ever growing population of urban poor. New infrastructures, residential areas, industrial sites and large scale commercial establishments are being constructed at an unparalleled speed often with little or no regard for the constraints of the existing urban landscape; the quality, character, limitations and sustainability of the existing resources.

In this process of fast and often unplanned urbanization, it is the existing qualities of a city, its ecological, historic, aesthetic, social, cultural, religious and also its traditional economic qualities that are unarguably falling behind and losing significance. The historic urban landscape stands at the threshold of being devoured by illegal construction, inconsiderate overuse of resources, and a greedy, thoughtless, and shortsighted focus on economic growth. This onslaught does not only result in the physical loss of traditional buildings, materials and the historic fabric of the place, but also takes away in its stride, the traditional wisdom of their construction techniques, skills of craftsmanship, as well as the social practices and cultural traditions of the people living within the historic areas.

The need to raise the awareness about the qualities of Indian cities, to protect their wealth of heritage, social fabric and cultural traditions is therefore more pronounced now than ever before. There is an urgent need to build up the awareness among urban planners, architects, the government and the contractors, and last but not least the population at large in how to recognize, respect, plan and conserve the qualities of Indian cities while developing their assets and fulfilling the needs of a 21st century living.

But what are these resources, the heritage, the historic urban landscape of Indian cities? How are they discovered, recorded, characterized, sustainably used and protected for future generations?

3. Urban Heritage and Urban Conservation

Heritage is a term that has often been used to represent monuments and antiquities. In recent years, awareness has grown in India to understand that heritage includes many more aspects. Heritage, in the context of cities, needs to be defined in a very encompassing way to include both intangible and tangible elements.

Urban heritage consists of the natural and cultural physical (tangible) elements, and the intangible aspects of a city. In the Indian context one may explain that it includes the place where the city is built, the sacred geography underlying its physical fabric, the natural and man-made water systems, the *ghats*, ponds, tanks and water harvesting systems; the street patterns, pathways, *bazaars* and *chowks*; the private and public buildings, gates and walls, birdfeeders and statues; the parks and gardens; the temples, mosques, and churches, urban historic fabric and the related *yatras*, pilgrimage ways and congregation places; the trees; the views to and from the city; the way people live, work and own the city as their space for life and death. It includes traditional crafts and festivals, oral history, indigenous knowledge systems, social practices and the performing arts.

Urban heritage is however not simply the addition of all these elements. It signifies the interplay between all the above elements, the way they interact, grow and form each other. Only when we understand how the different elements interlink and depend on each other do we understand the heritage of our cities. Cultural heritage cannot be defined by age or typology alone. The city of Chandigarh is as much part of the urban heritage of India as are the mills of Bombay. It remains finally to emphasize that urban heritage, by the above definition, includes not only public property and spaces, but also consists of privately owned buildings and spaces. This is a key challenge when considering urban development and conservation efforts.

With the above definition of Urban Heritage, the urban conservation approach needs to take a more dynamic perspective as opposed to the one generally prescribed for monuments and antiquities. Urban Conservation deals with the living environment, multiple ownership, variety of legal and planning provisions, different layers of governance, administration and management. It must be focused on the socio-economic development, the regeneration of the historic city, on housing and mobility, the linkages between the core and the periphery, while keeping alive the historic, natural, social and historic resources. Urban Conservation is closely intertwined with Urban Regeneration. The tools of urban conservation are much more varied than the tools for monumental conservation and the number of stakeholders is much larger. This adds to the complexity but also increases the opportunities for urban conservation.

4. The Indian Heritage Cities Network

In order to help retain the sense of balance between nature and society and in an attempt to reconcile the conflict between tradition and modern in historic Indian urban landscapes, the Indian Heritage Cities Network (IHCN) program was established by the UNESCO New Delhi office in 2006. The Network over the past few years has been instrumental in promoting heritage-based sustainable urban development in the country. Its mission is to highlight the Indian city as a Living Cultural Resource; foster the safeguard and sustainable use of the unique and diverse urban cultural heritage of India; promote the physical natural and cultural heritage, traditions, crafts and creativity as driving forces for urban development, and the generation of employment for a balanced socio-economic and cultural development.

The IHCN constitutes a Network of Urban Local Bodies, Governmental and Non-Governmental Institutions and NGOs, and dedicated individuals. The Network and its members, in general, aim to foster sustainable socio-economic and ecological development of Indian historic cities and towns based on the strength of their traditions, cultural identity and social networks. They encourage local community participation and help to create partnerships between people, technical experts and administration and in the process build the capacity of Indian cities and towns to protect and conserve their cultural and natural heritage. IHCN also facilitates national and international cooperation between governmental and non-governmental stakeholders and works towards adapting the existing planning, policy, legal and regulatory frameworks and existing government schemes and programmes to the heritage context in which they are implemented. IHCN aims to evolve models for enabling institutional frameworks for community information, consultation and participation in heritage conservation activities such as neighbourhood heritage committees or the creation of Heritage House as a centre for cultural activities, awareness generation, information exchange, technical assistance and facilitation of heritage conservation and heritage-based development.

In particular, IHCN and its members conduct research, create pilot schemes, develop tools and methods, prepare manuals, guidelines, tool-kits and other material which is published and disseminated to broaden the base of knowledge, expertise, experience and good practices of the members, governmental and non-governmental institutions, and any interested individual or group. The Network prepares educational material and conducts courses, trainings and other activities for the capacity building of elected representatives, bureaucrats, technical staff of governmental and non-governmental institutions, professionals, faculty, professional and craft people, and any other group or individual engaged with the historic urban and rural environment. Besides, it conducts exposure visits and creates a platform to match offer and demand of technical expertise. In collaboration with its partners, it also develops a service for appraisal, monitoring, advice and evaluation of projects at national, state and local levels.

Since its inception the Network has had a growing membership base and currently comprises of twenty-two Indian member cities, seven French cities and regional partners, seven national university and institutional members and a number of NGO partners, with many more Indian and European cities, regions and universities expressing an interest to join. Through the immense support gained from its members and active partners, IHCN has been conducting successful activities, events and undertaking projects promoting integrated conservation.

5. 'Moving Towards Heritage-Based Urban Development'- A Joint Project Between UNESCO-IHCN and JNNURM, Ministry of Urban Development, GoI

The Ministry of Urban Development (MoUD), Government of India and UNESCO New Delhi Office have developed a partnership to help safeguard and promote the sustainable use of India's unique and diverse urban cultural heritage, through a joint project 'Moving towards Heritage-based Urban Developments'. It primarily aims to mainstream the concern for heritage protection and conservation and the sustainable use of cultural resources in the Jawaharlal Nehru National Urban Renewal Mission (JNNURM) and ensure that the preparation of City Development Plans (CDPs) and Detailed Project Reports (DPRs) by the Mission Cities shall in no way compromise the valuable historic areas of the Indian cities.

In this project, a body of Indian experts from various relevant fields shall under the umbrella of UNESCO, revise the 'Draft Toolkit for the Preparation of a City Development Plan' with special view to heritage concerns; revise City Development Plans (CDPs) of four Mission Cities (Mysore, Varanasi, Srinagar and Madurai), prepare a Heritage Toolkit for Detailed Project Reports (DPRs) for all Mission Cities; prepare a training manual and the content development for a capacity building workshop for ULBs to be jointly organized by MoUD and UNESCO in October 2009.

The joint UNESCO-MoUD project is a continuation of the interventions and inputs since 2005 of the Indian conservation community to convince the JNNURM Directorate and the Ministry of Urban Development in general that heritage is an important part of the urban environment and that it cannot be neglected in any urban development initiative in any Indian city.

Mainstreaming Heritage

While defining 'Urban Heritage' and 'Urban Heritage Conservation' (see above) within the contextual dynamics of growing Indian cities it becomes clear that heritage cannot be treated in isolation. Urban Heritage Conservation should be a part of every effort of planning and development in a city. *In as much as it is rooted in tradition, culture has sometimes been regarded as an obstacle to modernization.*[3] In the case of inhabited historic towns the difficulties are numerous, largely

[3] *The Challenge to our Cultural Heritage, Edited by Yudhishthir Raj Isar, UNESCO Paris and Smithsonian Institute, Washington DC, 1986, Pg 21 (Article- Collision Course: Heritage Preservation versus the Demands of modernization) – Y S Isar*

owing to the fragility of their urban fabric and the runway speed with which their surroundings are being urbanized. But the holistic approach to urban conservation as advocated by IHCN wishes to place the modern Indian city's traditional cultural core, tangible and/or intangible in nature, at the centre-stage of any development process. The aim is to help preserve the cultural identity of the city's historic areas and project these as the socio-cultural capital of the city and as vital and undisputed elements to help achieve the historic city's development goals. The underlying force for this is also to develop the dynamic inner city historic areas as livable and humane environments, fulfilling the contemporary demands of its residents whilst respecting its cultural traditions.

The *Toolkit for the Preparation of a City Development Plan* (CDP toolkit) has recently been revised by the Technical Cell of the JNNURM, MoUD, in order to integrate the lessons learned from the first two years of the Urban Renewal Mission. The revised document has merged a number of earlier separate documents into one, and thus is much more comprehensive than the Toolkits first published in 2005. It also makes a serious attempt to integrate heritage into the CDP.

The working group under UNESCO acknowledged the efforts made by the JNNURM towards making the CDP Toolkit more comprehensive and integrative, even including a chapter on heritage. It did however emphasize that an even more integrative approach was needed to assure that the projects sanctioned under the JNNURM would not be harmful to the historic resources of the Indian cities.

Heritage is a cross cutting theme that needs to be addressed in all sectors of city planning. It can easily be compared to ecology or poverty alleviation, two other subjects that are inherent to all planning aspects in a city. Heritage, or the traditional natural and cultural resources, must be integrated in all assessment, visioning and planning efforts. UNESCO therefore suggested including heritage considerations while, for example, assessing water systems, poverty alleviation, housing, or any other aspect of the CDP.

The UNESCO revision of the Toolkit aims to mainstream heritage concerns so that the guidelines given do not lead to destruction of valuable heritage resources, but instead protect and preserve them. These resources can and will lead the way to localized solutions to generate urban employment; to restore historic buildings with modern amenities; to protect the watershed for future generations; and will finally lead to balanced socio-economic and cultural development. It introduces the concept of a resource-based approach to urban development, respecting throughout all planning and development processes, the existing natural, cultural, social and historic resources of a city. These existing resources must be recognized, analyzed, valued, integrated in the planning efforts and conserved and maintained for future generations. This applies to all sectors, including water, drainage, sewerage, transport, and others. In many cities, the historic water system, for example, is the very reason for the city's existence, and not just an aged and irrelevant part of the infrastructure that can be disposed off.

Natural and cultural resources are the basis of the existence of a city; they determine why the city was built in that place, how it survived over the centuries, and also give valuable clues on how to develop it for the future. These resources also play an important economic role as they are closely linked to the most needed services (such as water) and to the livelihood of the people (such as the craft sector) or tourism. Many of these resources are non-renewable and must for all these reasons be recognized, assessed, preserved and used in a sustainable manner for the future of the city. The natural environment, including the natural heritage, provides cities with resources which it needs for its survival. These natural resources must therefore be preserved and used in a sustainable way so as not to exploit and destroy them irreversibly. While assessing the socio-cultural and economic environment, it is essential to cover social infrastructure, cultural traditions and lifestyle and economic base in the context of the development environment. An assessment of cultural environment of the city in terms of data on the traditional communities living in specific areas, and their history, traditional crafts villages and areas that are part of the city and cultural heritage aspects like festivals, performing arts, cultural practices, religious practices, rites and rituals, the use of public spaces during festivals etc. are all important to understand the urban development context. Only such an approach will lead, if applied thoroughly, to sustainable urban development.

The effort should be towards adaptation of the existing resources and heritage in cities, to meet changes in economic, social and environmental requirements, rather than their demolition or abandonment. These should be viewed as elements of urban regeneration which ought to be brought together to help improve the socio-economic conditions and the infrastructure of the urban landscape in which they exist, in turn aiming to improve the quality of urban living. The concept of *urban renewal* has often guided efforts to rebuild or redesign the cities to accommodate contemporary demands, wherein renewal invariably implies removal of the old to make way for the new. Urban Regeneration as advocated by IHCN aims to retrieve the intrinsic values of the place and attempts to synthesize cultural values with economic opportunities and social benefits.

IHCN enforces the cities to look at their historical values and to treasure them as it believes that preserving cultural continuity is perhaps the only way to achieve socially sustainable development. Any planning process must be based on the mapping, documentation as well as condition and value assessment of the natural and cultural environment, and its many aspects. This may include the topography and geology, traditional water systems, traditional road and transport systems, the historic buildings and open spaces, the trees and vegetation cover, etc. Over and above these aspects of the physical environment, a documentation of living traditions and intangible heritage should also be conducted. This includes festivals, *yatras*, etc. All these aspects must form the basis for any sectoral planning, be it housing, road infrastructure, water and sanitation or economic planning. In CDPs too, therefore, Heritage cannot be reduced to and addressed through the Heritage Sectoral Plan only. It was suggested that every Sectoral Plan should, in the future, have a heritage component.

Furthermore, UNESCO suggested that the CDP toolkit needs to outline a clear link from establishing a vision for the city, to creating Sectoral plans and developing DPRs. In between the CDP, which is essentially the vision document, and the DPR, there needs to be a stronger emphasis on the intermediate planning level at the sector level. This level shall help, on the basis of the CDP, to prepare the required detailing to develop the DPRs. For the heritage sector such a plan may be called the Heritage Management Plan. UNESCO also emphasized the need to establish the inter-sectoral and intra-sectoral linkages before developing the sectoral plans.

The JNNURM Technical Cell is currently finalizing the CDP Toolkit with the above mentioned revisions as suggested by the expert team under the umbrella of UNESCO-IHCN. There is a growing realization that all cities in India have a significant heritage component. It was therefore decided that the (new, revised) general CDP Toolkit shall be inclusive of 'heritage resource based development' for all cities. The JNNURM Mission Directorate now proposes to ask all 63 cities (including the 11 heritage cities) to realign their CDPs as per this toolkit since all earlier CDPs were found lacking in several aspects, heritage being one of them.

Next Steps

UNESCO-IHCN is currently pursuing the other stages of the joint project, this includes the preparation of the Toolkit for heritage related DPRs and the CDP Reviews of four Mission cities. The proposed Heritage DPR Toolkit shall be generic in nature and relevant to all Mission cities. It aims to ensure that no project within or in the vicinity of heritage areas in any city should damage the heritage resources. Besides that, the review of CDPs of four Mission cities is also being undertaken, to provide UNESCO and the JNNURM with more data on the question of how heritage has so far been integrated in the JNNURM process. The evaluation of the four CDPs and the Heritage DPR Toolkit shall be presented at the proposed capacity building workshop to be jointly organized by MoUD and UNESCO for the Urban Local Bodies (ULBs) later this year.

6. Beyond the JNNURM

The CDPs and DPRs of the JNNURM provide a first great opportunity to integrate heritage into the aspects of urban development and planning. It is however necessary that heritage becomes a part of all elements of the Mission. This includes the administrative reforms prescribed in the JNNURM for all cities. The various experiences of Indian cities to include heritage officers or a Heritage Cell, coupled with a Heritage Committee giving technical advice, is of great importance to learn how best to integrate the protection, conservation and management of natural and cultural heritage resources in the administration of a city.

The JNNURM is a programme that will one day be over. What remains is the regular planning system and, on the basis of the 73rd and 74th CAA, the decentralized and community based governance. Heritage awareness, tools for protection and management, technical and administrative capacities must therefore be built in each state and each city. The JNNURM may lead the way, but more energy is required to develop heritage legislation, appropriate amendments to current legal and administrative frameworks, and heritage friendly Master Plans.

A large majority of India's unprotected cultural heritage lies at the mercy of the insensitive national heritage legislation that does not look beyond monument centric objects, artifacts and antiquities. Adding to this complexity are the narrow-visioned Town and Country Planning Acts, a State activity whereby Master plans and other supporting plans (like Zonal and Local Area Plans) are drawn up by the recognized Development Authorities.

The District Planning Committees (DPCs) created as per the Constitution of India for planning at the District level, is a key tool to promote decentralization in the country. The DPCs entail the preparation of integrated development plans for infrastructure, keeping in view the available physical and natural resources of the place.

Successful changes in a heritage rich country like India can only be undertaken if significant changes in the state level programs and policies are introduced, which are in tune with national priorities and vice versa. A cultural approach to development whereby heritage becomes an integral component of these planning documents, as well as heritage sensitive legislation that prevents freezing of historic sites is the need of the hour. It is imperative that heritage experts be included in the processes involved in the formation of these Plans, thereby ensuring holistic and integrated development and conservation of the concerned areas. Consistent efforts should also be made to improve the capacity of the ULBs, the development and planning authorities, the departments of tourism and culture etc. to inculcate heritage sensitivity in all aspects of their work.

Session 3

Focus on Legal, Financial and Managerial Issues

Urban Management Issues: Mumbai

Ms. Abha Narain Lambah - Conservation Architect

The urban fabric of Mumbai is held together by the tenuous warp and weft of historic buildings and modern in fills, strained with the overlay of the needs and aspirations of its millions, virtually bursting at the seams. In this bustling metropolitan city where the historic fabric is also the centre of the downtown business district, the upmarket residential areas and the focus of dizzying real estate values, the pressures of urbanization constantly influence the fundamental equation between the old and the new, threatening to change the delicate balance between conservation and development. This dichotomy of the past and present is an unavoidable reality and yet, it is this interface between the past and the present, the historic and the modern, that makes for the intriguing dynamics within the city.

In 1995, Bombay established itself as the first Indian city to adopt heritage regulations for the protection of its urban heritage. As per the Heritage Regulations for Greater Bombay 1995, 633 entries listed architectural heritage ranging from monumental public buildings to neighbourhood landmarks and entire urban precincts, protecting them from demolition and regulating the developmental interventions to their built fabric. The urban fabric was further delineated into heritage precincts like the Fort area and Banganga, defining entire neighbourhoods as areas of urban significance and historic value, therefore worthy of preservation.

The Heritage Regulations for Greater Bombay were framed and gazetted on 20th February 1991. This was the first gazette for inviting objections and suggestions, and finally published in 1995. As per the Maharashtra Government Notification No. DCR 1090/3197/RDP/UD – II dated 21st April 1995, a publication titled "Heritage Regulations for Greater Bombay" enumerated buildings, structures, fountains, open spaces and precinct under various categories of Grade I, II and III, for formal protection by the state. The regulation came into force on 1st June 1995 and with subsequent notifications, now includes 574 buildings, 1 public open space, 14 milestones and 18 precincts that qualify for protection under the regulation.

The regulation was thus successful in not only protecting vulnerable historic building stock, but also in acknowledging colonial heritage and urban grouping of buildings as worthy of preservation. Moreover, it recognized the need to continually reconfigure a city, along with the reality of its living, breathing buildings, that were unlike many cities that confined monuments to museum pieces, functioning public structures such as railway stations, courts and libraries.

The regulation thus did not place a complete freeze on the listed heritage, but allowed for a grading procedure whereby structures placed in the elite Grade I list merited "strict preservation" both to their internal and external features, those under the Grade II category allowed for some internal modifications while Grade III structures had a greater degree of flexibility for alterations. To monitor these changes, the Heritage

Committee, an advisory body consisting of experts from a range of fields such as urban history, conservation, archaeology, engineering and architecture, was established to judge each case on its merits, with reference to the grading and significance of each structure.

Given the position of Bombay as the financial centre of the country, this had tremendous repercussions for the Fort precinct and many such historic quarters located in south Bombay. These areas had the highest real estate prices in the country and thus were under the greatest pressure of urban development and modern skyscrapers, threatening to entirely engulf, if not obliterate the fragile historic fabric. The Heritage Legislation was thus successful in accomplishing a colossal task, enabling the preservation of a considerable amount of building stock that would have been lost to the pressures of urbanization.

Much remains to be done to make the conservation movement a success in the city when we take stock of the situation ten years into this pioneering regulation. Today we have a well structured regulation in place, but what seems most lacking, is the political will and administrative backing to support this regulatory framework. Heritage listing protects listed buildings from demolition, but it cannot prevent a building from ruination through sheer neglect, if not willful destruction. The heritage regulation acknowledges and protects the vernacular built heritage and private buildings, but there are no fiscal incentives to help private owners to restore and maintain their heritage properties. While the Heritage Committee is an advisory body to review development proposals concerning heritage buildings, it has neither basic infrastructure of staff, website or permanent office to undertake much needed vigilance, nor budgetary allocations to make financial grants in support of deserving projects of conservation in the city. And, though guidelines for heritage precincts such as Khotachiwadi, Bandra, Marine Drive, Opera House and

Mahalakshmi have been prepared years ago, bureaucratic red tape has prevented these from being notified to make them operational and effective.

For any conservation policy to be effective, it is imperative to create a balance between issues of architectural concern and those of urban infrastructure through the co-ordination of various involved agencies, planning and legislative bodies and government organizations. This also needs to have an amply broad public base to ensure its implementation at the grass-root level. A well defined Management Strategy for each area supported by public-private-partnerships in implementation would help create a support system for the more concentrated efforts at individual architectural restoration, involving local participation to assist the efforts of the specialist conservationists. While some NGOs have prepared individual management strategies for areas like Ballard Estate, Horniman Circle and Kala Ghoda with the help of the local citizen groups, much more needs to be done to take this to a level of city wide policy and implementation.

A vision for the city's heritage would begin in fact with the way development plans are sanctioned in the city. Transparency in civic governance should be the first priority – where a citizen can check on a website, any information on development rules, building permissions and where a *babu* has kept his file without being made to run in circles. This would ensure a clear transparency on what building is proposed to be demolished, which new addition is coming up in an old area, whether this will impact the infrastructure of that locality, or the aesthetic quality of that streetscape. Moreover, citizens should be given greater powers to take action in their local areas.

A critical next step should be that of incentivizing heritage preservation and creating economic policies to support conservation. Innovative tax incentives for restoring heritage buildings, funds for heritage preservation and financial mechanisms such as soft loans are the need of the hour for the vast bulk of the city's buildings constructed before 1947. The idea is to understand that historic stock is an asset, not a liability and merely requires innovative financial mechanisms to make it economically sustainable. Tax breaks for restoring private buildings and financial tools for restoring and retaining heritage would ensure a greater public involvement in restoration and a trend towards innovative reuse of heritage properties rather than demolition and reconstruction.

Innovative urban level schemes and pilot projects are also needed to revitalize the city's urban assets. Iconic urban plazas such as those around Flora Fountain, Horniman Circle and Nagar Chowk offer a tremendous opportunity for pioneering urban innovations and pilot schemes for revitalization. The historic Crawford Market has a remarkable potential for adaptive reuse and revival along the lines of Boston's Quincy Market and schemes of re-invigorating areas such as Ballard Estate after office hours should be taken up on the anvil for a holistic economic revival of the historic inner city. Innovative urban solutions such as night bazaars in heritage precincts, illumination of Victorian streetscapes and well designed hawker plazas as seen in Singapore and Bangkok are possibilities that require enormous brain storming and public debate but could also offer solutions for economically sustainable urban solutions. Initiatives in the field of alternative transport systems and pedestrian zones in areas such as Bora Bazaar, Rampart Row, Banganga should be explored and pilot projects to assess their viability should be initiated.

While cities like Shanghai, Bangkok and Kuala Lumpur in Asia have adopted an aggressive, all out policy to woo tourists and tourism dollars, Mumbai is still rather laid back in tapping this immense economic potential. Even with two world heritage sites of Victoria Terminus and

Elephanta, it is still largely perceived as a financial and business destination unlike other cities that use a UNESCO World Heritage Site listing as a major advertising and earning opportunity through heritage tourism.

In 1999, an amendment to Development Control Regulation 33 (7) rendered nearly 300 Grade III buildings on the Heritage List and precincts out of the protective ambit of the Heritage Regulation. This allows a Cessed building to be demolished without requiring Heritage Committee clearance and to be replaced with a modern building with extra FSI, severely threatening the survival of historic areas such as Khotachiwadi and Marine Drive where 50 to 65% of the buildings are Cessed. Repeal of this amendment along with sensitive repair guidelines adopted by the MHADA Repair Board would give a new lease of life to the hundreds of vulnerable buildings threatened by imminent destruction today.

The decentralization and Panchayati Raj model is perhaps best suited for our metropolitan city, at least in the field of civic improvement. Local Area Management Committees and citizen associations such as Kala Ghoda Association, Bandra Welfare Association, D.N. Road's Heritage Mile Association, Horniman Circle Association have demonstrated the efficacy of community driven models in fund raising, maintaining, restoring and improving local neighbourhoods. So, why not give them greater powers to co-ordinate efforts of the various service providers in the area and strengthen this system with adequate legislation.

Heritage and Urban Renewal–Legislative and Policy Requirements

Shri Shyam Chainani - Secretary, Mumbai Environmental Action Group

Urban Destruction

What is happening in India is not urban renewal but urban destruction.

Government departments, other agencies and NGOs who are involved in issues like garbage disposal, cleaning their localities, improving infrastructure and so on are silent when the whole of their towns and surroundings are being ripped up.

We have not yet understood how the on-coming massive urbanization will affect us, It will hit us with a bang. What is worrying is the sheer irreversibility of it all. People seem completely unworried about their and their children's future.

The very character of our towns has changed – irrevocably. City after city, town after town, hill station after hill station have been ravaged and the process is going on at full speed. Before we discuss renewal, we must first fully understand the problem and hence a discussion of some towns is necessary.

Bombay

The example of Bombay, the Gateway of India, and the country's leading city, is relevant. I mention it in some detail since similar situations prevail in other cities and towns.

Many years ago, in the United Services Club Library, I stumbled across the autobiography of James Halliday, a British officer of the Indian Civil Service (ICS), who in 1938 had acted for a few months as Municipal Commissioner of Bombay. I was astounded when, in his autobiography "A Special India", I read his description of Bombay. After talking of the physical comforts and pleasures of Bombay after years spent in districts he says "Apart from such worldly and carnal satisfactions, and in fact more than them, I enjoyed my job. Bombay was a well-ordered place, and in many ways independent from the rest of the Province and of India. Its climate was not good: humid and hot, or humid and wet. But, except for that, it seemed to me the nearest thing to a Greek City State that the modern world could show. It was not only its beauty, set like a jewel in the surrounding waters of the Indian Ocean, and the wooded beauty of its harbour; it was its internal organization also that gave the impression. It had its own magistracy; its own sheriff; its own very fine police force, distinctively uniformed in blue with yellow turbans, under a separate Commissioner of Police; its own Port Trust; and its own town services which functioned under the direct control of the Commissioner and under the remoter, policy-making supervision of the Mayor and Corporation".

James Halliday describes Malabar Hill's Mount Pleasant Road, as it was in the early 1940s, as being "one of the precipitous roads that fell from the ridge of Malabar Hill to the sea in a cascade of wisteria, hibiscus and bougainvillea flowing over stucco garden walls. One gets glimpses of such roads in old Sam Remo or Estoril."

James Halliday's descriptions were perhaps valid for the next decade and a half. Till the mid 1950s Bombay, (or parts of it), could still perhaps be described as a beautiful city. With fine buildings, broad streets, leafy roads, infrastructure that worked, beautiful suburbs like Bandra and Juhu, and a generally civilized atmosphere, it was the envy of most. Malabar Hill and Cumballa Hill were still places in which one could stroll for pleasure, as I used to do.

However, in the last four decades the pace of construction (and destruction of heritage and environment) has gone on without check.. The bungalows, heritage structures, trees and gardens which gave a special character to Malabar Hill, Cumballa Hill, Bandra, Juhu and many other beautiful areas – areas which were far more attractive than the standardized Lutyens Delhi – were virtually totally and ruthlessly demolished and replaced by unplanned high rise concrete jungles, which are characterized by pollution, traffic congestion and no open spaces. The resemblances to Sam Remo and Estoril were obliterated. All this happened without a whimper of protest from the citizens. In the case of Lutyens Delhi, Prime Minister Rajiv Gandhi issued tight written conservation directives in February 1988; these directives have preserved its unique character. In Bombay there was, sadly, no Chief Minister or official whose conception extended to anything remotely like that. The same process has taken place in and devastated other historical and garden cities and towns in India – Bangalore, Poona, Hyderabad, Calcutta, Simla, Dehra Dun and so on. James Halliday would get a terrible shock if he was to visit Bombay today.

Poona

I know this city very well. I was five, when at Independence, my father became the first Indian Divisional Commissioner. It was a garden city. At an altitude of 1800 feet, well away from the coast, without the humidity of Bombay and surrounded by hills, it has a climate and ambience quite different from that of Bombay. Nights in winter are quite chilly and the rainfall is far less than that on the coast. The Pune A to Z says that it has 'the bracing climate of a hill station'. Its climate was such, that for the army, it was a 'non-fan' station – where fans were not authorized. It was called the pensioners' paradise. With its lovely bungalows, large gardens, broad roads with large old trees and quaint central streets, it had a hill station atmosphere specially in the champagne monsoon weather of the Deccan Plateau, because of which it was the monsoon capital of the Bombay Presidency. Till a couple of decades ago, it was one of the hill stations of Bombay, and it was very common for people to go to Poona for a change of scene and climate. My family used to do the same. I used to love going there.

Today, Poona is very different and makes one want to weep. It is no more a hill station or a non-fan station. Except for the Cantonment, it has less open spaces than Bombay. Its hill slopes, hill tops and river banks which gave it its character, are being fast built up. Its character is like one of the many nondescript Bombay suburbs. It has the disadvantages of a small town with few of its advantages. I have to go there for work and I try not to stir outside the cantonment.

Bangalore

It was a garden city, with houses perhaps even finer than those of Poona. It, too, used to be a hill station Many people used to go to Bangalore to escape the heat. At an altitude of 3300 feet, Bangalore was described by Sir Mirza Ismail, Dewan of the former princely state of Mysore for many years as having "an equable climate all the year round which could be described briefly as one requiring neither fan nor fire". He wrote of its two monsoons "with an annual rainfall of 35 inches which keeps it green almost throughout the year, except in the months of March and April." He describes: "The flowering trees in their gorgeous colours – the blue and mauve jacaranda, the pink and red cassias, the yellow peltophorums, the pink largestrocmias, the plumirias, and the gold mohur, its whole top crowned with a mass of red flowers." Not surprisingly, Bangalore was also a pensioners' paradise.

Today the situation is quite different. Bangalore is one of India's five metropolitan cities with huge population. Most of the private gardens have been built over, the bulk of the civic heritage which gave Bangalore its charm has been destroyed, and what remains is fast being overshadowed by high rise construction. According to Maya Jayapal, the number of tanks has gone down from 262 in the 1960s to 82. The drive to 'modernise', make it an I.T. city and so on have destroyed much of Bangalore's environment. It can hardly be called a hill station any more. While one guidebook says that "it continues to be the summer resort to many", others say the opposite since the massive constructions and industrialization have raised the temperature. Maya Jayapal writes "Once a retreat for pensioners, and the summer-weary from neighbouring Tamil Nadu and Andhra Pradesh, it now has its residents fleeing to cooler climes in the summer months of March, April and May." If I had known Bangalore as well as I had known Poona, I am sure my tears would have been even more copious. However in spite of the obliteration of most of its heritage, and the change in its climate, it is still a pleasant city.

Delhi

In 1911, I wonder whether the Viceroy, Lord Hardinge and the British Government realised the impact on Delhi when they decided to shift the capital there from Calcutta.

Many of us remember Delhi as recently as 30 or 40 years ago. What has happened here is scandalous, with many of its priceless Moghul and pre-Moghul monuments either having vanished or having gleaming residential colonies built cheek-by-jowl with them. The process is continuing.

What happened in the past was bad enough. What is happening now is far worse. The building of the Metro Rail is going ahead apparently without any concern or regard for archaeological damage. In its various incarnations, Delhi has been an imperial capital for several centuries with a still surviving built heritage on the ground of at least 800 years vintage. What is below ground is likely to be of still greater vintage. The very least that can be done is to have a proper archaeological survey before digging so that these irreplaceable priceless heritage artifacts and remnants of our history and culture are not needlessly obliterated.

What has happened in the Ridge, with twelve 5 Star hotels being planned, in an area of 1000 hectares is scandalous.

What has happened in Lutyens Delhi, where our revered leaders and others are making unauthorized extensions and changes, is well known.

Hyderabad

This fabled historical city of the Asaf Jahis was known the world over for the Nizams, its exquisite buildings, its lifestyle and its cuisine.

The last ruling Nizam died in 1967, the lifestyles have vanished, and it is tragic that all that now survives of the Hyderabadi style is its cuisine. Much of its centuries old Qutb Shahi and Asaf Jahi period heritage has been demolished. Several of the lakebeds, including those of lakes dating from Qutb Shahi times, have been built over by housing societies. In addition several of the lakes have been converted into municipal parks. Much of its topography, including the rocks and boulders which mark its terrain, has been flattened. Will the remaining physical heritage survive to tell the history of this famous, fabled, once royal capital?

Former Andhra Pradesh Chief Minister Chandrababu Naidu has been the darling of many for his initiatives including turning Hyderabad into "Cyberabad". No one realizes or cares that all this has completely changed Hyderabad's character. Barring a few areas, it resembles any other large modern city.

Bhopal

Bhopal was a beautiful royal capital of the state bearing its name. Pre independence, Bhopal was a city of heritage buildings and lakes. The prominent Motia Tank had channels leading to a second lake which had channels leading to the lowest one, the Hussaini Tank. It must have been a sight to see.

To its great misfortune, Bhopal became the capital of Madhya Pradesh when that state was formed. It is heart rending to see that comparatively little survives of its character. Many, if not most, of its princely era heritage buildings have been destroyed. As regards the water bodies, the fountains have long stopped working, the overflow channels between the lakes are now blocked, and the lakes themselves are being gradually and illegally filled up.

Dehra Dun

Dehra Dun, at a height of 2300 feet is 32 kilometres from Mussoorie and is the gateway to the famous hill station.

Lord Hardinge, Viceroy of India from 1910 to 1916, described Dehra Dun as being "a beautiful and most delightful place at the foot of the Himalayas with snow-capped mountains only a few miles distant". He added that "Dehra Dun is the place that I liked best in India, and of which I have the happiest memories." A quarter of a century after Lord Hardinge, Lord Linlithgow thought similarly of Dehra Dun, with his son and biographer describing it as having been "a favourite haunt of his".

When the new state of Uttaranchal was formed, there was much jockeying between the two distinct regions of Kumaon and Garhwal as to where the state capital should be located. To its great misfortune, Dehra Dun was chosen.

There was a cry from the heart by G.R. Vora in his letter of *12th April 2003 to the Times of India:*

"It is with horror that we observe the systematic obliteration of the greenery and the natural topography of the once pristine town of Dehra Dun since it became the capital of the new state of Uttaranchal three years ago. What was the need to nominate this town, replete with greenery and wildlife, as the state capital? Wasn't there any other town that could host our not-so-honourable politicians and their entourage for going about the business of managing this state?

"The beautiful jacarandas, the narrow winding lanes lined with lush green trees and chirping birds, old canals – the heritage landmarks from the 18th century, the water mills and the lichi and mango orchards will soon vanish from Dehra Dun's skyline. No amount of flower shows by the governor's office in the attempt to evoke love for the environment is going to undo the mass destruction unleashed upon Dehra Dun in the name of development by the powers-that-be."

Ranchi

The case of Ranchi is interesting. At an altitude of 2100 feet, during the British Raj, it was the summer capital of Bihar and the Headquarters of the Army's Eastern Command. It was considered to be a health resort. In books on hill stations, it is mentioned as one. Apparently, people from Jamshedpur, from Calcutta and elsewhere used to go to Ranchi and Hazaribagh – 107 km north of Ranchi – for holidays.

Ranchi too has become a capital city – that of Jharkhand state. One can only hope that Ranchi, in its new *avatar,* will be spared the fate of Dehra Dun. However the signs are not good. *The Sunday Express of 15th June 2003* mentions the obvious differences – removal of potholes from the roads, better air connectivity, plans for a five star hospital and so on. However the press item goes on to say that "to a large section of the city's populace, all this is window-dressing. 'It was never so bad even during Laloo Raj", says Anju Chatterjee, an octogenarian born and brought up in the city. "The civic facilities are abysmal. Filth and garbage lie about everywhere." In addition land prices have doubled."

Raipur

With the creation of Chhatisgarh state, Raipur from, a Revenue Divisional Headquarters, became the state capital.

When I went there in 2001, the first impact was beginning to be felt. Among other things, heritage buildings were being destroyed and out of 120 water bodies, only 20 survived.

Accidental Protection

We think our towns are lovely – but the few remaining beautiful areas are protected mainly by accident. To give one example, in Bombay, though the historic core – the Fort and its environs – still retains much of its character, this is not because of any great concern for heritage or any environmental consciousness on the part of the hard-headed commercial community which owned/controlled/worked in the Fort but purely accidentally because of several factors.

These factors included:

a) Rent Control

If a landlord could not get his tenants out, he could not redevelop or demolish his building. Whatever the merits and demerits of Rent

Control there is no doubt that it was, to a large measure, responsible for saving by far the most important part of Bombay's built heritage.

b) Floor Space Index (FSI)

Most, if not all, the buildings in the Fort area had consumed more than the permissible FSI. The permissible FSI at that time in the Fort, Ballard Estate etc. was 2.45 whereas most of the buildings had already consumed an FSI of 3, 4 or even higher. If these buildings had been demolished and re-built, they would have had to be re-built to the prevailing lower FSI – a highly uneconomic proposition.

c) BMRDA Notification of 10th June 1977

The Bombay Metropolitan Region Development Authority (BMRDA) issued a notification on 10th June, 1997 by virtue of which

(i) the FSI throughout Greater Bombay was (with a few exceptions) fixed at a maximum of 1.33 or to that permitted in the Development Control Rules (whichever was lower).

(ii) Construction or reconstruction of buildings to house offices and commercial establishments was prohibited in the island city. It is difficult to assess how far this notification went to prevent the destruction of heritage buildings, but it was certainly a further disincentive to demolish heritage buildings in the Fort and adjacent areas.

d) Lease Conditions of Bombay Port Trust and Other Lease Conditions

In the early 1970's, the Royal Bombay Yacht Club (not to be confused with the Old Yacht Club building which belongs unfortunately to the Department of Atomic Energy) had a plan to demolish their club house (now listed at Serial No.92 in the Bombay Heritage List as a yellow stone building of 1898 having both architectural value and value as part of a group of buildings and therefore listed as Grade II-A). The proposal as mentioned by the Club President at an Annual General Meeting was to demolish the building, replace it by a high rise commercial building and relocate the public rooms of the Club on the top two or three floors. This plan was, fortunately for Bombay's heritage, not proceeded with; this was not because of any concern for heritage, but because the building is on Bombay Port Trust leased land, which apparently made the whole scheme unviable (The BMRDA notification referred to above would have also probably squashed the scheme). However, times change; the Royal Bombay Yacht Club and its members are now very proud of their old building, and view its period nature as a precious asset; the Club is one of the few organizations which engaged a conservation architect to prepare a master plan.

e) Public Ownership

Public ownership of many of the buildings and the innate conservatism of and lack of funds with Government agencies also helped to slow down the demolition of publicly owned heritage buildings. But even here there were signs of 'progress'.

The Fort Precinct, the vast art deco Marine Drive Heritage Precinct (which consists of large areas in addition to Marine Drive and which has been rated as one of the finest art deco collections in the world), the Heritage Precincts of Gamdevi, Khotachiwadi, Matharpakhadi, Opera House, Gateway, Majestic, Museum, University, Esplanade, Fountain, Horniman Circle, Ballard Pier, Bazargate, V.T., B.M.C, Crawford Market, Oval and many other areas all survive because of these restrictions.

These restrictions were, however, designed for other purposes and with their removal, heritage demolition is proceeding apace.

In addition to the vanishing accidental protection, what is needed is protection by law ie. regulations for conservation of heritage, both built and natural, together with other measures such as reduction in the permissible FSI.

Urban Renewal

One dictionary definition of the word 'renew' includes the word 'restore' However, what is going on under the current Urban Renewal Schemes is not restoration but large schemes savouring more of concretization. The 'renewal' projects include large sewage disposal projects, road construction, road transport systems, bus terminals, multi-storied car parking, road widening, slum clearance and so on.

It needs to be clearly understood that our towns and cities cannot be saved without developing our rural areas. The money that is being poured into our urban areas – slum housing, roads, other infrastructure – will only attract more people into our towns and cities, is no solution at all, and may well make matters worse. Grandiose schemes, such as making Bombay the financial capital of India or a second Shanghai will only make it the slum capital of India.

The objective should be to improve conditions in our rural areas and take jobs back to the rural areas to reduce, then halt, and eventually reverse the migration from rural to urban areas. Non capital intensive schemes such as wasteland development, contour bunding, soil protection, erosion prevention and so on will create jobs, and prove to be a desperately necessary investment in the country's agricultural infrastructure, along with improving the environment. Similarly there should be stress on drinking water, sanitation, rural housing and so on.

The Jawaharlal Nehru National Urban Renewal Mission should expand its focus to cover rural improvement as well. The name should be changed to Jawaharlal Nehru National Human Settlements Mission.

On the one hand we claim to be 'renewing'; simultaneously many policies are destroying our urban fabric.

Under road widening schemes, many heritage buildings have been destroyed and heritage precincts devastated. Similarly many of the other facilities affect heritage buildings and precincts. Under the guise of slum clearance, large swathes of our history are being wiped out as has happened in several areas, with Nanded being a prime recent example.

It is said that the JNNURM is not about infrastructure, but about reforms. What sort of reforms are they imposing? Some suggested conditionalities are mentioned below.

What needs to be done now in the urban renewal process (specially in the Jawaharlal Nehru National Urban Renewal Mission) is that measures to protect heritage need to be taken on an urgent basis. The most important of this is the enactment of suitable legislative measures to protect our heritage.

Under the JNNURM schemes, Government of India often makes stipulations on subjects in the 'State' list of the Constitution, such as reviews of the property tax regime, removal of rent control legislation and so on. It would be far more appropriate for Government of India's ministry of urban development to take up the matter with the state governments requesting them to enact heritage regulations in their states. Urban Development ministry must also make enactment of heritage regulations a mandatory condition for availing of grants under the JNNURM Scheme.

Floor Space Index (FSI) / Floor Area Ratio (FAR)

More than 20 years ago, when the Ajit Kerkar committee was set up to consider the question of slums and FSI in Bombay, Maharashtra Government Urban Development Secretary L.C. Gupta made the point that FSI / FAR is a planning tool and not a numbers game by which FSI can be increased at whim to please vested interests. Tinkering with FSI will have the most serious consequences.

The high permissible FSI in our own town centres, particularly in heritage precincts, is resulting in a great deal of heritage demolition. This FSI needs to be drastically reduced if not frozen, to what is currently consumed. The plot owners can be recompensed by grant of TDR (Transferable Development Rights). Under no circumstances should the permissible FSI / FAR, especially in inner cities and heritage areas, be increased. This should be a specific condition laid down.

De-congestion

If we are concerned about, and spending so much money on urban renewal we must at all costs stop the further growth of our megapolis and large cities.

Traffic Congestion

Though this is the age of high technology and I was educated at three "high tech" universities, I have not heard of any technique by which one can compress human beings. Yet we continue to build more and more in smaller areas without thought of how people will move. My friends keep telling me that New York and London work with high FSIs and high densities. However both those cities have efficient underground railway systems, efficient bus networks, and systems that work. Can the same be said about Bombay, Delhi, Calcutta, Patna, Meerut and so on?

In New York, massive demolition of buildings took place for creating freeways. In Bombay, my city, it is impossible to demolish high rise buildings in order to widen the road. When a flyover was planned on Peddar Road – which is one of the two north-south traffic arteries of Bombay – even though no buildings were to be demolished, there were huge citizens protests. Lata Mangeshkar threatened to leave India. The local residents felt that they were being made to suffer for the benefit of other commuters.

A few years ago there was an article in the Times of India which was entitled *"Now, Kurla shopkeepers hum Lata's road tune – Say proposed Santa Cruz-Chembur Link Road Will Ruin Them"*

I repeat the first two paras of the press item. This says:

"Mumbai: If singing legends Lata Mangeshkar, Asha Bhosale and their neighbours could block the proposed viaduct passing through Peddar Road, residents of Kurla's Gazi Nagar feel they can do the same with the 11-km Santa Cruz-Chembur link road (SCLR) project.

Threatened by the prospect of losing their livelihood under the Mumbai Urban Transport Project (MUTP), around 250 shop-keepers in the area have come together under the United Shop Owners' Association and urged the Mumbai Metropolitan Region Development Authority (MMRDA) to stall the project. They have cited the case of the Pedder Road viaduct which was scrapped at the behest of Lata and Asha. In fact, Asha had threatened to relocate to Dubai if the project was not halted.

As more and more buildings are built, with ever higher FSI being permitted, and buildings (like the famous World War II fighter pilot Douglas Bader) reaching for the skies, how will people move? We may well reach a situation where going by car will be slower than walking. These huge megalopolises are extremely vulnerable and have exceeded their limits of growth.

Regularizations

We can never hope to have a decent urban environment if we continue to regularize illegal structures and unauthorized extensions to buildings. Delhi takes the cake in this regard. We can never hope to regulate slums if illegal housing colonies of the affluent (like Sainik Farms) are regularized.

In 1983-84 Bombay was rocked by the FSI fraud scandal. By various ingenious methods, the builders managed to get extra FSI by fraudulently purported to increase the area of their plots. On the principle that one must go for the heart, we filed writ petitions against five such buildings. We were successful in getting demolition action in the case of three buildings located in the most expensive areas of Bombay. One was the famous Pratibha building where the top eight floors of a thirty six storey building were ordered to be demolished. At that time there was much talk about how so-called national resources were being wasted and the builders should be let off with a fine and so on. However six storeys were demolished; till the remaining two are demolished, the bottom 28 floors cannot be occupied.

A few years later, we got an order for the demolition of an entire building called Arihant (at the bottom of Peddar Road) which had been built in the open space of another building. The Supreme Court upheld the demolition action. Very shortly thereafter, holes were made in the ceilings and the building made unusable. I will never forget what happened thereafter. At the Bombay Gymkhana, one of my sister's friends whom I barely knew, said that her liftman was very happy with the Arihant demolition. I was puzzled and asked how he was concerned. Apparently the liftman had said that everybody was demolishing their 'jhopdis' (huts) which they accepted. This was the first time that action had been taken against 'amir log' (rich people). She said that I should never think that the message has not gone through.

When structures are regularized, the reverse message goes through.

The position was beautifully summarized by the Supreme Court. Dhananjay Mahapatra writing in the *Times of India on 28th August 2009* in his article entitled *'Ruling class is protecting builders : SC'* reported that 'Stalling of the demolition and sealing drive against illegal buildings and encroachments in Delhi by a Parliament enacted a law came in for sharp criticism from the Supreme Court, which said the protection given to wrong doers by the ruling class has irreparably harmed planned development'.

"Because of the encouragement and support from the state apparatus, the powerful construction lobby has shown scant regard to repeated anti-encroachment orders of the Supreme Court and the High Courts and also to the master plans and zonal development plans", said a Bench of Justices B N Agarwal and G S Singhvi.

"As when the courts have passed orders or the officers of the local and other bodies have taken action for ensuring rigorous compliance of laws relating to planned development of the cities and urban areas and issued directions for demolition of illegal / unauthorized constructions, those in power have come forward to protect the wrong doers by issuing administrative orders or enacting laws for regularization of illegal and unauthorized constructions in the name of compassion and hardship', the Bench said.

Writing for the Bench, Justice Singhvi said such protection has irreparably harmed the concept of planned development of cities and urban areas.

"It is high time that the executive and political apparatus of the State take serious view of the menace of illegal and unauthorized constructions and stop their support to the lobbies of affluent builders and others, else even the rural areas of the country will soon witness similar chaotic situation," the Bench said.

Non regularization of illegal structures and developments needs be made a condition for disbursement of a JNNURM grant.

Location Specific Tax

Since nowadays great reliance is placed on the market and the JNNURM, surely the market can be used to save our towns. To prevent further congestion and strain on civic amenities, we have for long recommended a Location Specific Tax. This would have several simple indices.

The first index would be the location. A city can be divided into several zones with the most congested area (or the one causing maximum strain on civic services eg. Nariman Point in Bombay or perhaps Connaught Place in Delhi) having the highest rate of tax. The second index would be the area occupied by the office/industry. The third index could be the number of people occupied in that locality. The fourth, a more complicated one, could be the value added.

This Location Specific Tax would serve as a disincentive for people to locate commercial and industrial activities in congested parts of urban areas and should be coupled with an incentive to locate units in other areas.

What is Heritage?

Monuments and heritage sites

There seems to be considerable misunderstanding as to what constitutes 'heritage', more specifically 'physical heritage'. In most peoples' minds, built heritage consists only of 'monuments' – as if there is no other form of built heritage. To see the situation in the correct perspective, it would be instructive to look at just two figures. In England, there are over 19,000 'Scheduled Monuments'; as opposed to that there are 500,000 listed buildings and 10,000 Conservation Areas which enjoy statutory heritage protection. The USA would have relatively few monuments, but as compared to that they have listed 1.40 million 'contributing resources' in their National Register.

A few examples would illustrate the distinction between monuments and heritage sites.

The Taj Mahal, Red Fort, Elephanta, Khajurao to Ajanta, Ellora are monuments. Rashtrapati Bhavan, North Block, South Block, Connaught Place in Delhi, Raj Bhavan, the Maidan and Chowringhee in Calcutta, Marine Drive in Bombay, Marina Beach in Madras are not monuments, they are prime heritage sites.

Natural heritage sites must not be forgotten. In many places, like Kashmir, the hill stations of Munnar, Ranikhet, Landour, Pachmarhi, Mahabaleshwar, Panchgani, Matheran and the backwaters of Kerala, there are natural heritage sites that are more significant than man-made heritage.

World Heritage Sites

The emphasis of international bodies such as UNESCO, World Monuments Fund and so on is only on key monuments such as on the approximately 700 sites and areas which have been designated as 'World

Heritage' sites – ignoring the more than 99.99% of heritage that has not been so designated. Thus a participant from the Philippines at an international seminar in Japan said repeatedly that her country had five 'heritage sites'. She was of course referring to the five World Heritage sites in her country. It had to be pointed out that her country's heritage consisted of far more than that.

Minimum Age

It would perhaps be best to define the physical heritage that we seek to preserve. I keep getting asked as to how old a building has to be to be classified as a heritage building. To clarify a misconception, there is no minimum age for a building to be classified as a heritage building. The India International Centre would definitely be a heritage structure. Some feel that Le Corbuser's Chandigarh is a heritage ensemble. In London, Battersea Power Station is a prime heritage site. Many of New York's skyscrapers, a freight terminal and the TWA Terminal have been designated as 'Historic Landmarks' (Heritage buildings).

Heritage Definition

It is not just man-made artefacts which are heritage sites but also natural sites of environmental significance and sites of scenic beauty. A good definition could be as adapted from the latest definition approved by the Maharashtra Government. *This adapted definition would read as:* 'buildings, artefacts, structures, areas and precincts of historic and/ or aesthetic and/or architectural and/or cultural significance and natural features of environmental significance and/or of scenic beauty including but not restricted to sacred groves, hills, hillocks, water bodies (and the areas adjoining the same), open areas, wooded areas etc'.

Heritage Protection In India – Current Status

India's record in heritage protection is very poor. Monuments are supposed to be protected by the Archaeological Survey of India (ASI) and the various State Departments of Archaeology. Between them all these Departments of Archaeology protect (theoretically) only about 7000 monuments. Though the ASI is one of the largest archaeological departments in the world – we protect perhaps only 1 to 3 % of the estimated number of monuments in India. As opposed to that England has over 19,000 'Scheduled Monuments', representing over 36,000 archaeological items. Having regard only to India's size – leave alone its richer and far more varied history – we should have at least 475,000 protected monuments.

Coming to non-monumental heritage, our record is even poorer. The USA, a young nation with comparatively little built heritage, as on June 2006, registered 1.40 million "contributing resources" in their National Register of Historic Places. A decade ago, they had about 2,400 towns with "historic building" regulations. This figure would have increased substantially by now. To give the example of just one city, New York City had, as of July 2007, 1160 "Historic Landmarks" and 89 "Historic Districts" covering over 23,000 properties with an area of over 3,000 acres under the protection of their historic building regulations.

As mentioned earlier, England protects 500,000 listed buildings, and 10,000 Conservation Areas. Since we are 25 times the size of England, we should be protecting over twelve million heritage sites and 250,000 heritage precincts. If we consider our far richer history, the number should be even higher.

Other than archaeological sites, the Archaeological Survey of India (ASI) and the various state Departments of Archaeology do little (if anything) to protect heritage sites. Currently, the number of protected heritage sites in India would barely be a few thousand with heritage protection being confined only to Bombay, Hyderabad, Poona, Nagpur, Calcutta to a limited degree, Delhi, to a limited extent, along with the hill station towns of Mahableshwar, Panchgani, the non municipal areas of the Mahableshwar Panchgani Region, and Matheran.

Features of Heritage Regulations

Some of the features of a Model Heritage Regulations and a Heritage List are given in Annexure-I. (Refer to page no. 281)

A Model Regulation for Conservation of heritage sites, both built and natural is at Annexure II. (Refer to page no. 287)

It needs however to be briefly clarified here itself that inclusion of a building in the heritage list, or as part of a heritage precinct, does not prevent changes in its use or from it being sold, leased or otherwise disposed off. It also does **not** mean that its ownership vests in Government; nor does it mean that Government or the municipality has to acquire the property. Most importantly, it does **not** mean that changes to the property are banned.

All that inclusion of a property in the heritage list implies is that changes to the property need the prior approval of a multi disciplinary expert group appointed by Government.

What Heritage Designation Can Protect

Bombay

This will best be illustrated by several examples from Bombay.

The area of Marine Drive and the buildings in its vicinity are part of one of the finest art deco precincts in the world. The heights and elevations of buildings are controlled. Though in India, it is the IAS that rules, when a 12 storeyed residential building for Government officers was planned opposite the Brabourne Stadium, its height had to be halved so as to not exceed the precinct height.

When an overhead water tank was planned at Raj Bhavan, it was feared that the view from Marine Drive, would be affected; the tank had to be re-sited to the ground level.

The Reliance Group wanted a gleaming new building in Ballard Estate, reputedly the finest surviving Edwardian precinct in the world. They were told that with this design the building would have to be located elsewhere; in Ballard Estate they would have to conform to the heritage precinct norms.

The Navy wanted to demolish the old buildings of the Naval Hospital (INHS Asvini). They had to preserve the key heritage buildings and redesign the hospital around them.

The Air Force planned to demolish a heritage bungalow and build a high rise. They were informed that the height had to be reduced so as not to exceed the height of the neighbouring Assaye Buildings (Maharashtra and Gujarat Area Headquarters). In addition they were told that they would not be given the permission till they produced a conservation plan for the old so called dilapidated bungalow.

Delhi

Had heritage regulations been applicable in Delhi, the building close to Jantar Mantar would not have been permitted. The LIC building, which has disfigured Connaught Place, would not have been permitted there and would have had to be relocated. The high rise or cement concrete buildings which have come up in low rise heritage precincts would have had to be sited elsewhere.

Other Towns

If heritage regulations had been in place, the gardens and bungalows in Poona, Bangalore and other places would have been saved and both these cities would have remained as garden cities. Dehra Dun too would have had at least some of its leechee orchards, heritage structures and character preserved. Bhopal would have retained its lakes and pre-independence Nawabi character. Hyderabad would still be the beautiful city which the Qutb Shahis and the Asaf Jahis had built and which has been destroyed since independence.

Heritage & Urban Renewal in Indian Cities

The JNNURM[1] context and some broader issues.

Shri S. P. Shorey - Director, Urban Management Resource Group at the Centre for Good Governance, Government of Andhra Pradesh, Hyderabad

The 2005 National Conference by INTACH

In May 2005 the Indian National Trust for Art and Cultural Heritage (INTACH) held a National Conference on 'Heritage Conservation and Urban Development' at Hyderabad. The conference made detailed recommendations on the following aspects:

1. Strategies for urban heritage conservation to be adopted at National Level
2. Strategies to be adopted at State / Local level
3. Natural heritage conservation.
4. Role of INTACH
5. Specific recommendations for Andhra Pradesh-Hyderabad, the host city.

The conference also proposed the following strategies at National Level:

1. A Heritage Conservation Commission (HCC) to be set up.

[1] *Jawaharlal Nehru National Urban Renewal Mission, a nationwide project was launched by the Ministry of Housing and Urban Poverty Alleviation, Government of India in 2005. The project identified 63 Mission Cities in India which could access financial assistance from the central government for key infrastructure development with urban poor as the special target group. Assistance from the centre is subject to the State Governments and the concerned urban local bodies carrying out certain prescribed "Reforms" such as repeal of Urban Land Ceiling Act and modernising accounting systems.*

2. Model Heritage Law and Regulations to be adopted by States.
3. Listing of properties and creation of a National Register of Heritage.
4. Annual 'State of Heritage Reports' to be placed in the national Parliament .
5. Advisors on heritage to be in place in ministries.
6. Training of officials and setting up of heritage cells in important departments
7. The proposed Heritage Conservation Commission (HCC) to formulate financial strategies for urban heritage conservation.

The strategies proposed at the State/Local Level included:

1. Heritage to form integral part of local urban development plans.
2. Legislation/regulations should extend protection to heritage properties.
3. Elected local representatives and local population to be involved in listing process.
4. An 'urban renewal plan' to be worked out as an action plan.
5. Every local body to have a heritage cell.
6. Awareness building programme at local level.

Progress made post 2005 can be summarized as follows:

1. JNNURM is launched. A general improvement of infrastructure in cities should augur well for heritage too.
2. "Mission Cities" include a few Historic cities.
3. Heritage Toolkit added in the JNNURM formats to assist local bodies in framing schemes for heritage conservation.
4. A few cities joined Mumbai & Hyderabad in introducing heritage conservation as part of town planning regulations and system in general.
5. An "Indian Historic Cities Network" was launched to create awareness.

Urban Renewal

Avoiding mass destruction of historic areas and applying a brake on the demolition of individual historic buildings are the two immediate concerns in Indian cities. One may however take a quick look at the theories and definitions of urban renewal in the international and American context. The Encyclopedia Britannica, 2009 Ultimate Reference Suite described Urban Renewal as follows:

Urban Renewal: Comprehensive scheme to redress a complex of urban problems, including unsanitary, deficient, or obsolete housing; inadequate transportation, sanitation, and other services and facilities; haphazard land use; traffic congestion; and the sociological correlates of urban decay, such as crime. Early efforts usually focussed on housing reform and sanitary and public-health measures, followed by growing emphasis on slum clearance and the relocation of population and industry from congested areas to less-crowded sites, as in the garden-city and new-towns movements in Great Britain. Late 20th-century criticisms of urban sprawl prompted new interest in the efficiencies of urban centralization. Each country approaches 'Urban Renewal' according to its means and its political and administrative systems. One of the chief activities of urban renewal is redevelopment, which is achieved through the clearance and rebuilding of structures that are deteriorated or obsolete in themselves or are laid out in an unsatisfactory way. Other aspects of urban renewal involve the reuse of the land for new purposes, rehabilitation of structurally sound buildings that have deteriorated or lost their original functions, and conservation—a protective process designed to maintain the function and quality of an area, for instance, by requiring or assisting adequate maintenance while preventing inappropriate development or uncharacteristic changes in the use of land and buildings.

Urban Renewal in the US and Other Countries

The American term 'Urban Renewal' often meant wholesale re-building of old areas causing major population dislocation and other social and ethnic problems. Urban Renewal in the US therefore faced criticism in the sixties and seventies.

The following extract from Wikipedia is of interest :

Reactions against Urban Renewal

"In 1961, Jane Jacobs published *The Death and Life of Great American Cities*, one of the first—and strongest—critiques of contemporary large-scale urban renewal. However, it would still be a few years before organized movements began to oppose urban renewal. In 1964, the Civil Rights Act removed racial deed restrictions on housing. This began desegregation of residential neighborhoods, but redlining continued to mean that real estate agents continued to steer ethnic minorities to certain areas. The riots that swept cities across the country from 1965 to 1967 damaged or destroyed additional areas of major cities—most drastically in Detroit during the 12th Street Riot. By the 1970s many major cities developed opposition to the sweeping urban-renewal plans for their cities. In Boston, community activists halted construction of the proposed Southwest Expressway—but only after a three-mile long stretch of land had been cleared. In San Francisco, Joseph Alioto was the first mayor to publicly repudiate the policy of urban renewal, and with the backing of community groups, forced the state to end construction of highways through the heart of the city. Between 1956 and 1966, more than 12% of the people in Atlanta lost their homes to urban renewal, expressways, and a downtown building boom turned the city into the showcase of the New South in the 1970s and 1980s. In the early 1970s in Toronto, Jacobs was heavily involved in a group which halted the construction of the Spadina Expressway and altered transport policy in that city."

To quote from Wikipedia again:

Urban Renewal around the world-"The Josefov neighborhood, or Old Jewish Quarter, in Prague was leveled and rebuilt in an effort at urban renewal between 1890 and 1913. Other programs, such as that in Castleford in the UK and known as The Castleford Project seek to establish a process of urban renewal which enables local citizens to have greater control and ownership of the direction of their community and the way in which it overcomes market failure. This supports important themes in urban renewal today, such as participation, sustainability and trust - and government acting as advocate and 'enabler', rather than an instrument of command and control.

During the 1990s the concept of culture-led regeneration gained ground. Examples most often cited as successes include Temple Bar in Dublin where tourism was attracted to a bohemian 'cultural quarter', Barcelona where the 1992 Olympics provided a catalyst for infrastructure improvements and the redevelopment of the water front area, and Bilbao where the building of a new art museum was the focus for a new business district around the city's derelict dock area. The approach has become very popular in the UK due to the availability of lottery funding for capital projects and the vibrancy of the cultural and creative sectors. However, while the arrival of Tate Modern in the London borough of Southwark may be heralded as a catalyst to economic revival in its surrounding neighborhood, some civic authorities in the UK - for instance Newcastle-upon-Tyne and Gateshead have been accused of investing in cultural facilities at the cost of other programs and projects.

In post-apartheid South Africa major grassroots social movements such as the Western Cape Anti-Eviction Campaign and Abahlali baseMjondolo emerged to contest 'urban renewal' programs that forcibly relocated the poor out of the cities"

The Indian Experience of Urban Renewal

Urban Renewal as understood in the US and Europe was in a limited way practiced in pre and post-independence India as part of beautification projects and by the setting up of 'Civil Lines' in many Indian cities. For instance, re-building efforts after the devastating Musi flood of 1908 in Hyderabad, India led to imposing an entirely new road network over old neighbourhoods. In colonial cities like Calcutta (Kolkata) massive clearance of old areas and reconstruction took place after each battle to keep the native population away from the rulers and also purportedly in the interest of health and hygiene of subjects. This made Patrick Geddes advocate his famous principle of 'Conservative Surgery'. Unlike in the US, large scale remodeling of old and historic areas in Indian cities before or after independence did not evoke any response either negative or positive from citizens. Urban Renewal in the Western sense did not become an issue in India.

Indian Town Planning Before and After Independence: The National Commission on Urbanization.

Town Planning in India largely meant the requirement of obtaining a building permission from the municipality or the construction of roads, bridges, drains and other city infrastructure by Improvement Trusts, Municipal bodies and in later times also by Urban Development Authorities set up in larger cities. The Indian town planning system had by inheritance adopted British Laws. Curiously however decision makers in post independence India omitted the provisions of conservation of listed buildings and trees that were very much part of British town planning laws in 1947.

Only since the mid 1970s there was re-thinking about the approach to dealing with old cities and localities. By this time an "Urban Conservation" movement had picked up momentum in Europe. However heritage conservation appeared in official documents in India only through the 'Report of the National Commission on Urbanization' (1988) The Report devoted a full chapter on conservation[2].

Principal recommendations of the National commission on Urbanization (NCU) were:

1. Conservation as integral part of town planning process.
2. Density and building norms in 'Conservation Areas' to encourage repair and upkeep of heritage buildings.
3. Sensitive traffic management policies for historic quarters.
4. Retention of original streetscapes and pedestrianisation of old quarters.
5. Training of conservation experts and public awareness building.
6. Encouraging recycling of old buildings and areas.
7. Government agencies to effectively maintain and protect historic buildings under their ownership and use.
8. Tourism to be judiciously used for promoting conservation.
9. Fiscal and other incentives for owners of historic buildings to overcome resistance to restrictions.
10. Transfer of Development Rights as an additional incentive to promote conservation.
11. Urban Heritage Committees at local and national level to guide conservation of historic buildings and areas.

Emergence of the Indian National Trust for Art and Cultural Heritage (INTACH) in 1984 and the NCU Report are the two significant influences on urban heritage conservation in subsequent years.

The Place of Conservation in Public Mind: No Prejudice Against Heritage Conservation.

It is often said that the population at large of even the most historic Indian cities is indifferent to history and culture. One may take heart

[2] *National Commission on Urbanisation: August 1988. Government of India. Summary of recommendations on urban heritage conservation in chapter 12 of volume II*

at the fact that the common man does not have anything against historic buildings or areas. The population is equally indifferent to civic discipline, concerns of health and hygiene and the need for planned urban development in general. This could largely be so because of our colonial past, poverty and illiteracy but it is also due to the general disregard for the rule of law. For example sixty years of persuasion has not succeeded in enforcing the simple 'Helmet Rule' for two wheeler riders in most cities and towns. People do not have any special bias against historic preservation. They have little concern for civic issues.

The Jawaharlal Nehru National Urban Renewal Mission JNNURM (2005-2012)

Launch of the Jawaharlal Nehru National Urban Renewal Mission in 2005 was a significant event for urban heritage conservation because for the first time in India a project of such vast financial outlay included urban heritage conservation as a component for which the Government of India grant assistance is available. Whether a Mission City receives such assistance and how much it receives primarily depends on the particular city.

The Jawaharlal Nehru National Urban Renewal Mission has an outlay of Rs 100 000 crore (US $ 20000 million) to be spread over seven years inclusive of 50% funding from institutional and local sources. The scheme offered funding to 63 cities across the country to improve drinking water supply, drainage, solid waste management, public transport, housing and slum improvement with poverty alleviation as a major underlying objective. These are precisely the issues for the common man to be worried about in any old city of India. But even after four years the progress at the level of local administrations has been grossly inadequate. A news report is quoted here :

"Few takers for JNNURM: Only a third of central allocations utilised". *Business Standard - New Delhi July 09, 2009*

Four years after the launch of the Jawaharlal Nehru National Urban Renewal Mission, or JNNURM, to upgrade the infrastructure in cities, just above a third of the central funds allocated under the scheme have been used. With the scheme slated to end in another three years, only 32 out of 463 projects sanctioned under the Urban Infrastructure and Governance (UIG) head have been completed. According to Minister of State for Urban Development, Saugata Ray, the Centre may call a special meeting of the states soon after the current Parliament session is over. "We need to assess the situation. After all, it is our flagship programme and we must make it successful," he said. The Union Urban Development Ministry's statistics show the Centre has released only Rs 8,252 crore till date as Additional Central Assistance (ACA) under the UIG head, as against the Rs 23548.33 crore that was available till date. The total cost of the 463 sanctioned projects is Rs 49,743 crore. The government launched JNNURM on December 3, 2005, for seven years with a total planned investment of Rs 1,00,000 crore, with a committed central government share of Rs 50,000 crore. The states, along with the urban local bodies, are to cough up the other half.

"We always release the first installment quickly. But the subsequent Central release depends on the progress of the work and the release of the matching contribution from the states," Ray told Business Standard.

The Heritage Toolkit and Allocation of Funds for Development of Heritage Areas

As part of the Jawaharlal Nehru National Urban Renewal Mission, the Government of India also made special provision for improvement of the heritage components of historic areas. A Supplementary Toolkit on City Development Plan with focus on heritage was drawn up in Nov

2006 with the following components :

a. Heritage: setting the boundaries
b. The existing status and assessment of Urban Heritage
c. Formulating a vision for urban heritage
d. Defining strategies
e. Financing plan and financing strategies

The status of funds released for heritage areas is reflected in the following report:

"JNNURM funds for heritage areas" *July 02, 2009 Press Trust of India.*

Two projects for development of Heritage areas have been sanctioned under Urban Infrastructure and Governance (UIG) component of Jawaharlal Nehru National Urban Renewal Mission (JNNURM), namely 'River Front Development North Bank Zone-3', Nanded, Maharashtra for Rs. 43.13 crore and 'Construction of Heritage precincts along EVR Periyar Salai', Chennai, Tamil Nadu for Rs. 6.10 crore. In Hyderabad, Andhra Pradesh a project "Road Widening on Outer Ring Road and Inner Ring Road under Charminar Pedestrianisation Project", at cost of Rs. 35.10 crore has also been sanctioned.

This information was given by Shri Saugata Ray, MOS Urban Development in reply to a question by Shri Mohd. Ali Khan in Rajya Sabha today."

The Sector-wise release of funds under Jawaharlal Nehru National Urban Renewal Mission is given in the following table.

As seen from the table, the funds released for heritage areas are therefore a negligible 0.42%. For this the primary responsibility lies with the local bodies and the state governments.

Sub Mission for Urban Infrastructure and Governance.			
Sl.No.	Sector	Funds released Rs in lakhs	% of funds released
1	Drainage/Storm water drainage	103023.46	12.40
2	Roads/Flyovers	73753.04	8.88
3	Water Supply	332287.33	40.00
4	Sewerage	169678.46	20.43
5	Urban Renewal	6309.37	0.76
6	Mass Rapid Transport System	95469.42	11.49
7	Other Urban transport	10328.39	1.24
8	Solid Waste Management	33791.55	4.07
9	Development of Heritage Areas	3503.85	0.42
10	Preservation of water bodies	1813.73	0.22
11	Parking	700.00	0.08
Total		**830658.60**	**100**

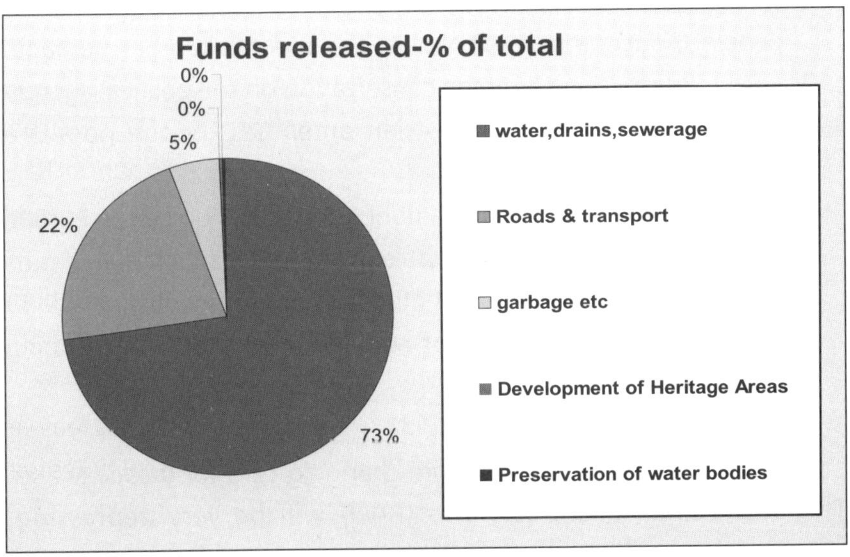

JNNURM to Make Special Provision for Urban Heritage as in the Case of Urban Poor.

While the present situation may seem discouraging, it must be borne in mind that without the constant efforts made by NGOs like INTACH and the support from a part of the bureaucracy and judiciary most urban heritage would have disappeared from India by now. Many urban historic buildings stand today because of judicial intervention. Many historic areas escaped being bulldozed and redeveloped simply because the authorities ran short of funds or the governments changed. Limited success stories of urban heritage conservation in Mumbai, Kolkata, Bangalore, Chennai etc need to be publicized and public opinion further strengthened. Poor people know that large scale re-development affects them most. They must be organized and made vocal by local leaders and professionals.

A few questions that arise in this context are given below:

1. How to create a broad based vested interest in urban heritage conservation. Presently vested interest in conservation seems confined to a handful of architects and planners who must secure employment.
2. How to overcome the mounting indifference among common people about civic issues in general and specifically urban heritage.
3. How to place urban heritage conservation on the political agenda when even the basic pedestrian amenities for the poor are considered trivial issues.
4. How to inculcate local pride among urban local bodies. In Europe the tradition of former City States means every small town has its own flag, Court of Arms and other symbols of identity.
5. Legislation and integration of heritage in to the town planning system.

The rapid pace at which cities are changing calls for drastic action. The Business as Usual Scenario (BAU) will be very depressing.

Conservation of both cultural and natural heritage must reach the political mainstream. There is enough money for conservation, what is needed is the will and priorities. The Mumbai and Hyderabad examples of urban heritage regulations have shown that there are no legal hurdles either.

The key to getting out of the stalemate is that in better examples abroad, urban conservation always improved amenities for local residents in their day to day lives. The Jawaharlal Nehru National Urban Renewal Mission has the capacity to link infrastructure development in poor localities with heritage conservation.

The JNNURM requires that certain percentage of funds in every Mission City must be spent for the urban poor. Similarly it should be mandated that in all Mission Cities at least 20% of total funds must be spent for reviving old neighbourhoods in respect of their architectural heritage as well as livelihood and employment generation. This must include pedestrian amenities and public transport dedicated to old areas.

Session 4

Case Studies

The Old City of Lucknow: A Case for Urban Renewal

Prof. Neeta Das - Professor of Architecture at BBDNITM, Lucknow

Heritage areas of cities, like that of Lucknow, have a problem of cluttered narrow lanes, problems of parking, water shortage, and poor services. These problems have forced more and more people to move out of these old areas. Many buildings are therefore neglected and some have also collapsed. If the people are not shifting out they are bringing down and renovating their shops and houses. The new shops now offer new wares in a new look. Closed derelict houses, the merciless change of morphology and socio-cultural systems have slowly started the collapsing of the area which is a rich resource of art and architecture. Presented below is a documentation of this area with the purpose of highlighting the important features and areas which should be considered for conservation.

Presently, this area, which comprises of the old fort, Machchi Bhawan, and the residential area of *chowk* is not even a designated heritage zone, nor does it have any relevant bye laws or legislation for its conservation and future development. Initiative needs to be taken by both the government and the property owners. Other than legal issues, the government needs to put in place some sort of a 'conservation process' (instead of projects). This process should take into consideration - (1) empowerment of the property owners by education relating to fund raising, re-hab and re-use, and technical training; (2) including the conservation budgets within the building maintenance funds of both public and private organisations; and (3) training more personnel for the field of conservation including engineers, architects, artist, scientists, contractors and craftsmen.

When Nawab Saadat Khan came to Lucknow in 1723 it was like any other medieval town i.e. accretive, concentric, and aggregarian. Like most other towns it was situated next to a river, in this case, Gomti. The town had an old fortified palace, the Machchi Bhawan, located alongside the river and near the highest mound named Lakshman Tila. To the southwest on the periphery of the fort was *Chowk,* the main trade route and market place of Lucknow. Around it on both sides was the residential area now referred to as 'old' Lucknow.

The Machchi Bhawan Fort

In 1590 Sheikh Abdur Rahim, the ruler of Lucknow before Saadat Khan, took up residence near Lakshman Tila (also known as Shah Pir Muhammad hill) and built his residence there called Panch Mahal or five palaces. He fortified it and erected the Shaikhan Darwaza at the south entrance. It stood just inside the north wall of the fort and was visible from the river. This building was either demolished or severely altered, as it does not feature as a major building after Asaf-ud-Daula came to power. By 1766 Panch Mahal had become the most prominent feature of Lucknow and was later called Machchi Bhawan. The fort palace probably got its name for two reasons: one, because the fort had two fishes on each of its twenty-six arches, hence, *Machchi* or fish. The second reason could be that the Sheikh had been awarded the title

Mahi Maratib or 'The honour of the Fish' by the Mughal emperor.[1] The emblem of two fishes facing each other was the insignia of the Sheikhs, and the Nawabs and the British alike, later adopted the same. Even today, the fish emblem can be seen on many buildings and government seals of Lucknow.

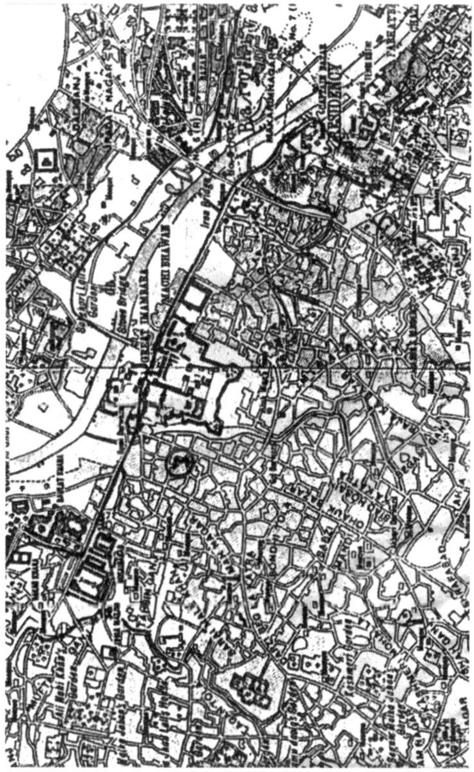

Fig. 1.1

Under the Nawabs

When Nawab Saadat Khan came to power, he rented some of the existing buildings from the Sheikhs, most important being the Panch Mahal, and improved it greatly. He added another gate called the *Naqqar Khana* near or instead of the earlier gate. Nawab Safdar Jung later purchased the Machchi Bhawan from the Sheikhs and further fortified it.[2] More additions were done by Nawab Shuja-ud-Daula.[3] When Asaf-ud-Daula shifted his capital from Faizabad to Lucknow, he started living in this fort and further enlarged it. Three years after his shifting to Lucknow, his grandmother Sadun-un-nisa Begum was not happy with the changes and complained to the Mughal emperor in Delhi that, 'the Nawab has entirely ruined the house which Nawab Shuja-ud-Daula raised to the highest pitch of splendour'.[4] Later Asaf-ud-Daula built the Asfi Imambara within the

---

[1] *U.P.Gazetteers, Vol. XXXVII, Lucknow, pg.32*
[2] *R.R. Kidwai. Lucknow, The Lost Paradise, pg. 36*
[3] *Banmali Tandan. The Architecture of Lucknow and its Dependencies, 1722-1856, pg. 76*
[4] *Rosie Llewellyn Jones. A Fatal Friendship, pg. 172*

complex. Thus, all earlier Nawabs, Saadat Khan, Safdar Jung, Shuja-ud-Daula, and Asaf-ud-Daula took interest in the old fort and greatly improved upon it. Pre-1857 maps show it to be quite a large fort (Fig. 1.1).

The fact that the British Commander during 1857, Sir Henry Lawrence, proceeded to dynamite a part of the structure for fear that it might become an impregnable stronghold for the Indian rebels, shows that the site and its subsequent development were entirely apt for defence. None of the later palace complexes paid more than a lip service to the notion of defence.[5] Apart from it's important position on the highest mound in Lucknow, the Machchi Bhawan fort commanded three essential points of communication in Lucknow: Two roads from the north, and the other from the west which led from Kanpur and Chowk, converged in front of the palace as did the approach from the Gomti bridge. Thus, this palace controlled the major crossing points over the Gomti. There are no records of quays or landings stages here although there was a considerable amount of river traffic especially from Calcutta.[6] There are many descriptions of the fort by travellers such as William Hodges, Martin Gubbins, and Lt General MacLeod, to name a few. Early pictures of this area, including views and etchings by

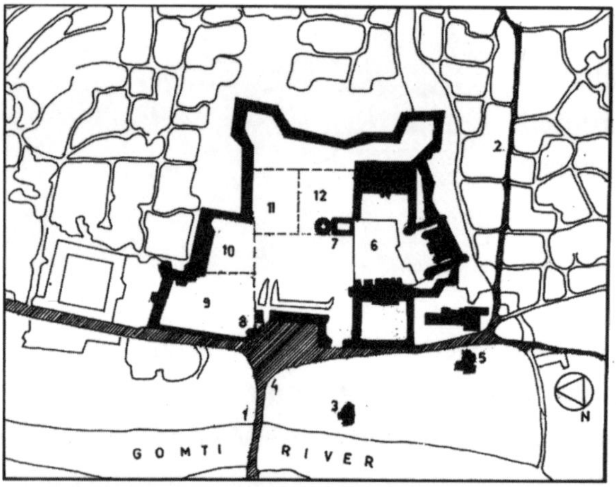

1.2 Reconstruction of the Machchi Bhawan fort

[5] Ibid. pg. 170
[6] Ibid. pg. 172

1.3 Approach from river, Aquatint of Machchi Bhawan by Daniell and Havell

William Hodges, Thomas and William Daniells, and Joseph Tieffenthaler[7], show that the chief characteristic of this complex was that of defence, emphasised by the massive buttresses rising from the hillock. It was the only fortified palace complex of Lucknow ever to be built (Fig. 1.2 and 1.3)). There is, however, a written record of another fort in south Lucknow called Jalalabad Fort, built by Nawab Safdar Jung, to protect the city from any invaders from the south.[8]

Many contemporary travellers have described the Machchi Bhawan fort. An 1858 description of the fort narrates:

"The Muchee Bhowun…has an imposing appearance. It comprises three plateaus, of which the lowest was little above the level of the road, and the highest towered above the neighbouring buildings. The high road skirted the whole length of the position, and followed the level of the ground, which rose naturally from the lowest eastern plateau to the highest on the west side. From the road on that, i.e. the west

---

[7] *Tandan, pg. 77*
[8] *Ibid. pg. 75*

extreme of the position, a short but steep ascent led to the main gateway. The highest plateau was covered with the 'bhowuns' or pavilions originally built by the Sheikhs of Lucknow, which were in a very dilapidated condition, and contained the modern residence of one of the ex-King's brothers, Newaub Yuheea Ali Khan. On the second plateau stood a handsome baraduree...and a few smaller buildings. The lower plateau was an open space surrounded by low ranges of masonary sheds. There was no gate leading directly from the outside into the second plateau; but two opened into the lower, one at the east end, the second from the main road on the north side".[9]

Description by William Hodges of the area in *Travels in India during the years 1780,81,82,83* mentions Machchi Bhawan as:

"...Constructed in the form of a chateau, surrounded with walls and high towers. There is a lofty gateway, and a great fore court, that stands before a tall building with arcades, designed for sounding the tambour (ceremonial drums)...the exterior of the building is not to be commended: it reminded me of what I imagined might be the style of a Baron's castle in Europe, about the twelfth century".[10]

Mr. Martin Gubbins, in *Historic Lucknow,* after 1857 writes:

" Machchi Bhawan was made on three raised mounds. The highest one has the main building, which is in dilapidated condition. On the second mound which is at a lower level, there is marble baradari and few small buildings, the third side has a wall with window".[11]

Lt General James MacLeod Innes while surveying the area in 1895 wrote:

" Machchi Bhawan comprised number of buildings and existed as a fort. The fortifications are made of stones and mortar. It is quite

[9] *Ibid. pg. 76*

[10] *Jones, op. cit., pg. 11*

[11] *Kidwai, op.cit. pg. 38*

high all round and interjected by round *burjis*. There is a gate on the western side towards the city where guards are mounted. Nearby are two pavilions on raised grounds having verandah on all the four sides on the north side; towards Gomti, there are vaulted halls with arches".

An English traveller in Gladwin's *Asiatic Miscellany*, contained in the *Asiatic Annual Register*, dated October 1785, gave a further detailed account. It mentions that the fort lies towards the east side of the city and along the edge of the river. It has six principal courts. The complex was entered through entrance gates into the first court, which had the Panch Mahal, and a room called *'naubat khana'* to sound the drums. This court was for the king's 'equipage and attendants'. The second courtyard consisted of the state apartments encompassing a square garden with a step well or *baoli*. The step well was also used as summer palace and has been described by Viscount Valentia when he stayed there as a guest. Parallel to the *baoli* was the *Sungi Dalan* or Stone hall, comprising a grand hall surrounded by a double arcade and crowned by four gilded cupolas. To the north of the *Sungi Dalan* was another garden court containing the public offices where probably the *durbar* or court was held. The fifth consisted of the *'zenana'* and the buildings were known as *Khurd Mahal* and *Rang Mahal*. The sixth and last court of the Machchi Bhawan complex was an area to the east called *Husain Bagh* which was described as a flower garden at the river's edge, enclosed with a brick wall covered with vines.[12] Accounts of early travellers also state that there was a building called *Aaina Khana* (mirror house) on the east of the Machchi Bhawan which housed 'an absolute confusion of treasures' collected by Asaf-ud-Daula.[13]

---

[12] *Tandan, op. cit., pg. 86*
[13] *Jones, op. cit., pg. 174*

Reconstruction

It is difficult to reconstruct the Machchi Bhawan fort because of several reasons. Firstly, very little of the original fort remains both in terms of the buildings and the mounds frequently mentioned by travellers. Secondly, the descriptions of the contemporary travellers give very conflicting views of the area especially if they are based on cardinal directions. Finally, the maps, drawings, and photographs have been made or taken at different periods. In the meanwhile, the same building might have been reconstructed or renamed as it changed hands from one owner to another over time.

However, a tentative reconstruction of the area can be proposed considering all the above-mentioned evidence. For this reconstruction the direction of the mosque, which is in the east west axis, will be considered. It is quite sure that the Machchi Bhawan fort was alongside the river and not abutting it. The Lakshman Tila with the Aurangzeb mosque was on the banks of Gomti and was near the fort. The fort was placed on the highest land of the hillock on which it stood. The hillock was undulating and had three mounds. This area today has the hostels of the Medical College and the Hussainabad Inter College. The Panch Mahal was probably located on the

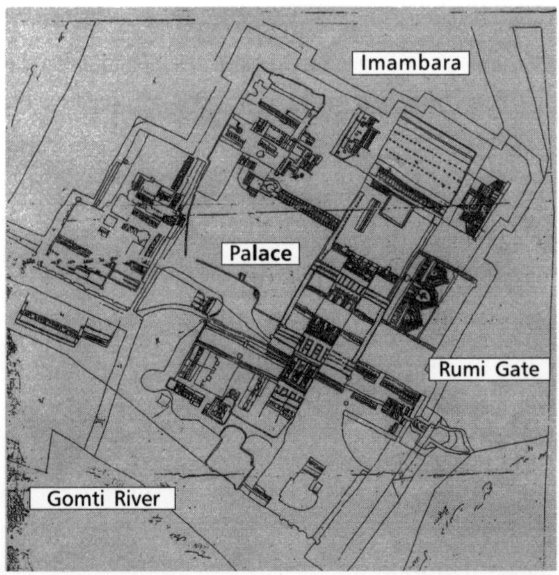

1.4 1863 Board of revenue pictorial map indicates the clustering of building around court in the Machchi Bhawan fort

southern end of the complex and the palace grew towards the north from there. (Fig. 1.4)

The road from *Chowk*, which also led to Kanpur, and the Stone Bridge, the route to Faizabad, met in front of the fort-palace, which formed a rectangular forecourt. The traveller would have to climb up a hillock to reach this court. From here was the entrance to the fort. One would pass through the '*Naubat Khana*', which was a part of the entrance gate, to the first court referred to as the offices of the Nawab. Clustering from the map and drawings would show this to have many buildings. Being the oldest part, this was probably altered a lot and many additions made. One would then pass through to the *durbar* or court of the Nawab. Then would be the *zenana* or the queens quarter and the highest area would be for the Nawab along with the baoli. The *zenana*, like the entrance court had many buildings. Again, this idea is taken from the clustering pattern shown in the map. This hierarchy of moving from the public to the more private areas is common to most Indian palaces. Large open areas within the fort premises were probably the slopes of the hillock, which were not used. Later, Asaf-ud-Daula constructed the Imambara complex on the northwestern end of the fort, which was much lower than the rest of the area and bound it's north edges by the *Rumi*

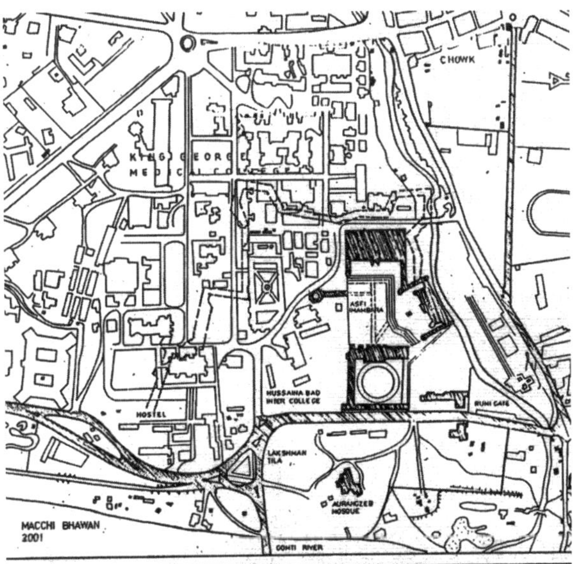

1.5a The Machchi Bhawan locality before demolition

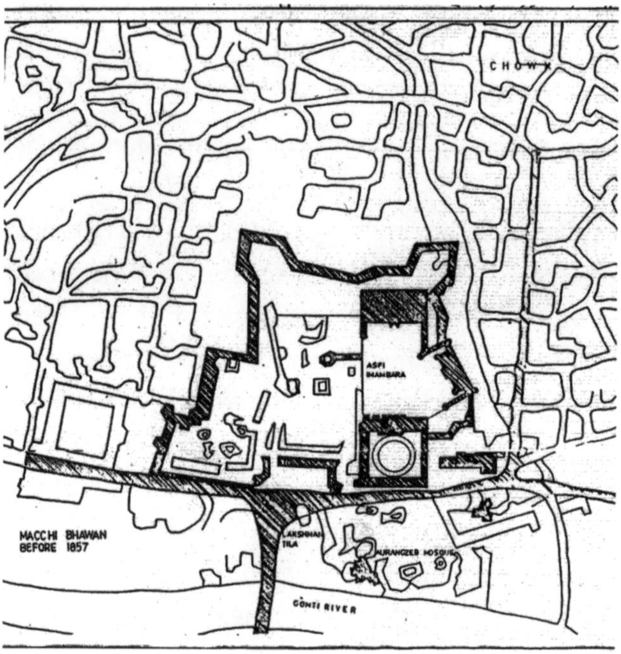

1.5b The Machchi Bhawan locality after demolition

Darwaza. The eastern end had a retaining wall, which segregated the *Lakshman Tila* from the complex. Parts to this wall can be seen today.

Before the First war of Independence (Sepoy Mutiny) the Machchi Bhawan complex bought by the British. The British stationed their army here. After the war in 1858 the whole fort was blown up, as were many other Nawabi buildings, which posed a threat to the British. In 1905, King George V laid down the foundation stone of a medical college in the same area. (Fig. 1.5) It was known as the King George's Medical College and later renamed as Chhatrapati Shahuji Maharaj Medical University. Of the old Nawabi buildings in the Machchi Bhawan only the Imambara complex, the *Baoli*, and the Aurangzeb mosque exist. Archaeological excavations might reveal more of the old structures and the fort wall.

Chowk

Below the the Machchi Bhawan fort to the west of it, the 'old' city of Lucknow grew around *chowk*, the main trade route of the city. Various *abadis* or settlements were established at different times according to

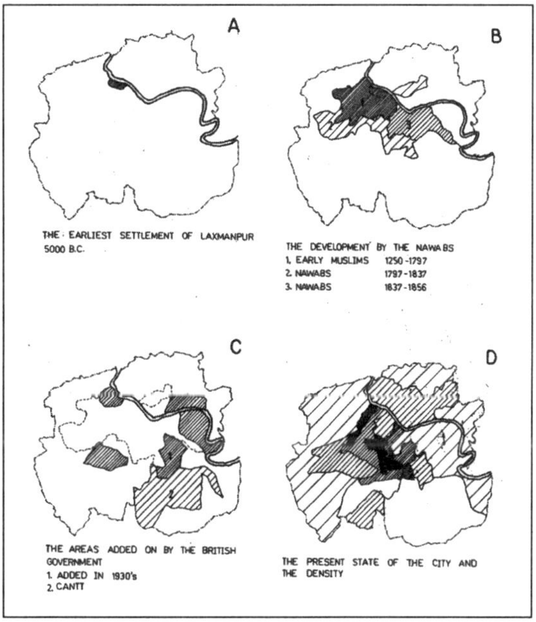

2.1 Development of the city of Lucknow

the needs of the people and the whims of the rulers and nobles. Lucknow started developing when Sher Shah Suri developed a silver and copper mint in Lucknow around 1539.[14] He also developed several areas to the south of *chowk*. Lucknow continued to grow around this area in the reign of Akbar (Fig.2.1). Due to his tolerance towards the Hindus, many Hindu colonies like Bajpai *tola*, Katari *tola*, Sindhi *tola*, Banjari *tola*, and Ahiri *tola* came up.[15] Mirza Mandi was established during the reign of Prince Mirza Muhammad Salim.[16] By 1640, in the reign of Shah Jehan, Lucknow became a brisk business centre of sugar, Indigo, and Calico produced by British factories in Awadh.[17] Fazil Nagar and Mansur Nagar were developed and named after the sons of the Subedar of Awadh, Mirza Fazil and Mirza Mansur. At the same time a *risaldar*, Ashraf Ali Khan founded Asharfabad. His brother Musharaf Ali Khan established Musharfabad today known as *Nau Basta*. During the time of Muhammad Shah Rangila, Raj Girdhar Bahadur and his wife founded the Bahadur Nagar and Rani Nagar. [18] After Asaf-ud-Daula shifted his capital from Faizabad to Lucknow the city continued to grow

[14] *H.N. Wright, op. cit., pg. 101*
[15] *History of Lucknow Cantonment, op. cit., pg. 64*
[16] *Lucknow Gazetteer, 1904, pg. 144*
[17] *There was one East India Company factory in Lucknow in mid 17th century, but it was a warehouse where goods produced in Awadh were collected before exported through Surat. The British weren't manufacturing anything themselves, therefore term factory used in a modern sense.*
[18] *History of Lucknow Cantonment, op. cit., pg. 64*

under the later Nawabs and by the first war of independence in 1857, the 'old' city extended from the *Chowk* street right up to Charbagh.

This city was very dense and much later when the British were trying to prepare a map of Lucknow; the 'old' city remained uncharted barring a few thoroughfares, and was labelled 'dense'.[19] Like other pre-industrial cities, the residential part of 'old' Lucknow displays a morphology in which commerce, residential living, and socio-religious institutions are intermixed and grew by accretion.

Morphology

The rulers of Lucknow being Muslims since the sixteenth century, 'old' Lucknow, in its dominant form and culture, was essentially Islamic with a dense and labyrinthine urban fabric in which were embedded courtyard houses as the basic domestic form. The residential area around *chowk* was divided into areas occupied by people of different communities, castes, or guilds. These areas were called *tolas* if they arose before Persian words became fashionable with the advent of the Mughals and *mohalla* if it did so later. The areas were named after the caste or occupation of the residents, like *Rastogi Tola, Kashmiri Mohalla*, and so on. The nobility built their own residential palaces and *mohallas* with their own mosques and markets and named them after themselves.[20]

The residential streets were radially arranged from the fort with secondary lateral streets connecting them. These streets or *galis* were narrow, irregular, and labyrinthine in character with blind curves and cul-de-sacs as a safety devise to confuse the enemies. The lace like and cellular form of the streets evolved in a cohesive pattern, flowing into each other, and the width of the roads varying with function, location, and importance. Streets served principally as areas where people mingled,

---

[19] *Veena Oldenburg. The Making of Colonial Lucknow. pg. 28*
[20] *Ibid. pg. 14*

and socialized, where hawkers lined the curbs, where goods and services were bought and sold, and where traffic, which chiefly comprised pedestrians or beasts of burden, was slow moving and yielded to those standing and transacting business. In 'old' Lucknow the custom was, and is, often to go to the street and not to get anywhere; the street itself was a destination and an event.

Whereas the street of *chowk* was the main spinal market cutting across the city, the speciality markets or *bazaars* were scattered among the winding *galis* or streets of the residential areas. Because people of a particular occupation generally lived in a single locality, *bazaars* were usually extensions of the *mohallas.* The shops of one of the lanes, usually the widest, in the *mohalla*, constituted the speciality *bazaar* and were called *gunjes, mandis*, and *katras*. The Sanskrit word *gunj*, was generally confined to a grain market, though several *gunjes* expanded into retail centres for a variety of goods. *Mandi* or wholesale market was usually the word associated with bulky items of low value such as vegetables, timber, grass or coal. The name *katra* was given to a bazaar that sold small cheap goods, but it originally denoted the quarter dominated by artisans of a particular guild. [21]

Although Nawabi Lucknow could be described as 'dense', the city was never enclosed as an entity and the dense, narrow, and meandering streets offered safety to the city. There is no evidence, either historical or archaeological, that Lucknow had external walls as many pre-industrial cities in Europe and Asia did. While the ruling families maintained defences of their own, in large citadels, other groups were left to fend for themselves. There were, and some exist even today, many large gates to close and protect specific complexes and localities, but none of them were 'city gates'.[22] The *chowk* street for example could be

---

[21] *Ibid. pg. 13*

[22] *Keith Hjortshoj. Urban Structures and Transformations in Lucknow- India, pg. 44*

shut down by gates on both ends, Akbari Gate and Gol Darwaza. Some scholars say Qazi Mahmud Bilgrami, deputy of the subedar of Jawahar Khan of Awadh at the time to commemorate the visit of Akbar, built Akbari gate as a customhouse gate.[23]

House Forms

In the 'old' city, dwellings were and still are organized as connected rows along these streets, both for the conservation and protection from heat, and to restrict the area of the city. The houses are similar in character, as there was little distinction between the classes of people, and are all introverted with a court in the centre. The inner court, sometimes more than one, however, is an extension of the house. It is used extensively by the women for household chores like washing and drying in the mornings and for relaxing in the evening. The courts have wells, which were the main source of water. Most of them are dry and in disuse now. Larger courts were sometimes indoor gardens with lots of trees and fountains. Both terraces and courts are used for sleeping at night during the hot summer months. The court is surrounded with covered and semi-covered multifunctional rooms around it.

The house presents to the outside world high, windowless walls, interrupted only by a single entrance door. The court is the main source for light and ventilation for all these houses. The entry is mostly on one end of the house and indirect to provide maximum privacy from outsiders. Most houses have at least one room opening on to the street, which is used as a shop or a drawing room to be used mainly by the men. By and large there are two bays of rooms on two sides of the court with a semi-covered veranda preceding a room. The inner rooms are dark and usually without light and ventilation and used mostly for storage and less for living. The verandas are the most frequented place of the house. No rooms are marked for any particular activity. The use

[23] *R. R Kidwai. Lucknow, The Lost Paradise. pg. 35*

of these verandas and rooms change with the seasons and the changing movement of the sun, sunny spaces being used more in winters and shadier spaces being used in summers.

The other two sides have only one bay and house activities like the staircase, the kitchen and toilet, with some area being demarcated for animals and their fodder, storage space for wood and coal. All these spaces are located near the entrance whereas toilets are located on the side of service lanes for easy accessibility. All toilets have a separate bathroom and a separate latrine. Most latrines of this time are dry and are raised above the plinth height of the house. This additional height gives space underneath the seat to keep a bucket to collect the soil waste, which is then removed and cleaned by a sweeper from the service lane. All water from the bathroom and kitchen is drained out into the open

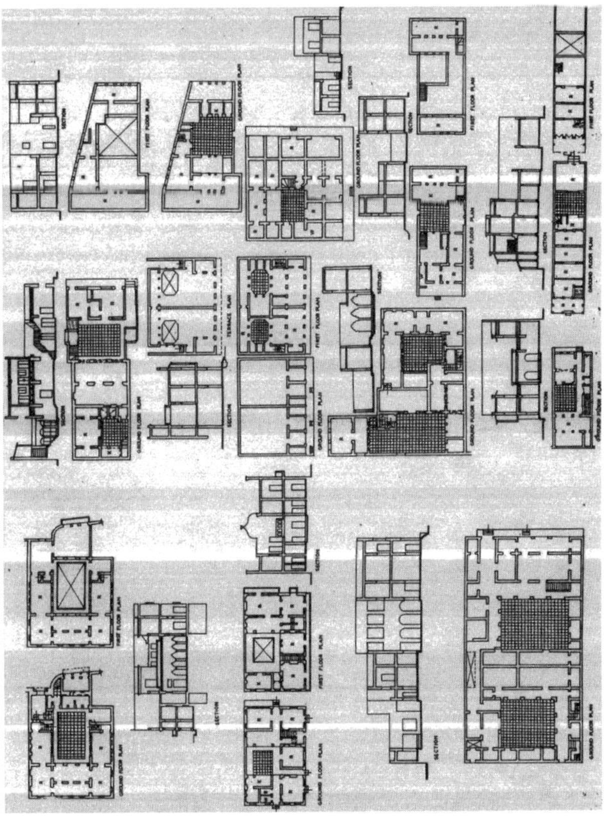

2.2 Collection of drawings of court in the old city
1 Shops on the ground floor of houses abutting the street
2 Bigger houses with two internal courts
3 A house in chowk with indirect entry
4 Early twentieth century house in Narhi

drains along the streets. It is noteworthy that the development of the old city has been such that all water drains flow away from the settlements, through *nullahs* into the river. The first floor of the houses usually replicates the plan of the ground floor. Some differences can be observed in the planning of corner houses and houses facing main streets. The ground floor of the houses abutting the street is totally dedicated to shopping activities (Fig. 2.2).

Although Lucknow always had a larger Hindu population, Muslim influence has been greater on all its architecture. Strictly there should have been a marked difference between the house forms of the two communities because of varied lifestyles, but the overall structure of the house is fairly similar. The main difference lies in the size of the inner courts and the entry. Since Muslim women observe more *purdah* the entries of the Muslim houses are more indirect with some extra transitional spaces. Also, their courts are much larger and are usually greener. Other than that only the religious spaces like *puja* spaces, mosques or *imambaras* are any indication of the religion of the owner.

Public Spaces and Public Buildings

The residential areas of Nawabi time predominantly had a singular religion, caste, or creed. The identity of any *mohalla* was transformed into Hindu or Muslim, by the presence of a mosque or a temple square complete with a *pipal* tree and well. There was no other difference amongst the areas, which were only segregated by streets or natural barriers. Today the segregation is not as strict. Beyond the private court, which is brightly sunlit, is the narrow dimly lit lane of the *mohalla* and the bustling *bazaar* street. There is a progressive loss of privacy and increase of public identity as one moves from the house to the main street.

A total lack of a central space is apparent and generated by a mere widening of the streets as it turns a corner or joins another street. Other than these, social and communal activities are centred around religious places like temples, mosques, and imambaras, which are embedded within the residential areas or *mohallas.* Mosques and temples are built in the centre of large courtyards or open areas within these dense masses. There are some more public buildings like orphanages, *serais*, and hospitals. Schools are usually a part of the religious complexes. All these buildings are similar in character and planning to the courtyard houses, only built covering a much larger area. Like the houses, these public buildings have a court in the centre with covered and semi-covered spaces around it. They are all joined to the adjoining buildings by common walls making them into one monolithic mass.

2.3 The chowk street with Gol Darwaza on one end and Akbari gate on the other and an inset of Firangi Mahal area

One example of a public building is the Firangi Mahal, which is a complex of structures embedded within the *Chowk* Street [24] (Fig. 2.3). Other important structures along the *chowk* street are Saudagar ka Imambara, Ram Mandir, and Darul Shafa. Some very important Imambaras embedded within the other parts of the 'old' city are Imambara Malka

---

[24] *See: Francis Robinson, The 'Ulama' of Farangi Mahal and Islamic Culture in South Asia*

Jamania, Imambara Moghul Sahiba, and Deputy Saheb ka Imambara. Even the later and larger Imambaras like Asfi Imambara and Hussainabad Imambara retain this character of a built form which is carved out from a dense mass with blank outside walls and spaces built around a central courtyard.

Later developments to the south of the city show on close inspection that the density of the built mass of the city decreased and it became more geometrical with roads becoming wider and linear. The houses also become more geometrical and longer. However, other than that the morphology of the 'old' city remained unchanged with common walls and living spaces organized around a court with toilets opening onto a service lane is a character that continued to be used till the early twentieth century in the much later colonies like Narhi and New Hyderabad, with the only difference that the street structure and the plot sizes became more geometrical and regular with streets opening onto square gardens, a concept brought into Lucknow by the British. The oldest settlements do not have a regular or geometrical shape and often all the houses have a different shape and size as they developed organically as and when needed and depending on the space needed by the owners. However, this concept was totally abandoned by the planners of independent and modern India who developed the concept of plotting and tenements.

Conservation and Urban Renewal Apropos of Commonwealth Games 2010, New Delhi

Shri A.K.Jain - Architect – Town Planner, member of the UN Habitat Research Advisory Committee

Delhi is a unique repository of traditional urbanism. The built heritage of Delhi is an irreplaceable and non-renewable cultural resource, which needs to be protected, nourished and nurtured by all and passed on to the coming generations. It enhances Delhi's environment, giving it a unique identity. The heritage resources include symbols of successive civilizations and cities that came up over the millennia, historic buildings and complexes, historic gardens, canals, bridges, water engineering structures, forts, palaces, citadels, places of worship, tombs, historic villages, unearthed heritage, etc. During the last decades, Delhi's runway growth had been overtaking its rich heritage. In the recent, there have been some significant developments, viz., the launch of Jawahar Lal Nehru Urban Renewal Mission (JNNURM) and Delhi as the venue of XIX Commonwealth Games, 2010. Delhi Master Plan 2021 (MPD-2021) dedicates a separate chapter on Conservation of the Built Heritage of Delhi. The surveys conducted by the DDA and INTACH listed 1203 historical monuments, sites and buildings in Delhi, which include the Archeological Survey of India notified 155 protected monuments. In addition to these, the State

Archaeological Department has notified 20 heritage buildings. The Delhi Master Plan 2021 provides a mandatory policy framework, area was heritage conservation action plans. It is an opportune time to develop the strategies and action plans for a time bound 'Urban Renewal and Conservation' taking advantage of Commonwealth Games 2010 and JNNURM. Certain pilot projects can be initiated, which have visibility and public appeal. These could trigger a series of follow up programmes.

The GNCTD in its CDP prepared for the JNNURM has projected an investment plan for Rs.582 crore for conservation of heritage during 2007-12.The Govt. of Delhi has also signed an MOU with the INTACH as its partner and for professional support. Looking at the time and financial constraints, it is necessary to work out the priorities and identify the key result areas. As Delhi is often taken as an example by other cities in the country, it is necessary to focus upon the process, institutional framework and capacity building for the co-ordination, convergence, public participation, partnerships and documentation for the conservation and management of the heritage resources.

Institutional Framework for Integrated Heritage Management

The existing institutional framework for protection, conservation and management of the heritage resources of Delhi is characterized by administrative and technical sectorisation. As mentioned in MPD 2021, there is a necessity for co-ordination and convergence and formulation of locally based conservation and urban renewal programmes, which include up-gradation, regeneration and provision of essential infrastructure in potential areas of heritage resources. A number of agencies in Delhi are involved in the development, conservation and heritage management, which need to be intrinsically linked. Accordingly, the mandate and responsibilities are to be defined and a common platform need to be created to bring all these agencies together. For certain dedicated projects, it will be worth while to create special purpose vehicle (SPV).

Inventory of Heritage Resources

It is necessary to have a common heritage database and inventory of heritage resources, which is comprehensive and reliable. Cultural Resource Information System for heritage resource should indicate exact location and legal boundaries of each heritage resource on maps to a scale appropriate for preparation and implementation of local area heritage conservation plans. This is a primary requirement for integration of the heritage resources into the city development process. The INTACH/DDA list needs to be updated and expanded together with delineation of all heritage resources (sites, structures, monuments, conservation areas, precincts, historic urban villages and water bodies/structures, etc) on GIS, digitized maps. This involves the classification, compilation and updation of the inventory of each heritage resource, correlation of authentic statistical data and preparation of maps at appropriate scale for formulation of comprehensive conservation and heritage management plans. In the case of monuments, buildings and sites protected by the ASI and the GNCTD, Department of Archaeology, it is necessary to demarcate the extent and exact boundaries of the designated protected area, as well as the properties within the prohibited area and the regulated area surrounding such monuments /complexes.

Prioritizing Heritage Projects

In view of the time and resource constraints, it is essential to prioritize the heritage conservation projects. The priority projects should be simple to design and execute, with lesser complexities and no legal hassles. Accordingly priority projects can be identified which can be taken up with the help of the JNNURM funding and within time frame. Such projects may include selected heritage sites in the old city of Shahjahanabad, such as Jama Masjid, Red Fort, Chandni Chowk, Salimgarh, Turkman Gate, Ajmeri Gate, Delhi Gate, Lahore Gate, etc. Redevelopment of Nizamuddin – Sunder Nagar -Humayun Tomb complex has already been taken with the help of Aga Khan Foundation, which should be developed linking major areas of concentration of built heritage. The facelift of heritage area/buildings and provision of well designed signages, lighting and putting the dangling cables underground in such areas can transform their chaotic ambience.

As stated in MPD -2021, the development of green corridors can be taken up along the canals and city drains. Work on South Delhi Greenway project along Barapulla drain had earlier been initiated by the Delhi Tourism &Transport and Development Corporation (DTTDC). A key area of focus could be the development of a series of boulevards, pedestrian precincts and heritage spaces of daily use. Chandni Chowk and various other areas in old city and new city can be developed as the boulevards and exclusive pedestrian precincts. A number of pedestrian corridors can be developed leading to riverfront, along the drains and bridges on the river. The development of heritage parks had been earlier taken up at Lodi Garden and at Mehrauli. Heritage parks can be developed in other areas, such as Tughlakabad, Adilabad, Red Fort, Jama Masjid, Hauz Rani, Hauz Khas, Chirag Delhi, Wazirabad, Shalimar Bagh, etc. Along the river, few bio-diversity parks could be planned and developed.

Urban Renewal and Conservation of Shahjahanabad (Old City, Jama Masjid, Red Fort, Chandni Chowk and Salimgarh)

The necessity of conservation and heritage management within the Walled City of Shahjahanabad and its extensions (2600 Ha-Special Area) is overdue. As recognized in the MPD-2021 and the Zonal Development Plans, the conservation areas have already been identified. The entire Walled City is a Conservation Area. A study of the heritage typologies, resources, and issues related to local community is necessary as the basis of formulating the Special Area Conservation Plans. A detailed inventory of the traditional housing stock, historic *havelis, Katras, Kuchas* and *mohallas*, and their demarcation on area maps, together with an indication of their value as heritage resource are necessary The Municipal Corporation of Delhi has initiated the work on Redevelopment of Jama Masjid area and have invited bids for preparation of the conservation plans of Old City (Special Area). The Integrated Heritage Management of Jama Masjid and other heritage areas within the overall plan of Walled City of Shahjahanabad should be linked with community development, regeneration, infrastructure upgradation and tourism development. In view of Infrastructure inadequacies in the Special Area /Old city, the upgradation and infrastructure retrofitting should be integrated with the value of the heritage planning. Water supply and sewerage lines will require argumentation while Social Infrastructure requirements could be partially met by adaptive reuse of heritage properties.

Historic Urban Villages

Urban villages as the traditional settlements encompass both, vernacular residential community structures, as well as religious buildings and historic monuments. They display varied characteristics depending on their location, inhabitants, their historical role and relationship to the city. Out of 165 odd urban villages, several villages such as Nizamuddin, Chirag Delhi, Khirki, Sarai Shahji, Begumpur, Kalu Sarai, Kalkaji, Sheikh Sarai, Adh-chini Said-ul-ajaib, Mehraulli, Hauz Khas, Shahpur Jat, Tughlaquabad, etc. have a major concentration of heritage resources. At the time of their incorporation within the urban limits, the land earmarked for village settlements, including *Gaon Sabha* lands (common land of the villages) encompassing the "*abadi*" area were shown in red ink, known as the 'Lal Dora'. This area, in the past, had been exempt from municipal byelaws and restrictions leading to very high densities, incompatible land uses and the location of noxious and hazardous industries within the settlements. Most of these urban villages, which have a concentration of heritage resources, are included within the conservation zones identified by the INTACH/DDA.

Historic urban villages are threatened today by increasing over-densification, uncontrolled and illegal constructions, encroachments and non–conforming uses, which overpower and engulf the significant heritage resources of the traditional settlements.

Locally based, participatory, integrated conservation and management programmes for the heritage villages with a thrust on infrastructure upgradation and historic buildings rehabilitation through comprehensive conservation plans, which support and stimulate local handicrafts need to be taken up. The programmes should provide the linkages between poverty alleviation, environmental improvement and conservation. Pragmatic and community based programmes should be formulated with the objective of regeneration and conservation of the historic villages, which can be part of the thematic heritage tourism circuits. The revenue generated through heritage tourism can be utilized for the environmental upgradation of the settlement for the benefit of the local community.The provision of essential infrastructure and adaptive reuse of heritage areas could be of great potential for heritage tourism, whereas the provision of community facilities, and for generation and diversification of employment opportunities for the benefit of local community.

Canals, Drains, Lakes and Traditional Water Management Structures

Components of the historic and traditional water management systems of the city, such as the canals, drains, rivulets, *bunds,* sluices, reservoirs, *baolis,* tanks, village ponds etc. have the potential to supplement the city's water resources through water harvesting, as well as play a significant role in groundwater recharge. These heritage resources, such as Ugrasen's Baoli in Connaught Place, Baoli in Nizamuddin, Jharna and Hauz Shamsi in Mehrauli, Hauz Khas tank, etc., are vital functional, recreational and educational resources. Some of the larger reservoirs, such as the water body associated with the Shikargah or Hunting palace at Jaunti, the *Bund* and the *Baoli* associated with Talkatora Garden, Adilabad, Najafgarh lake ,etc. are of immense ecological value and have considerable potential for heritage tourism.

Heritage Tourism

Planning for heritage tourism linked to the city's vast range of heritage resources for environmental and community benefits should be developed with adequate safeguards and according to the conservation framework/ charters for cultural tourism. Identification of thematic cultural tourism circuits within Delhi may include heritage trails, nature and historic walks, pilgrim circuits and the programmes for 'heritage festivals', linked with the cultural resources of the city and its traditional festivals and celebrations. The designation of a category of 'heritage hotels' can encourage the tourism and heritage conservation. Strategies for transportation linkages, parking, adaptive re-use, up-gradation and provision of state-of-art infrastructure in heritage conservation areas should be developed within the overall heritage management framework. Preparation of heritage management plans and conservation plans should be undertaken for the identified heritage resources by qualified conservation professionals, with the objective of developing organizational capacity for heritage management.

It is necessary to formulate Conservation Guidelines for the areas associated with protected monuments, sites and buildings as well as for other areas with a concentration of natural and cultural heritage resources. The development plans for areas in proximity with World Heritage Sites beyond the official 100m prohibited area +200m regulated zone should be prepared, alongwith their impact assessment on the heritage. This should be mandatory, so that long term and cumulative impacts are mitigated. This will help in ensuring that the valuable heritage resources are not lost but utilized for the benefit of the community in the improvement of the environment of heritage areas and the visual corridors are not obstructed.

Making Conservation and Urban Renewal Work

Multiplicity of organizations and lack of effective, coordinated action, non-preparation of Urban Renewal and Heritage Management Plans have been the main reasons for the backlogs in the heritage and urban renewal. In this regard the JNNURM can act as a major resource for urban renewal, heritage conservation and rehabilitation. This can bring a turnaround and accelerate the conservation efforts. This also necessitates building private-public partnerships and using the rehabilitation process to alleviate poverty and mitigate negative environmental impact.

Currently, funds earmarked for conservation of heritage resources are woefully inadequate and mechanisms are required whereby innovative funding could be generated for restoration, conservation and management of heritage resources. The mobilization of adequate resources for effective conservation and heritage management should be linked with processes of economic regeneration. The incentives for conservation could be given in the following manner:

- By direct financial grant to the owner of the heritage resource by the Central/State/Local government.
- Providing the building owner access to credit, tax relief, property tax exemption, land use relaxation (heritage hotel) and other concessions.
- Cross –subsidies for maintenances of listed heritage buildings.
- Development Control Incentives, such as Transferable Development Rights (TDR) for heritage buildings and Accommodation Reservation (AR) for community buildings, road widening in villages/ old city.
- Direct action by the authorities through upgradation of infrastructure, restoration and maintenance of buildings and provision of essential utilities and community facilities.

Encouragement should be given by the public authorities to the locals in conservation and rehabilitation activities and in formulation of community based heritage management plans in a participatory manner. The initiatives to encourage Public-Private-Partnership in the heritage conservation and management sector will bring the Business Organizations, N.G.Os, Residents Welfare Associations, Public Sector Undertakings and Government Departments in the endeavour.

The JNNURM funds can be accessed under the Sub-Mission on Urban Infrastructure and Governance, for Urban Renewal, which includes the redevelopment of old city areas, conservation of heritage area/ structures, widening of streets, shifting of non–conforming activities, replacement of old and worn out services (water/ sewerage/drainage/ solid waste disposal, etc.)

The Govt. of India (Ministry of Youth & Sports), DDA, CPWD, Government of Delhi, Sport Authority of India and other organizations have taken up various projects for the prestigious 19th

Commonwealth Games, to be held in Delhi during October 2010. All the sports complexes (11) and other venues have been planned as 'Green Projects', which include Commonwealth Games Village (DDA), training venues, transport and other infrastructure. The image of Delhi as a green and clean city is a key concern, which involves a synergy at various levels of planning, design, and conservation of heritage. This is an opportune time to showcase the unique built and natural heritage, which makes Delhi a unique city.

Ground Breaking Decisions by the Chief Minister of Rajasthan

Ms. Faith Singh - Founder, Jaipur Virasat Foundation

Decision: 2009 June 30th: The Government of Rajasthan Department of Urban Governance announced through the state Hindi language media it would pursue a holistic four-year strategy of heritage resource management throughout Rajasthan in six cities and nine cultural regions, working with expert NGOs and professional organizations.

Decision: 2009 July 8th: The Chief Minister of Rajasthan, Mr. Ashok Gehlot, announced in his budget speech as Finance Minister,

- A State Heritage and Development Council chaired by the Chief Minister
- A new State Heritage and Development Authority
- A budget allocation for the above of 10 crore rupees

The development of a regional and urban planning and management strategy at policy level is the outcome of seven years field work by JVF with its partner organizations and supporters, following on ground work done through the 80s and 90s by INTACH. On June 29th, 2009, Jaipur Virasat Foundation, members of the JVF partner consortium, and key representatives of Jaipur citizenry made a presentation under the title Vikas and Virasat (Progress & Heritage) in the State Secretariat Conference Hall to Minister for Urban Governance, Mr. *Shanti Dhariwal; Minister for Panchayati Raj,* Mr. *Bharat Singh, representatives of the state administration and various agencies for urban affairs and town planning, and the Minister for Tourism Art & Culture Ms. Bina Kak.*

The new Authority is integral to the strategy. Its function is to coordinate the work of heritage resource management across the sectors to benefit the people and alleviate poverty in the state, and to foster an inclusive economy of creative (culture-based) industries and cultural tourism. The Authority is to be instituted and made statutory through a Town and Country Planning Bill (being currently presented before the State Assembly). The Authority will be an independent agency housed in the Rajasthan Town Planning Office in Jaipur, the state capital, and attached to the Department of Urban Governance.

Vikas & Virasat strategy integrates seven component programs rooted in the people's heritage resources, to foster a creative economy that is inclusive, pro-poor, and sustainable.

- Programs One, Two and Three address planning and management of the historic built heritage including: application of a regulatory framework to preserve the character of Rajasthan's heritage settlements; development of management tools and management capacity to conserve and develop the historic built environment; a series of "acupuncture" projects in six cities of Rajasthan to kick start the program and give visible results, to stimulate wider engagement.
- Program Four creates new heritage based livelihood opportunities for traditional communities from the region's traditional skills,

knowledge, crafts and arts. It revalorises intangible aspects of heritage by linking them to economic and social development, fostering participation and ownership of the Vikas & Virasatstrategy by the maximum number of people.

- Programs Five & Six stimulate and strengthen the growth of a creative economy as a new development paradigm, through creative and community festivals, through promoting best practices in heritage based commercial activity, and through marketing pro-poor, cultural tourism for Rajasthan, worldwide.
- Program Seven applies an adaptive management strategy to the Vikas & Virasat strategy. It co-ordinates, monitors and disseminates the program as an integrated whole and invites expert development partners and funding for the program.

Decision: May 2009: To develop Jaipur as a world class city by the Government of Rajasthan, giving public recognition to the need to conserve and respect Jaipur's core historical character while providing the amenities of the modern world class city.

Vikas & Virasat has emerged from frequent meetings and dialogue between JVF professional partners and associates with senior members of the state administration, elected members of government (including a brief meeting with the Chief Minister) and national level experts. Since the new Congress government took office in January 2009 and at the national level in May, JVF's efforts have been to work with the government to develop a pragmatic strategy applicable to regional and local conditions. JVF and its partners welcome the Rajasthan Chief Minister's ground breaking decisions as indicative of political will, vision and concern, supported by progressive administrators committed to good governance and to applying new strategies to address poverty, inequality, and loss of regional identity and cultural diversity.

Looking Back

In the 80s and 90s, INTACH laid the foundations. JVF started its work in 2002 and through creative festivals and work with rural folk performers across the state, JVF has connected the term *'Virasat'* with a dynamic, living heritage, a source of pride, potential livelihood and progress. The function of creative festivals is now better understood; the Jaipur festival - and particularly Jaipur Literature Festival, started by JVF, is a world renowned brand, a signature event; JVF with partner Mehrangarh Museum Trust has created the annual Jodhpur RIFF brand as an international festival of folk music promoting Rajasthan to the world. Rajasthan Government has in 2009 committed to establish the new authority and as a first for India, has allocated funds for integrated heritage management in its budget. Could this, we ask, be the beginnings of a future National Ministry for Traditional. Knowledge and Livelihoods for inclusive development, specific to India's character?

Looking Forward

India is bursting with energy to modernise and has a rich resource of capable professionals. People are desperate for a better life and they want to see results from their government. With appropriate leadership, support from both public and private sectors, and professional management and capacity building, our abundant heritage resources can support livelihood for thousands of people in Rajasthan. Unlike the oil based economy that has set unsustainable expectations that threaten the existence of the planet, human and heritage based progress is of minimum environmental impact, renewable and indefinitely sustainable.

The challenges for Vikas and Virasat are threefold:

- To apply the mission as dynamic human resource management for social and economic development, rooted in the living knowledge of the people, not simply the restoration of historic monuments disconnected from most people's daily lives or cultural activity for an elite that is divorced from poverty alleviation and development.

- To ensure that the best professionals in the country are enabled to deliver their skills and experience to the people of Rajasthan through the new Authority.
- To focus on *aam aadmi* as Vikas & Virasat's prime beneficiary

Heritage based growth can transform Rajasthan if it becomes the self-perpetuating outcome of culture-based economic activity, owned widely by the people. India needs a growth paradigm that is rooted in its people's own understanding, strengths, and time tested skills and knowledge. The need is critical. Rajasthan has made a start. We see this as the beginnings of a new phase for progressive management of India's heritage, where India charts its own development strategy, taking the best from the experience of the industrialized developed world and conserving its own highly developed civilization.

God Bless Rajasthan! Thanks to Rajasthan's Chief Minister, Mr Ashok Gehlot, for leading in this ground breaking step!

Jaipur Virasat Foundation (JVF) was registered September 2002 to pursue a ground-up, community based approach to heritage management as an equitable, inclusive strategy for the benefit of India's modernising democracy. Trustees -Basantt Khaitan, Gajsingh Jodhpur, John Singh, ML Mehta, Mahavir Sharma, Paras Kuhad, Rathi Vinay Jha, Rima Uooja, Vikram Golcha. International Patron -URU Prince Charles the Prince of Wales (UK)

Reviving Heritage-Centric Urban Development of Udaipur-Status and Futuristic Action Plan

Shri S.K.Verma I.F.S. (Retd.) - Regional Convenor INTACH Udaipur

Heritage Fabric of Udaipur:

'Heritage' is anything transmitted from the past, which is perceived by our multicultural society as having a quality or significance that makes it worth preserving for its own sake and for the appreciation of current and future generations and it should be based on hard, scientifically tested, facts and not on vague notions born out of cultivated ignorance. Mewar is a living treasure of glorious past and vibrant present. The Heritage Fabric of Mewar in general and Udaipur in particular is a complex weave of many different things. Numerous elements, both natural and man-made, interweave to give the settlement distinct character and cultural significance. It is of great interest to scan the literature, historical records and visit heritage sites of the Mewar's heritage. Mewar was a geographically secluded territory, the rugged terrain a distinctive physical feature of the Aravallie Ranges that helped to shape the State's history. Mewar offers so much tranquility, peace, happiness and satisfaction to even short-time visitors, who come here only for a short duration. To visitors from abroad or from distant corners of India, the very thought of Mewar gives images, vision and insight of Mewar as a land of valour, sacrifice, serenity, worship and is famous for its splendid natural canvass, filled with rich culture and fine arts. Thus, Mewar's historical and cultural heritage has a distinct identity due to its stoical adherence to traditions, despite several blows to its heritage and traditional lifestyle. India has always held this kingdom in high respect and a source of inspiration.

The Heritage fabric of Mewar in general and Udaipur in particular includes:

(a) The man-made elements- Buildings, artifacts, structures, Ruins, Palaces, *Havelies*, Forts, Fort Walls, Gates, Streets & Streetscapes, *Chowks*, Stepped Wells (*Bavdis* and Kunds), Places /structures of worship and its surroundings; Open Spaces and Gardens and precincts of historic, and / or aesthetic, and / or architectural.

(b) Abundant natural precincts and landscapes-both natural and man-made elements.

(c) Natural elements-landforms of environmental significance and / or of scenic beauty, including but not restricted to sacred groves; hills, and water bodies and their bio-diversity viz. medicinal plants and the wildlife. It includes rock formations, gorges, caves, points, walks, rides, waterfalls, lakes, pools, groves etc.

(d) Rural environment -full of hilly landscapes with scattered hutment, sacred groves, terraced fields and forests. In rural environment ancient Indian culture and art found an asylum in the territory and enriched the kingdom's own superb heritage. The bullock carts jingle, women sing folklore and children frolic.

(e) Complexes weave of many things viz. literature & stories of bravery, supreme sacrifice and devotion.

(f) Community structures other Residences and their cultural significance

(g) Living heritage namely (i) Performing Arts including music, dance, drama etc., (ii) Visual Art including painting, sculpture and graphics, (iii) Folk and Tribal Art, (iv) Handicrafts, Crafts, etc.

(v) Fairs and Festivals. The living heritage promises livelihoods for millions. Local communities act as service providers and act as a support system where tourism is developed. Culture & of cultural significance and character.

Background of Udaipur

Udaipur, the capital of Mewar was founded by ex- Maharana Udai Singh during the year 1559. The population (1881) was 38264 while it grew to 307682 (1991) and now it is expected to be 389317 (2001) and 830000 by 2022. Udaipur is located at an altitude of 600 Mts. MSL the annual precipitation is 67.26 cm. Udaipur attracts 15% of state's foreign tourists. It is now a tourist destination where the guests/ tourists arrival rose from 71958 nos. (2001) to 739,880 nos. (2005). It is a paradox that tourism in Udaipur can grow immeasurably, especially with improved communication and infrastructure, but tourism can dry up completely if the lakes are not saved.

Udaipur is picturesque with diverse tourist attraction like lakes, heritage, religious places and garden and with a congenial natural setting. Udaipur, the city of lakes, is a lovely city whose cultural significance and character does not depend only on its heritage fabric, but also on its sense of tranquility, serenity, congruence and a quality of timelessness. Generally even a common man of Mewar is proud of their cultural heritage and is knitted in a social fabric of compassion and mutual respect for each other. Udaipur and its surrounding are a fascinating blend of sights, sounds and experiences of exquisite lake palace. Jag Mandir, Jag Niwas shimmer like jewels in Lake Pichola. It is a spectacle in white colours of built heritage. Its kaleidoscope of palaces, lakes, temples, gardens and narrow lanes strewn with stalls, carry the flavor of a heroic past, epitomizing valour and chivalry. The City rampart with its original eleven gates, of which only nine remain and the City Rampart 'Shaharkot', broken at many places to give way to traffic and communication network, is in a bad shape. The excellent forts and palaces stood tall with their rich heritage and exquisite architecture of forts and palaces. This glory survives today in the radiance and architectural heritage of intricately carved '*havellies*' (mansion) making this city a paradise for an architecture buff.

For a visitor from abroad there is an intense desire to see this enchanting natural heritage of lakes, forts and palaces and to buy works of pottery, decorative arts and handicrafts. It is also famous for 'Mulela' Pottery, tribal embroidery, folk painting on cloth, carved wood and carved statues of sandstone and painted wooden panels. Even the name of Maharana Pratap, Maharana Kumbha and his *Maharani* turned Saint Meera Bai and the tales of the sacrifice of Panna Dhai fills a sense of pride of the glorious heritage. Tourists are eager to visit the Haldhighati and Chetak Samadhi, the shrines of Eklingji, Nathdwara, Ranakpur, Rishabdev etc. to spend sometime to see the famous lakes and gardens.

The heritage attractions of Udaipur fall into three categories viz. (a) Headline places - Palaces, Museums, Lake views; (b) Secondary places – Gangaur Ghat, Jagadish Temple, Gardens, Parks, "Milk Tank" and, (c)The city itself – Streets, Markets, Community Places, Schools, Exhibitions, Restaurants, Shops, Cafes, Bridges, etc. The living heritage of festivals, fairs, folksongs and dance, traditional arts and paintings etc. is impressive.

A few of heritage attractions are: City Palace Complex, Fort/City Rampart and its Gates, Temples-Jagdish Temple, Amba Mata, Mahakaleshwar and Jain Temples, Memorials, Lakes & Islands-Pichola, Fatehsagar, Goverdhan Sagar, Swarupsagar, Badi, Madar, Udaisagar. Places of tourist interest Jagmandir, Jag Niwas, Arsivilas, Natni ka Chabutra, Mohan Mandir, Gangaur Ghat, Bagor Havellies, Purhoit ki *Haveli*; Embankments, Sites of natural scenic beauty, Heritage streets, buildings and *Havelies*; Mahasatiya & Gangukund and sites like Jagdish

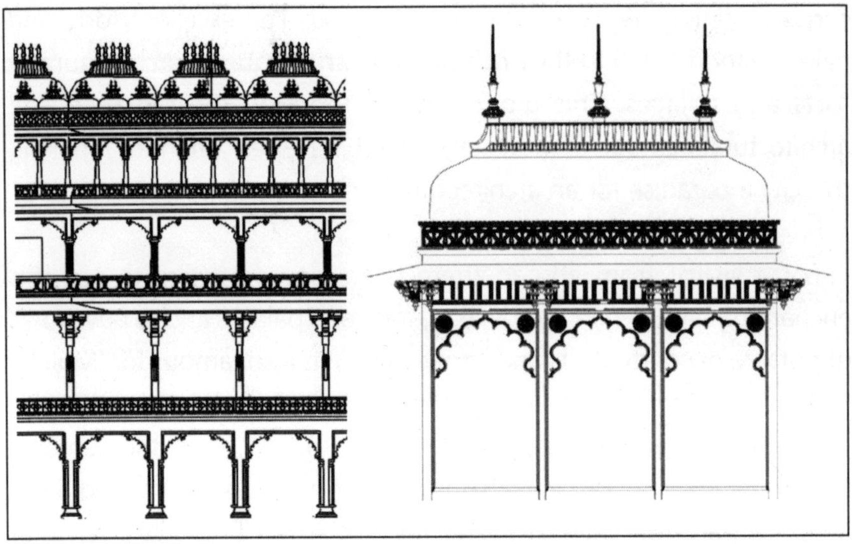

Temple Area, Gangaur Ghat Area, Ravji ka Hata Area, Bara Bazar, Sarrafa Bazar and Motichohata and surrounding Landscapes. The components of architectural heritage are Gates (Pols), *Chhatries* & Pillars, Projections, Grills, Doors, Carvings, Verandahs, Elevation Aspects, Facade, Material and Colour Component, *Chauk*, Open Spaces.

Existing Patterns of Urban Development

During 1997 Master Plan was prepared for an area of 9879 acres (1997), while now this has to be re-formulated to 27180 acres (2022). Thus , the vision should be expressed in quantitative terms, e.g., planning to raise the number of visitors from x to x+ 1 by 2011 or income from heritage from y to y+1. The vision may be qualitative, e.g., providing a life time experience to visitors.

Existing city growth pattern for urban developments is mainly towards the eastern part of the city. In the western part, the urban growth is limited due to physical constrains like mountains and lakes. Major urban developments are taking place towards Jhadol, Nathdwara and Airport.

The existing land use 1997(Area in acres) and the Proposed land use-2022(Area in acres)

S.NO.	LAND USE	Existing land use 1997 (Area in acres)	Proposed land use-2022 (Area in acres)
1.	Residential	4,988	13,380
2.	Commercial	548	1,220
3.	Industry	1,152	1,110
4.	Government	96	340
5.	Recreational	358	2,430
6.	Public & semi public	1,632	2,430
7.	Circulation	1,105	2,480
8.	Total Developed area	9.879	23,380
9.	Govt.Reserved	865	950
10.	Plantation	-	800
11.	Water Bodies	1.900	2000
12.	Agriculture Research farm	-	50
	Agri.& forest	285	-
	Other vacant land	9,672	-
	Grand Total	22,601	27,180

Major Concerns

As the city grows today, one of the major concerns is conserving the lakes, history and rich heritage, which attracts both national and foreign tourists. Most of our cities have a historical core and we need to conserve this core to reinforce the identies of our cities.

Major weaknesses of Udaipur City are: Insufficient Infrastructure facilities like Untreated Sewage being released into the lakes (45 drain spots); Ghats (73nos.) being used for washing and bathing purposes; Drainage and Solid waste Management coverage less than acceptable standards i.e. total solid waste being dumped annually (approx. 500 tons) and waste of 53 hotels and restaurants being dumped in lakes; and Heavy sedimentation in the lakes due to soil erosion on hill slopes and construction waste being dumped into lakes. Major commercial activities are concentrationed within old city area, causing severe congestion. Traditional houses in walled city risk demolition by their owners due to high maintenance/repair required for these buildings. Absence of efficient mass transportation facility within the city, lack of civic awareness on heritage and conservation and insufficient heritage management are severe constraints. Further the Ahar River has become a waste water drain and is heavily polluted as a result of raw sewage inflow and dumping of solid waste.

Emerging Trends of Urban Development

Usually the heritage properties in and around urban area are public and historic spaces in Heritage Zone; Streets with special heritage character; Renewal of inner city areas or heritage precincts; Areas containing groups of heritage buildings and related spaces; Natural heritage sites; Potential for adaptive re-use of heritage buildings and spaces and Functions which will enhance transit or pilgrimage potential of the city.

As such, opportunities exist for (a) Protection, restoration and overall environmental improvement of lakes to attract domestic and international tourists; (b) Developing existing heritage sites & conservation to attract more tourists; (c) Improving linkages of city through broad gauge railway network (to Ahmedabad) and efficient air service to trigger tourism, and; (d) Developing a tourist circuit connecting places of tourist interest which would involve development of related infrastructure.

Now it is appreciated that there is a need for modern 'Infrastructural Development and Planning for Heritage Identity. We should be able to look straight at our past in the eye. Only then, we can cope with the present and plan 'Future for our Past'. Develop a clear understanding of the problems and issues involved. Evolve future strategies whereby the general public, especially students and youth, town planners, architects and policy and decision makers can absorb this vision. It is important to maintain the diversity of our rich and varied cultural and historical heritage, which is more than 5000 years old.

Formulating a Vision for Urban Heritage

Our Heritage is a precious capital that has been built over the centuries and its destruction, even partly, will leave us poorer. Each generation interprets the past heritage differently and derives new inspiration from it. It is our solemn duty to sustain this legacy and to pass it on to the future. This approach, we are convinced, is the only meaningful course for development. Striking a right balance between traditions and the demands of today lies at the heart of successful and sustainable development and economic growth. Each one of us, young and old, can make a meaningful contribution to achieve this balance. A clear understanding of the problems and issues involved, will help us to evolve future strategies whereby general public, especially youth can absorb this vision.

Developing a vision for the city is key to the preparation of the CDP/ Conservation Plan. As indicated in the 'Toolkit for the Formulation of a City Development Plan', "a vision is a statement of what the city wishes to do, within a given time-frame, and is often expressed in terms of clear expectations. It defines the potential of the city and reflects its unique attributes in terms of comparative and competitive advantages, values and preferences of the city's residents, relationship of the city to the state, national and global economies, and of course, the history and physical characteristics of the city".

Usually the heritage properties in and around urban area are:-

- Public and historic spaces in heritage zone
- Streets with special heritage character
- Renewal of inner city areas or heritage precincts
- Areas containing groups of heritage buildings and related spaces
- Potential for adaptive re-use of heritage buildings and spaces
- Functions which will enhance transit or pilgrimage potential of the city

Following the main toolkit, the City Development Plan (CDP) with heritage focus needs to develop a vision for its heritage component: what is the city's vision for heritage? What does the city think about the future development of city's heritage? In what direction does the city want to develop and use its heritage? In developing the vision which, it must be emphasized, is a participatory process involving the key stakeholders, the Conservation Plan/CDP should address the following areas aspects i.e. the future role of city's heritage, both tangible and intangible, in city's socio-economic and cultural profile; the hidden or under-used potential of city's heritage and the extent to which the city wishes to tap it for city's growth and development; the possible economic contribution that heritage can make to the city's economy and other roles that heritage can play, e.g., creating networks and relationships. A clear vision is necessary for designing strategies and identifying relevant projects.

Futuristic Urban Development

We should also be able to address:

1. Urban Development-Objectives and status of urban growth, planning and legislation, Master plan vis-à-vis expectations of local communities & visitors and impacts of globalization.
2. Setting up of heritage zones and management of cultural and natural heritage through heritage action plan and heritage-centric regulations for in new urban habitations. Conservation of heritage in sites of conflict/encroachment.

3. Heritage tourism and site management: conservation and development (Built and natural heritage sites including Lake-systems)
4. Regional co-operation and funding of conservation projects ·

Legal Framework to Regulate and Conserve Heritage Properties and Sites

It is quite astonishing that Rajasthan, known for its heritage properties and historical sites, has no specific law to declare or regulate legal framework to regulate and conserve them till now. The State Government of Rajasthan has now realized the importance of heritage conservation and is planning to formulate Heritage Regulations (June, 2009). The new regulations are expected to provide legal framework for heritage conservation as well as to take action against people who tampered with such properties or their conservation. It will also provide for conservation of heritage properties and their precincts and natural area surrounding it. The regulations also moot a State level Monitoring Committee comprising of NGOs, architects, town planners etc. These regulations could be under the Municipal Act, either as a separate regulation or a regulation as a part of building bye laws.

A committee with the Chief Town Planner of Rajasthan as Member Secretary has been working to frame rules governing such properties for quite some time now. It is a happy sign that the first draft is ready and dis-cussion is being held at the highest level to finalize the Heritage Regulations.

It is a happy sign that after great persuasion for three years by INTACH Udaipur Chapter a Heritage Cell has been created in Municipal Council Udaipur. Similar action is yet pending at the level of Urban Improvement Trust and District Administration.

Usual Threats to Heritage Components

Rapid urbanization is causing unplanned growth. Changing use of building and its facade, increasing encroachments, dilapidated condition of the heritage art & culture, absence of bye laws and heritage regulations, lack of planning and co-ordination and financial resources, lack of infrastructural facilities and lack of public awareness, absence unified heritage authority are major concerns of the day.

We should take prompt action for the following:

(a) General Measures:

1. Study and evaluate the City Development Plan (CDP), which has already been prepared to identify the interface between the proposals made as a part of the CDP and the requirement of conservation.
2. A broad perspective plan of Master Plans, incorporate listings of buildings, sites, remains, ruins, monuments and landscapes of archaeological, historical, cultural, architectural and ecological value in the City Development Plan. Locate the heritage buildings and sites on the map.
3. An appropriate toolkit should be prepared for the formulation of City Development Plans for the historic areas of the cities. This is very much possible without losing the character and historic assets of the city with sensitive intervention and planning.
4. Citizen's participation will ultimately lead to laying out a vision for the city. After a series of stake-holder's consultations, a consensus can be reached on the issues of conservation and planning. Stake-holders are individuals, affinity groups and trusts and the State Government.
5. There is a strong link and symbiotic relationship between the built heritage and natural heritage. The ponds, the network of open spaces, forests and the landscapes are an integral part of the buildings of heritage value.
6. There is a strong link between the heritage buildings and the craftspeople who build them. Heritage conservation must include

the role of crafts people and the use of local materials and traditional building practices.

7. To achieve these objectives the citizens must be involved in decision-making so that conservation and development can be made a sustainable process.

Specific Measures

1. Conservation Master Plan: A futuristic plan should be developed and heritage scheme of Udaipur should be:

- Conserving heritage zones in and around Udaipur within the master plan area of Udaipur and all development schemes to be carried out in light of preserving historical monuments, natural streams, lakes and drainage courses.
- All future developments should be approved in heritage zones by the Heritage Cell.
- Effective implementation of Master Plan and heritage plan by the local bodies.

2. Creation of Heritage Advisory Committee & Heritage Cell:

A Heritage Advisory Committee should be established by District Administration with all authorities dealing with urban development like Municipal council, Urban Improvement Trusts, Town Planning, District Administration and departments dealing with lakes, drainage and traffic systems, tourism, forest, horticulture etc. The INTACH Udaipur Chapter should be invited as a Special Advisory to give a technical opinion on each project.

3. A Heritage Cell should be established in the offices of District Administration, Urban Improvement Trusts, Town Planning, Forest and Wildlife and Tourism Departments. No Heritage cell will be successful unless we have participation of citizens and local consultants.

4. Preparation of Heritage Bye-Laws:

Heritage regulations, bye-laws and policies should be drafted after identifying heritage zones, monuments, buildings, lakes etc. Norms, bye-laws and policy should be formed for these zones. The bye-laws should be formed in consultation with the heritage cell and they should be strictly adhered to.

5. Financial Management:

Efforts should be made to get a full support from the local bodies, MP's, MLA's for implementation of the above plan and regular grants on yearly basis. Also schemes should be prepared for individual projects and submitted to agencies like JNURM for executing the Heritage Projects regularly.

6. Planned Development of the city with improvement of city infrastructure along with

- Allocation of Annual budget
- Preparation & application of bye laws for the heritage buildings
- Creation of unified heritage authority & its powers.
- Involvement of local bodies for the protection and improvement and NGO's & public contribution & participation.
- Planning & strategies for the protection heritage site through identification of heritage zones & places, timely plan implementation, mapping & detailing of the heritage places. additional infrastructure facilities to the heritage zone.
- Identification of components, improvement of access to heritage sites, restoration of heritage buildings, delineation of heritage streets, under ground cabling & electrification, cleanliness, improvement of parking pPlaces etc.
- Zoning & planning of the heritage places.
- Public awareness / publicity of heritage places.
- Heritage regulations should be part of Development Controls in Development Plans.
- All Urban Renewal schemes must obtain the approval of Heritage Conservation Committee (H.C.C.) comprising of the local authorities, NGO's / CBO's and experts, especially such permissions /approval of development around protected sites or within heritage precincts, administered by local bodies. These permissions /approval should not be dealt as routine Building Permits but ought to be

considered through a H.C.C. Similarly all proposals of Tourism Development must be whetted by the H.C.C.

- All Urban Renewal and conservation schemes of built and natural heritage must invariably include the listing and documentation of all heritage structures and elements and mapping them clearly in statutory Local Area Plans of settlements and notifying the heritage list under the Urban and Regional Development Planning Acts or a separate Heritage Conservation Act.
- Jawaharlal Nehru National Urban Renewal Mission (JNNURM) ought to be realigned in consonance with similar missions for rural development so that migration in to cities, which could be mitigated through enhanced investments to projects in rural areas.

The sectoral goals of urban development of Udaipur are (a) Proper land use and spatial growth, (b) Regular maintenance and cleanliness of lakes, heritage sites and places of Tourism value, (c) Roads, parking spaces and transport facilities, (d) Water supply, (e) Proper sanitation and sewerage,

7. By a rough estimate of the year 2008 Rs 578.00 crores will be required for the following sectors:

Sr. No.	Sector	Investment (Rs Crores)	Sectoral Distribution
A	Water Supply	167	28.97%
B	Sewerage	117	20.18%
C	Drainage Works	17	2.91%
D	Traffic and Transportation	80	13.86%
E	Basic Services for Poor	66	11.43%
F	Solid Waste Management (SWM)	11	1.90%
G	Tourism and Urban Renewal	31	5.44%
H	Lakes Conservation	23	4.03%
I	Public Amenities	14	2.48%
J	Heritage Conservation	50	8.65%
	Total	**578.00**	**100.00%**

(f) Proper maintenance of drainage channels, (g) Solid waste management with composting, (h) Urban services for the poor and (i) Institutional strengthening. A thorough assessment of the proposed land use in tandem with natural heritage and tourism based development needs is essential.

We aim to enable urban development of Udaipur that provides for its residents an environmentally friendly, culturally rich, economically vibrant ambiance, by sustaining its heritage resources and providing a variety of opportunities along with a robust infrastructure that takes care of all of its citizens giving equal importance to urban poor of city. We need to protect our heritage for younger generations to enjoy and to enable them to comprehend Indian history with depth and understanding.

This is an opportunity to reassess our "Strengths and Weaknesses". Our strength is that every citizen of this great historic city has a great potential and capabilities to work for the sacred cause of conservation of heritage fabric. Our weakness is that all of us are not able to work together for the sacred cause of conservation of our rich cultural Heritage fabric of Mewar.

Remember our motto is "Fighting to preserve what is rightfully ours" and we have to conserve heritage which is based on the belief that "living in harmony with heritage enhances the quality of life".

Tranquebar History, Heritage and Development: A Model Heritage Village

Shri Ajit Koujalgi

Executive Summary

Tranquebar, a former Danish Colony on the East Coast of India, about 300km south of Chennai, has seen some positive work in terms of development of the town with heritage preservation as one of the main impetus. This has happened because of private initiative, involvement of organizations like INTACH and Tranquebar Association, positive support by the State and Central ministries of Tourism, National Museum of Denmark and

Land Gate-Entrance to the Old Town

the constant and unwavering support of Bestseller Foundation (a Corporate Social Responsibility arm of the Danish business house 'Bestseller').

This is an ongoing long-haul project which is materialising slowly. Its success will depend on many factors that are difficult to predict at this stage. No matter what the outcome is, the effort is well worth the try.

It is hoped that this example will help other heritage sites in India to take up similar action - provided corporates and governments come forward with finance and administrative and legal support.

Historical Background - Tranquebar Town

Tranquebar, known in Tamil as Tharangambadi (the 'place of the singing waves') has a rich multicultural history that influenced the coexistence and development of various communities over centuries along the Coromandel Coast.

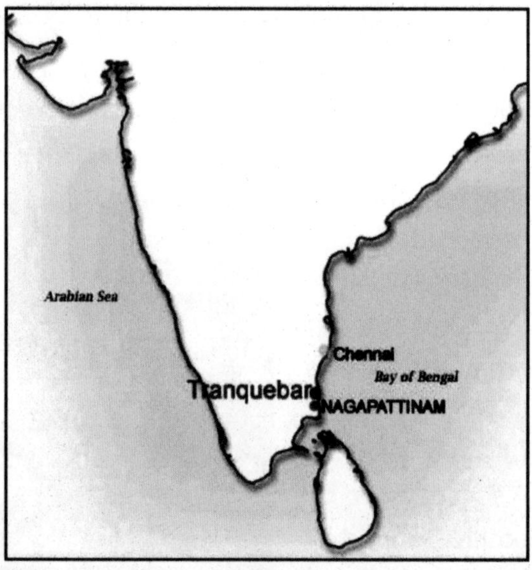

A part of the kingdom of Ragunatha Nayakar of Thanjavur in the 17th century, it attracted the attention of various foreign traders and missionaries. That included Muslim traders, envoys of the Danish East India Company, German theologians and missionaries, Moravian entrepreneurs, and later the British East India Company.

The Town During Danish Rule

Historically Tharangambadi was a part of the territory of the Nayaks of Thanjavur. The Danish king, Christian IV (1588-1618) in order to increase his country's overseas trade established the East India Company. He sent a fleet of four ships with the young danish admiral Ove Giedde as commander to India. The second in command, Danish captain Roland Crappe, arrived first in India in 1620 and on behalf of the Danish king entered into an agreement with the Nayak of Thanjavur.

The East India Company established a protected 'collection post' for the goods by building a fort called Dansborg. The work was mainly carried out by Ove Giedde who also became Tranquebar's first Commander (1620-1621). The fort quickly grew into the square citadel with four bastions which is still exists. Due to political unrest in the 1660s the whole town was surrounded by a fortified wall which was later extended to include the Dansborg as well. In 1677 the administration of Tranquebar was transferred to the Danish government and remained in their hands till 1845 when it was sold to the British East India Company.

Archiival image of King Street

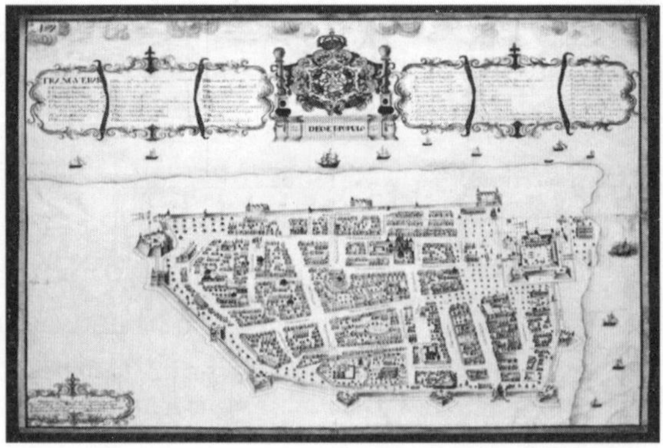

Archival map of Tranquebar during Danish rule

During the Danish period Tharangambadi experienced its biggest social and religious reform through the missionaries Bartholomaeus Ziegenbalg and Heinrich Pluetschau. The reforms included the introduction of the Lutheran Christianity, a printing press, schools for girls and an increase in the overall education status among the fishermen. Tranquebar is the living memory of the Danes in India.

The Town After Danish Rule

Tharangambadi was sold to the British East India Company in 1845 due to economic turmoil in Denmark since the spice trade was not lucrative anymore in Europe and the place had lost its commercial value for Denmark. The acquisition of Tranquebar by the British brought renewed importance and very soon it was accorded the privilege of becoming headquarters of the collector of Thanjavur between 1845 and 1873. But with the shifting of the district head quarters and the courts to Thanjavur in 1874, the town finally lost its importance.

Sketch of Dansborg

Tranquebar Today

Today, the historic town is inhabited by about 3000 people; it is well connected to prominent cities like Chennai, Pondicherry, Karaikal and Nagapattinam. It is frequented by tourists, researchers, pilgrims, etc. and is a popular destination among Danish tourists visiting South India.

View of the town above the shore

Tranquebar during weekends

Tranquebar during festivals

Tranquebar Town Development - The Heritage Context

Today when one enters Tranquebar through the Land Gate one has the feeling of stepping back in time and entering another world. The King's Street with its Danish pillared houses and churches lend it a special charm. But slowly one notices that most of the heritage structures, both Danish and Tamil, are not well looked after, neglected or have been changed beyond recognition with insensitive modifications. Over the years many heritage buildings have been demolished and even today buildings continue to disappear. This trend needs to be urgently reversed if the town has to keep its special character.

The process to develop Tranquebar as a heritage destination has been initiated through the preservation of architectural heritage as a motor of tourism and economic development. The town is perceived as unique because of its architectural character which is an outcome of a synthesis between Danish and local Tamil vernacular architecture.

Dansborg Fort

The movement to preserve and restore this heritage began with the restoration of the Dansborg Fort – the citadel of the Old Danish trading post - by the Tamil Nadu State Archaeological Department in collaboration with the Tranquebar Association in 2002. The fort now houses a museum and is visited by all those who visit the town.

Step two was the restoration and conversion of the utterly neglected and desolate former British Collector's Bungalow into a Hotel named the 'Bungalow on the Beach' in early 2005. Today it is a heritage hotel, run by the Neemrana Group of Hotels. Another old Danish-Tamil style building, the Gate House on King's Street was also restored and converted into a bed and breakfast facility by the Neemrana Group.

Bungalow on the Beach before and after restoration

Bungalow on the beach

The next impetus came with the appearance of the Danish Bestseller Foundation India after the Tsunami in 2005. Bestseller Foundation wanted to help Tranquebar overcome the traumatic disaster by taking up a number of social, educational, coastal protection planting, solid waste management and other employment generating schemes. To house some of these activities they decided to buy some derelict and damaged Tamil houses on Goldsmith Street and partnered with INTACH Pondicherry to restore them. Thus 5 Tamil vernacular houses were transformed to their former glory. The largest of them is now a guest house also managed by the Neemrana Hotel. Two are housing the INTACH and Solid Waste Management offices and a permanent exhibition on Tranquebar history and architecture. The other two will be devoted to a centre for the development of crafts in collaboration with Upasana from Auroville.

Five houses in Goldsmith Street before and after restoration (Panoramic View)

Inner courtyard-house 4

Five houses in Goldsmith Street before and after restoration (Panoramic View)

Listing of the heritage buildings in Tranquebar has been carried out so that the right moves from the concerned authorities could safeguard the existing beauty of the place and ensure its development in the right direction. At present there are no heritage regulations and it is difficult to prevent demolition or unsympathetic changes to heritage structures and prevent new architecture that is in total disharmony with the traditional architecture. However INTACH is in a continuous dialogue with the local bodies and the government to introduce controls, guidelines and incentives.

A Solid Waste Management programme, involving local households and the Panchayat, has been organized with funding from the Bestseller Foundation, making Tranquebar one of the cleanest towns in the area. This message is now spreading to other communities in the vicinity. Recently the Swiss Red Cross contacted INTACH to introduce the system in 3 more villages near by.

Soild waste programme daily cleaning activities

Some local people, the Panchayat and the District Administration as well as the Tamil Nadu Tourism Department are supporting the idea of protecting the heritage as a means to bring change and prosperity to the town. A Rs. 5 crore Destination Development Scheme funded by the central Ministry of Tourism to landscape the Parade Ground in front

Street-after cleaning

of the Dansborg, Goldsmith Street and providing separate parking for buses behind the Fort has been taken up. Other State Government agencies like the PWD and TNEB have promised to involve themselves in this development. The entrance area *Bazaar* will also be improved.

Thus the objective is to work towards an Integrated Development of Tranquebar, which will combine the heritage preservation with infrastructure upgradation and creation of new economic opportunities through development of tourism, crafts and cottage industry.

Parade Ground now and proposed

Kings Street view now and proposed

Private organizations like INTACH, Bestseller Foundation and the Neemrana Hotel Group with active support from the Tamil Nadu Tourism Development Corporation can partner with local, state or central agencies to work on making Tranquebar a premium heritage destination. Upasana from Auroville has taken up crafts development using local traditions and introducing design and marketing innovations.

Tranquebar Craft Resource Center (TCRC)

The Tranquebar Craft Resource Center (TCRC) is a community based entity that works with selected local crafts and craftspeople around Tranquebar. It aims to nurture a creative ambience for the artisans where they can interact with designers and tourists, infuse new ideas into their craft practices and access new markets. The main role of TCRC is

Upasana crafts' people at workshop

to provide skill & design inputs and create a branding platform for the local craft producers in the context of cultural tourism. Through these activities, we seek to transform the simple folk crafts into 'gifts of Tranquebar' and to simultaneously build the producers' capacity to sustain a viable enterprise.

Selected crafts: Bamboo basketry, Terracotta dolls, Palm leaf basketry, Woodcarving, Seashell and Coconut shell crafts located within 20km of Tranquebar town.

Tranquebar can form an important part of the tourist circuit together with Chidambaram, Pichavaram, Poompuhar, Karaikal, Vellankani and UNESCO world heritage sites like Gangaikondacholapuram, Darassuram and Thanjavur.

There is great interest in Denmark to help develop this place and the Danish National Museum is now funding the restoration of the Governor's Bungalow. They would like to take up more projects like refurbishing the museum etc. Thus the nongovernmental investment in the past 5 years and expected funding works out to about 1 million Euros and more will be coming. By bringing in support funding from the State and the Central Governments these efforts can be synergized to make Tranquebar a 'model heritage village' in Tamil Nadu.

Some Forthcoming Projects

- Governor's Bungalow's restoration has been taken up with funding from the National Museum, Denmark.
- Facade restoration and roof repair of all the houses in Goldsmith Street, with funding from the Bestseller Foundation.
- Matching Grant Scheme funded by Bestseller Foundation to restore some private buildings, wherein about 50% of the cost will be subsidised.

- Restoration of the Shore Temple will be taken up shortly and funded by the Government of Tamil Nadu – HR & CE.
- Restoration of the all building facades and landscaping the street like paving,lighting, etc,
- Proposal for Market Street: Improvement of road, pavement, lighting, restoration of the all building facades, etc,
- Restoration of Hotel Tamil Nadu (HTN).

Restoration of Governor's Bungalow

Governor's Bungalow - restoration has been taken up with funding from the National Museum, Denmark.

Governor's Bungalow now and proposed

Restoration of Façade and Roof Repair Works (about 20 buildings)

Facade restoration and roof repair of all the houses in Goldsmith Street - with funding from the Bestseller Foundation

Goldsmith street existing view

Restoration of Heritage Building of about Five Private Houses (Matching Grant Scheme)

Matching Grant Scheme funded by Bestseller Foundation to restore some private buildings, wherein about 50% of the cost will be subsidised.

Heritage building needing restoration

Restoration of Shore Temple

Restoration of the Shore Temple will be taken up shortly and funded by the Government of Tamil Nadu – HR & CE.

The Shore Temple

Restoration of King's Street and Landscaping Works

Restoration of the building facades and landscaping the street with paving, lighting, etc.,

King's street now and proposed

Proposal for Market Street

Improvement of road, pavement, lighting, restoration of the all building facades, etc,

Market street-now and proposed

Restoration of Hotel Tamil Nadu (HTN)

Hotel Tamil Nadu-now and proposed

Development Phases

Phases in the Development Of Tranquebar					
Phases	**Sl.No**	**Proposals**	**Activities Involved**	**Govt**	**Other**
PHASE - 1	1.1	**Bus stop on ECR, approach road and Parking**	Provision of bus stops for intercity traffic and reviving of the old causeway. Providing separate vehicular approach road on embankment of Uppan River leading to boat jetty and parking area and visitors toilets.		
	1.2	**Landscaping and Lighting**	Granite paved pathways, lighting, soft landscaping, restoration of facades		
		Parade Ground			
		Goldsmiths Street			
	1.3	**Matching Grant Scheme**	Heritage sensitive restoration of various buildings in Queens Street. Restoration of Graded buildings with a 50 grant from Bestseller Foundation and the rest 50 % from the owner of the building.		
	1.4	**Model Street and Façade restoration scheme**	Restoration of Goldmsith street façade		
	1.5	**Improving the existing Drinking water conditions**	The town is lacking in adequate drinking water facillities, the scheme to enhance and improve the existing conditions of the drinking water facillities inside the town.		
	1.6	**Rebuilding the causeway**	Rebuilding the old causeway on Uppan river and improving the connectivity		
	1.7	**Underground Cabling**	Providing Underground cabling in the heritage precint with improved better electrical equipments		
PHASE - 2	2.1	**Landscaping and Lighting**	Granite paved pathways, lighting, soft landscaping, restoration of facades		
		Beach Promenade			
		Queens Street			
	2.2	**Improving the Thirumullaivasal Canal**	Cleaning, dredging and lining so that the water flows through the canal from sea as well as the river and providing boat jetty along the river bank		
	2.3	**Model Street and Façade restoration scheme**	Facde restoration for King Street		
	2.4	**Façade renovation of buildings**	Façade renovation - plastering and painting activities		
		Girls Hostel -Kings street			
		Ziegenbalg Spiritual Centre			
	2.5	**Improving the Over Head Tanks**	Improving the over head tank in the parade ground		
PHASE - 3	3.1	**Landscaping and Lighting of Kings Street**	Granite paved pathways, lighting, soft landscaping, restoration of facades		
	3.2	**Market Street - Revival**	Provision of defined vehicular and pedestrian paths, parking, façade restoration, standardizing commercial Signage		
PHASE - 4	4.1	**Restoration of monuments**	Restoration at different levels such as building level and site level		
		Dansborg Museum			
		Old Mosque and tank			
		Tank behind Dansborg			
		Zion Church			
	4.2	**Matching Grant Scheme**	Heritage sensitive restoration of various buildings all over the town		
	4.3	**Signage**	Street Signage and building plaques		
	4.4	**Awareness Generation**	Awareness generation programme among students, public and professionals		

Conclusion

Many of these activities are made possible because the Bestseller Foundation has 'adopted' heritage preservation and development cause in Tranquebar and the Tamil Nadu Government is actively supporting the work. It is hoped that such an example will inspire other corporates and foundations to adopt other heritage towns in India.

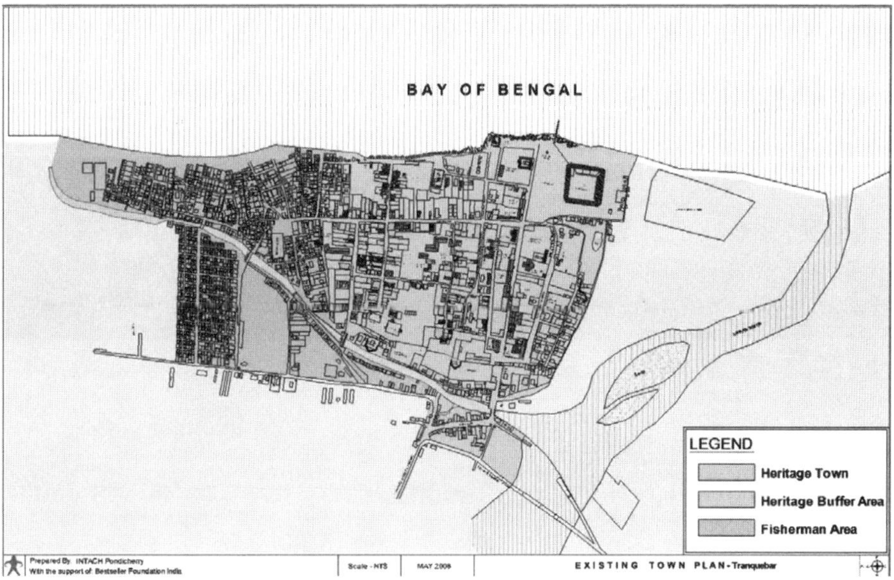

Map of Tranquebar

By bringing in support and funding from the state and the centre this effort and help can be synergized to develop Tranquebar as a "Model Heritage Village".

Session 5

Case Studies

Promoting Heritage-based Urban Development in India: Indian Heritage Cities Network (IHCN)

Ms. Shalini Mahajan - IHCN, UNESCO, New Delhi

UNESCO as the UN nodal agency for culture, architecture, urban planning and conservation has made heritage a key resource in its development oriented projects. The organization has shown through numerous examples the world over, that heritage is not an impediment to development, but a resource that can contribute to poverty reduction, employment generation, waste management and sanitation, improvement of water systems and environmental regeneration as a whole.

The Indian Heritage Cities Network (IHCN) was founded as a programme by UNESCO New Delhi Office at an international conference on 'Indian Cities of Living Heritage' in September 2006 at Jaipur, Rajasthan. Having been established with the endorsement of the Ministry of Urban Development, Government of India, with the support of the French Government and the *Association National des Villes d'Art et Histoire* of France, the Network now comprises twenty-two Indian member cities, seven French cities and regional partners (as of December 2009), several university and institutional members and a number of NGO partners.

The mission of the Indian Heritage Cities Network is to highlight the Indian city as a Living Cultural Resource; foster the safeguard and sustainable use of the unique and diverse urban cultural heritage of India; promote the physical natural and cultural heritage, traditions, crafts and creativity as driving forces for urban development, and the generation of employment for a balanced socio-economic and cultural development.

UNESCO New Delhi, through its Culture Sector, is maintaining the Secretariat of the Indian Heritage Cities Network (IHCN) to support Indian cities in their endeavour to safeguard and use the heritage resources for sustainable development through policy advice, capacity building, good practice exchange, awareness raising, technical assistance and the facilitation of partnerships between Indian and International Cities and Regions.

Some of the key activities of the Network include:

- Documentation & Communication: Setting up a *Cultural Knowledge Databank for Cities* and an *Expertise Locator*;
- Web Portal: Establishing an electronic communication network linking members through the internet facilitating partnerships and knowledge exchange, both in India and abroad;
- Public Campaigns: Organization of seminars, workshops, exhibitions, field trips, awareness drives, etc. for local communities, such as Heritage Walks, and partnering with Heritage Festivals;
- Publications: Publishing of a newsletter, information brochures, and workshop papers;
- Technical assistance: Provide technical expertise to cities in developing strategies for adapting existing state and municipal planning, legal and regulatory frameworks for heritage protection and conservation; assistance in planning interventions for heritage-based sustainable and balanced urban development;

- Partnerships: Brokering partnerships between members (Indian and International cities, regions; Institutions, NGOs and Individuals) to exchange experience and good practice in urban conservation and development;
- Training: Organizing training programmes for members of the Network through study tours, technical workshops for solution exchange and facilitating longer term training for capacity – building in urban heritage management and development;
- Thematic workshops and conferences: Organization of workshops and conferences with the participation of experts from both India and abroad;
- Education and Capacity Building: Develop a system of short term courses, mid term trainings, long term educational curricula for elected representatives, administrators, technical staff and professionals.

One of the successful ongoing Heritage Campaigns that UNESCO New Delhi has led is the:

"Revive Chettinad Heritage Project".

This project is a *technical cooperation towards heritage resources management* in Chettinad, including heritage conservation and promotion of cultural tourism. The project aims at developing heritage management both at the regional level of Chettinad as well as at local level for some key villages of the Chettinad region with special focus on spaces, built heritage and water bodies. Initially conceptualized at an international conference in Karaikudi, organized by UNESCO in collaboration with the Govt. of Tamil Nadu supported by the Chennai-based NGO, Architectural Heritage Safeguard (ArcHe-S), the project comprises of the following key activities:

(i) Development of Regional Heritage Master Plan and Regional Heritage Itinerary;

(ii) Development of local Heritage Plan;
(iii) Elaboration of Heritage Bill; and Building Regulation;
(iv) Establishment of a Heritage House;
(v) Awareness-raising of local population and District – local authorities on the issue of heritage preservation.

Before outlining UNESCO's consistent efforts in Reviving Chettinad's Heritage, a brief overview of the history of the region and its rich heritage and its present status is necessary in order to understand the state of urgency it is in.

Chettinad is a semi-arid zone of 1,550 square kilometers in the heart of Tamil Nadu, inhabited by some 110,000 Chettiars who are spread over two main cities (Karaikudi and Kanadukathan) and about 73 villages. Since the time the community was founded, the Chettiars have upheld a vision of urban planning and development which makes this area an outstanding heritage region.

This is a geo-cultural territory organized around nine clan temples. Each member of the Chettiar community belongs to a particular clan. Religious symbolism dominates the landscape of this region. The Chettiars belong to a lineage of wealthy traders and financiers who made their fortunes by extending their business to the whole of Southeast Asia, particularly during the 19th century when they were at the peak of their economic power. As a result of their travelling, the Chettiars integrated diverse influences into their traditions which contributed to their uniqueness. Their villages were constructed as per precise and sophisticated rules of urban planning, represented namely by orthogonal streets and specific water management system, which are also directly linked to the Tamil tradition with rectangular plots and houses with an inner courtyard.

Another interesting landscape feature seen in all Chettinad villages are the water tanks called *"ooranis"*. Each village comprises of at least three *ooranis,* each having a specific purpose like bathing, drinking etc. The roofs of Chettinad houses are so designed that the water falling down finds its way and percolates into these *ooranis.* This region is truly a cultural landscape, shaped both by nature and human activities. A typical element of the region is the *"Erys"*, which are surface water reservoirs that help irrigate the fields located between the villages. It is a very characteristic feature of this region showcasing sustainable water management practices.

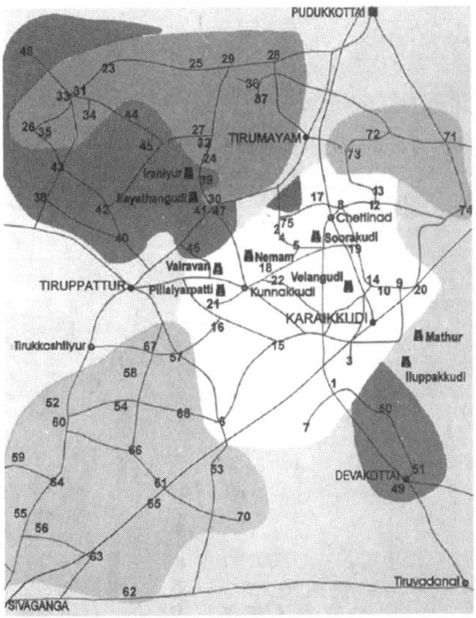

Map of Chettinad Region

Oorani

Ery: surface water reservoirs

Art Deco style dominates the architectural heritage of the region. The houses which evolved over two centuries are veritable palaces. On the ground floor, the architecture is typically Tamil, while one can see Western influences on the higher floors. This reflects the ways of life of the Chettiars who knew how to combine their vibrant traditions with the global economy. In order to build these palaces, materials and expertise from all over the world were used, only adding to the cultural

Typical Art Deco House in Chettinad

glory of Chettinad. These beautiful houses have their interiors adorned with intricately carved Burma teak columns, wall paintings and stuccowork.

The living heritage of the region is kept alive by the people involved in craft activities like tile making (Athangudi tiles), wood work, basket weaving, chariot-making etc and in traditional village festivities, dances and other art forms. Chettinad cuisine is infact famous all over, so are its typical weddings. Chettiars interestingly no matter where they are in

the world come back to their houses in the villages and get married there, thus keeping their tradition alive.

Current Situation in Chettinad

Once a glorious land of the Chettiars, this region fell into apathy in the middle of the 20th century. The marvellous architectural heritage left by the previous generations are silently but steadily disappearing under the threat of time and the lucrative business around the export of columns, windows, ceilings and decorative elements. Houses and entire villages are rapidly vanishing packed into containers headed for Western countries. Lack of local economy is another major challenge, besides the lack of any protection and regulatory controls existing in the area.

This region went into decline about sixty years ago as a result of major economic difficulties following the independence of Burma (Myanmar) and Malaysia. This in turn led to the gradual disappearance of the urban and architectural heritage. Today, besides a few palatial

Rampant urbanization as seen in Chettinad

Widespread demolition of traditional houses

homes which are still maintained by the families for the purpose of large important occasions and gatherings, a considerable amount of smaller houses have been already demolished, and those which have survived, whose exact number is yet to be determined, are in a critical state of conservation. Their total disappearance seems almost inevitable for various reasons, in particular the lack of financial means of the owners and a joint ownership, dismantling the houses for the purpose of sale. This could totally wipe out the living evidence of a way of life, of an extraordinary page in history, which constituted the cultural wealth of India. The dismantling of houses has led to a lucrative antiques business and many architectural elements, in particular pillars and doors have been exported all over the world from Kochi, Chennai, Mumbai and Delhi. In 1947, there were 96 villages in Chettinad. Today, there are only 75.

Revive Chettinad Heritage Campaign

UNESCO's association with Chettinad dates back to August 2006 when it held its first mission to Chettinad to assess the state of heritage and the feasibility of the program.

Alarmed by the vulnerable situation of the Chettinad region, Revive Chettinad Heritage Society was formed by leading Chettiars at the call of ArcHe-S, a Tamil Nadu-based French NGO to halt the further destruction of the Chettinad heritage. This was followed by the organization of an international workshop by UNESCO in May 2007 on heritage-based development of Chettinad, with the support of Govt. of Tamil Nadu, the Panchayats and Districts, ArcHe-S, Revive Chettinad Heritage Society, Anna University, Govt. of France and Ecole de Chaillot. The "Revive Chettinad Heritage Campaign" was launched and endorsed at this workshop by UNESCO, aimed at developing a long-term conservation and promotional plan of Chettinad heritage with the support of the Government of Tamil Nadu. A joint action plan was drafted that outlined the protection, conservation and development of the region highlighting the need to undertake listings, surveys, initiating the concept of Heritage House etc. Another significant development at this workshop was the setting up of collaboration between Ecole de Chaillot and Anna University.

Cultural Mapping Workshops

As a follow up to this collaboration, a workshop on Cultural Mapping was held in July 2007 wherein students of Anna University and the faculty of Ecole de Chaillot participated, undertaking a baseline study of Kanadukathan, largest village of the region. This, in January 2008, was followed by the organization of the Heritage Seminar in Karaikudi where in-depth documentation of heritage buildings of Kanadukathan was undertaken besides urban landscape studies of the region. These studies revealed how the settlement had grown over the years and how the skyline of these villages had been maintained and the need to preserve the same. The studies not only looked and documented the heritage building facades but did a thorough building typological analysis and its space organization and functional utilizations. It showcased how environment friendly these buildings are and the lessons one can learn from them even today.

Examples of Architectural Documentation of heritage buildings

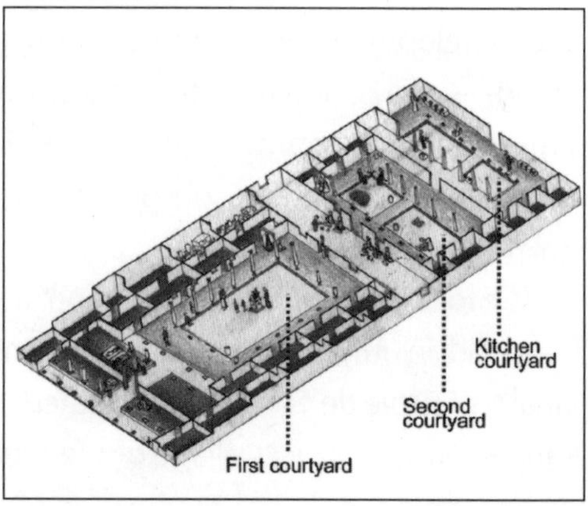

It was in 2008 that Chettinad was listed on the World Monument Fund's Watch List of 100 Most Endangered Sites. It was in the same year that a partnership was initiated between Chettinad region and the French Region Centre, supported by

UNESCO. The French confirmed their support towards French expert missions, financial support to ArcHe-S to help provide technical assistance, establishment of Heritage Studios and conducting village mapping.

In March 2008, the Govt. of Tamil Nadu through DC Sivaganga offered the use of one of its traditional buildings, to be converted into a Heritage House. Conceptually speaking a Heritage House is a way of setting up an administrative unit at the local level, that acts as an advisory service to the local population and to the authorities on all heritage related matters and also undertakes heritage awareness-raising and outreach programmes. It is usually a traditional historic building located in the historic core of the city, restored to the highest professional standards incorporating contemporary and modern interventions, thereby acting as a pilot conservation project in the area. Staffed with trained architects, urban planners and supported by people from relevant fields, the Heritage House undertakes activities like listing, surveys, planning, research and documentation, exhibition and awareness raising etc.

In Chettinad, an old school building called Alagappa Chettiar House in Kottaiyur was designated to be converted into a Heritage House for the region. The building had typical wood carvings and wall paintings of the region, thereby making it an ideal space to showcase Chettinad's rich heritage. Detailed studies, surveys and condition assessment of the building has been undertaken, identifying major restoration works to be carried out. These are currently underway.

The programme of the Chettinad Heritage House includes setting up of an office of the heritage team and visitor services along with an interpretation centre, handicraft demonstration and pedagogical

workshops, exhibition rooms, resource centre etc. It is currently also providing technical assistance to the DC Sivaganga in restoring the public spaces and in providing heritage-sensitive solutions for ongoing Govt. projects, e.g, improvements of ooranis, roads, parks, implementation of solar lighting etc. Currently, the survey team is in a process of compiling a heritage profile of some key villages of the Chettinad region, by plotting the existing traditional houses, thus identifying heritage zone or street in each of the villages to provide the basis for the authorities of Tamil Nadu to enact a heritage conservation plan of Chettinad region.

Since 2008, Chettinad has also been part of UNESCO's Heritage Passport Program, which is basically an attempt towards integrated regional heritage development. It looks at regional level and also at the local level whereby heritage-based itineraries are being developed e.g, Architectural trail, Temple trail, Art Deco Trail, Handicraft Trail,

Alagappa Chettiar House, Kottaiyur designated as Heritage House, Chettinad

Nature Trail, Sea shore trail, in an attempt to cater to the different and varied interests of the informed tourists. Fortunately today there is an increasing awareness about the future of Chettinad and it is attracting visitors who are keen to have an off the beaten track experience. It is not too late to take stock of the architectural, urban and ecological richness of Chettinad. This is what the first part of the 'Revive Chettinad Heritage Campaign' intends to accomplish.

In the second phase, the Campaign has an ambition to establish a multidisciplinary team of architects, jurists and mediators in Chettinad region itself, whose role will be to define a comprehensive strategy for the conservation of the Chettinad heritage region. The technical team will also provide legal and technical advice to the local inhabitants to suggest solutions for adopting the traditional houses to standards of modern comfort and to new activities in order to facilitate their maintenance. The project team of 'Revive Heritage Chettinad Campaign' is motivated by a passion to bring a new boost to the Chettinad region but also believes that there is no empowerment without recognition of heritage and history. With solid data and understanding on the heritage elements of the region, the team hopes to provide to the Chettinad region a tool to carve its future in resonance with its own tradition.

Humayun's Tomb – Nizamuddin Basti- Sundar Nursery Urban Renewal

Shri Ratish Nanda - Conservation Architect, works for Aga Khan Trust for Culture

Humayun's Tomb garden restoration, "is of course, the first privately funded restoration of a World Heritage Site in our country. The project has indubitably been an unqualified success, with the gardens, pathways, fountains and water channels of the Chahar Bagh having been brought close to their original perfection.

Looking at the magnificent work that has been undertaken here, we cannot but be grateful to the Trust for its support and help. This effort has been an instructive example for us in finding new and creative solutions to the age-old problem of allocating scarce resources in a developing country to the preservation of our heritage. I hope that more public-private partnerships can be evolved to maintain and restore the monuments of our ancestors, which often lie in neglected condition in our cities"

—Dr Manmohan Singh, Prime Minister of India, 27 November 2004

Public and official endorsement of the results of the collaborative project work by the Archaeological Survey of India (ASI) and The Agha Khan Trust for Culture (AKTC) in the rehabilitation of Humayun's Tomb Gardens (1997-2004) in Delhi prompted the Government of India and the Aga Khan Development Network (AKDN), of which AKTC is a part, to consider further possible partnerships aiming at the integrated physical and socio-economic development of cultural heritage sites in India.

After research into a number of possible sites, suggested by the Ministry of Tourism and Culture, Government of India, AKTC developed a recommendation for an area development project in the vicinity of Humayun's Tomb, focussed on the Nizamuddin Basti, further features of the Humayun Tomb site and the Sundar Nursery site, which, together with their unique cultural assets and heritage, would unify these three zones into an urban conservation district of considerable breadth and significance for the city of Delhi.

Conservation Area

The Humayun's Tomb complex and its surrounding areas covers almost 60 acres of land. Besides the Humayun's tomb-garden, the complex includes several significant monuments such as Isa Khan's tomb enclosure, Afsarwala tomb and mosque, Arab Serai, Bu Halima's Tomb and several monumental gateways. The World Heritage Site is presently limited to the walled garden enclosure of Humayun's Tomb.

The adjoining Sundar Nursery, a large, enclosed nursery on the north side of Humayun's Tomb, owned and operated by the Central Public Works Department (CPWD), is an integral part of the proposed project. This 27 hectare tract is a flat, expansive and under-used green space containing several Mughal-era monuments of which at least three are protected by the ASI. The area's position between Humayun's Tomb complex and the zoo to the north as well as its proximity to Nizamuddin provides the opportunity to create a larger area development project connecting with Humayun's Tomb and its outer precinct.

The Sundar Nursery could easily incorporate recreational zones. The existing south-central entrance allows for a shared entrance zone with the Humayun's Tomb complex; within this zone the parking area could be extended to serve both Humayun's Tomb complex as well as the Sundar Gardens. While enhancing the Nursery functions, part of the grounds could be developed for education and recreation, with the creation of an interpretation centre for the Humayun's Tomb World Heritage Site-Nizamuddin area. The park could be sensitively landscaped, additional attractions such as botanical gardens developed and turned into a major draw for Delhi's citizens and visitors to the city with zones for heritage interpretation, food and beverages, botanical gardens, crafts *bazaar*, all in the shadow of key Mughal period buildings.

The urban village of Nizamuddin Basti, west of Humayun's Tomb, is a compact, self-contained district with a high count of landmark structures dating to the Mughal and pre-Mughal periods. Shrines, mausoleums and *baoli* (step well) in Nizamuddin are located within relatively short distances of one another and are well integrated with a vibrant community centred around the dargah of the 14th century Sufi Saint Hazrat Nizamuddin Auliya. Nizamuddin is revered by Indians for its rich history and spiritual focus as well as its spirit of tolerance with visiting pilgrims representing a cross-section of society. The rare examples of religious pluralism that one can experience in Nizamuddin offers an important message of hope for India and the world.

Nizamuddin Basti, with its living culture, several dozens of listed monuments and a 15,000-strong population with below-average income levels, would require an integrated area development approach, emphasizing AKTC's experience as a prime coordinator of a consortium of consultants, NGO's and private sector groups involved in a comprehensive programme of preservation/ rehabilitation of a number of monuments as well as the socio-economic development of the *basti*.

Situated within each of the adjoining zones of Humayun's Tomb, Sundar Nursery, and Hazrat Nizamuddin Basti are several significant monuments spanning almost a millennium of Delhi's heritage. Since the 14th century burial of Hazrat Nizamuddin Auliya, several significant buildings were been built in this area, especially by the Mughals, and there are today over eighty listed heritage buildings in the Humayun's Tomb-Nizamuddin Area of which thirty-six are protected by the Archaeological Survey of India. In addition, significant monument clusters/ complexes such as Purana Qila, Lodi Gardens, Safdarjung Tomb and Golf Club are located in close proximity.

The Project Objectives

This Area Development Project would combine conservation and urban environmental rehabilitation works with a series of community-based socio-economic development initiatives designed to improve the quality of life and environment for the well-established communities within the project area. The success of the project will depend on a close degree of liasion and coordination amongst the three public parties, two private parties and other stakeholders such as interested professionals, potential co-funders, the private sector and the cooperation of the communities involved.

The Public-Private-Partnership MoU signed on 11 July 2007 between the Archaeological Survey of India, Central Public Works Department, Municipal Corporation of Delhi, Aga Khan Trust for Culture and the Aga Khan Foundation marked the commencement of the project. The PPP was signed following approvals by the three public parties, the Ministry of Tourism and Culture, Ministry of Urban Development, Ministry of

Law, Ministry of External Affairs, Ministry of Finance and Delhi Government.

The project is governed by a Project Committee that includes community representatives from Nizamuddin Basti. Co-Funding has been received from the Sir Dorabji Tata Trust, Ford Foundation, Sir Ratan Tata Trust, World Monuments Fund, J.M. Kaplan Fund, amongst other private parties.

The project hopes to fulfil the Master Plan objectives for the Nizamuddin Conservation Area; it hopes to set international standards for conservation, meet World Heritage Convention requirements for conservation, presentation, site management and primarily focus on improving living standards by environmental enhancement and improved access to health, education, job based vocational training, microfinance for the thousands who inhabit Hazrat Nizamuddin Basti.

The proposed project will link the various, presently segregated, heritage zones in the area together as part of a large urban renewal initiative which, located centrally in the capital city of Delhi, would be of immense strategic importance. The project will seek to improve living standards in the Nizamuddin Basti, considerably enhance visitor experience and, through rehabilitation of critical monuments and civic open spaces, enhance the area's value and significance in terms of history, places of spiritual importance and recreation.

The project is envisaged to be similar to the recently completed Azhar Park – Darb al-Ahmar Area Development Project in Cairo, Egypt where AKTC converted a derelict site into a major and self-sustainable urban park and carried out rehabilitation works in the historic yet impoverished and densely built-up district of Darb al-Ahmar that borders the park.

The project is envisaged to develop and expand as per the policy direction of the Committee (representing all five parties, representative of resident communities, and other stakeholders), yet to achieve conservation and urban development goals, the broad objectives of the project at the onset can be grouped under three distinct headings. These also help define the roles of the three public parties within their mutually shared objectives of carrying out a model project that would lead to conservation based development, improve quality of life for local communities, improve access and enhance cultural significance of this conservation area and provide additional attractions and facilities to Delhi's citizens and tourists to this unique heritage zone.

a. *CONSERVATION:*

Several listed heritage buildings, both protected by the Archaeological Survey of India and as yet unprotected stand within the project area. Conservation works will be guided by prevalent International and Indian Charters/Philosophy and be carried out by the Archaeological Survey of India. The project hopes to set international standards for conservation, exceed World Heritage Convention requirements for conservation, presentation, site management and enhance visitor experience. Conservation works would include upgrading existing facilities, creating new facilities where required and undertaking measures aimed at enhancing visitor experience taking into account local aspirations.

b. *URBAN DEVELOPMENT:*

The Nizamuddin Area is a recognized Conservation Area as per the Delhi Master Plan 2001. The proposed project would include the preparation of a Local Area Plan for the Nizamuddin Basti, carry out environmental development of the *Nullah* that flows along the *basti* and landscape the parks that surround the *basti*.

Revitalize the Sundar Nursery area with the creation of new attractions such as a Mughal Botanical Gardens, an Interpretation centre, greater public access and creating a new sensitively landscaped public park while enhancing nursery functions by providing required facilities such as greenhouses in Sundar Nursery. Similar works are also to be carried out in the areas adjoining Humayun's Tomb to the east, south and along Mathura Road, all in consultation with the Central Public Works Department.

c. *SOCIO-ECONOMIC DEVELOPMENT:*

The social development initiatives planned in partnership with the Municipal Corporation of Delhi will be implemented in the Nizamuddin Basti area comprising a resident population of approximately 20,000 and other beneficiaries identified during the course of establishing baselines. A synergistic, community centred and collaborative approach will be adopted to improve the *nullah*, develop public parks and strengthen urban basic services through interventions in three core areas of health, education and environmental sanitation.

It is hoped that the project, with its support to the local communities can demonstrate how conservation and revitalization of cultural heritage – in many cases the only asset at the disposal of the community – can provide a springboard for social and economic development.

Conservation works are presently being carried out on several significant structures in the complex and were preceded by a prolonged and sustained archival research programme, detailed measured drawing, structural assessments, outlining conservation philosophy, detailed conservation proposals and stakeholder discussion with independent experts, local community, and those from agencies such as UNESCO, ICOMOS, ICCROM and INTACH. Conservation works are aimed at enhancing the historical significance, restoring architectural integrity and ensuring preservation of the monuments. All works are guided by Indian and International conservation principles and draw upon the latest scientific technology such as High Definition Surveys using 3d laser scanning, ground penetrating radar surveys and traditional craftsmanship. Technical supervision of all works is a priority with conservation architects, archaeological engineers, and experienced conservation professionals constantly supervising all ongoing works. Training is a significant element of the project with over 15% of conservation budgets earmarked for training programmes in diverse aspects ranging from use of lime mortar to sandstone craftsmanship.

In a partnership project of this nature, centred at a World Heritage Site but including conservation of unprotected monuments and those that stand within dense settlements and have a strong community linkages, conservation solutions cannot be standardized.

Acknowledging the significance of the undertaking, European Union, in its recent report, acknowledged, *'ASI has only just begun to collaborate with the civil society. Its experience of working with the AKTC in a multi stake holder project to develop the Humayun's Tomb Gardens including a large community development component located in Nizamuddin Basti has been very positive and is likely to be strategic in determining the interest of the ASI in other civil society partnership in the future'.*

Case Studies

Though works are ongoing on several structures the following two case studies aim to illustrate some variety, in terms of challenges and solutions that are being undertaken. These do not illustrate the entire range of activities being undertaken on any one of these buildings, which space available here does not permit to explain.

Humayun's Tomb

The mausoleum of Mughal Emperor Humayun is well known as the pre cursor to the Taj. As the first major building built by the Mughals and due to its unique architectural style, craftsmanship, scale and setting the tomb the site has been listed on the World Heritage List. The ongoing conservation works, follow the John Marshall guidelines and as such, *'repair is attempted only in cases where its advisability is undoubted and where special funds can be provided for the purpose'*.

In order to retain and indeed enhance the cultural significance of the site it is necessary to reverse architectural details where these have been altered, such as with the use of modern materials such as iron grille doors and inappropriate stone detailing. In order to achieve this, over a million kilos of concrete has been carefully removed from the roof of Humayun's Tomb. Since 1924 successive layers of concrete have been laid on the roof to prevent water seepage but have instead put tremendous excess load on the building, blocked rainwater spouts and obliterated architectural elements. The works are 'inspired by the desire to recover the architectural integrity of the tomb building'[1] and have been characterized by high levels of documentation, supervision, craftsmanship.

Similar to the inappropriate works carried out on the roof, an additional layer of concrete was applied to the lower plinth, an important interface between the garden and the mausoleum. Originally, 'paved with large blocks of Delhi quartzite[2]' the lower plinth today distracts from the original architectural intention and disfigures the historic character. The concrete is now being removed and over 12000 sqm of stone blocks will be reset and exposed as the Mughal builders intended them to be.

---

[1] *Herb Stovel, in a written comment.*

[2] *Hasan, Zafar, List of Hindu and Muhammadan Monuments, ASI*

Hazrat Nizamuddin Basti *Baoli*

The project components in the Hazrat Nizamuddin Basti were focused on socio-economic activities at the onset, however in July 2008 a large portion of the 13th century *baoli* (or step well) collapsed. The *baoli*, built by Hazrat Nizamuddin Auliya in the years 1321-2, is considered holy by millions of pilgrims and is the only *baoli* in Delhi still with underground springs still supplying very pure water that had been heavily polluted with leakages in the sewerage system and waste disposal by adjoining households.

Following the collapse several meetings were held with the Hazrat Nizamuddin Dargah Committee and local residents remain involved in ongoing works which will continue through 2009. There has been significant community participation and support with desilting the well being a principal request of the *Pirzadas*, or keepers of the shrine.

In order to commence necessary studies, the water had to be continuously drained out and it was revealed that sewage pipes were leaking into the *baoli* and the Municipal Corporation of Delhi being a project partner allowed 100+ m of sewerage lines at 8 feet depth in a narrow Nizamuddin lane to be replaced as part of the project.

A High Definition Survey using a 3D laser scan of the *baoli* was carried out as was an exhaustive ground penetrating radar survey – both of these were used in India for conservation for the first time. The GPRS allowed structural engineers to understand the underlying soil conditions and plan conservation works accordingly. Once the water had been drained a 3-5 cm thick epoxy layer was found to have been applied consistently on the wall surfaces; which, it was learnt was applied in 2002-3 and was causing severe structural stress as the ground water was not able to seep into the *baoli* and visa-versa, as it had been doing for centuries. This epoxy was carefully removed by hand chisel, in a pain staking process by master stone-cutters.

Community support enabled the principal access to the Dargah to be kept closed to pilgrims for almost a month and AKTC built an alternate dwelling for the one structure over the collapsed portion that was required to be demolished to enable conservation works. These included rebuilding the collapsed portion and adjoining portions after partially dismantling wall surfaces that had suffered severe buckling.

For the first time, in several centuries, the *baoli* was cleared of all rubbish to its original foundations, 80 feet below ground level; this required over 8000 man days of work as it had to be done manually due to the compacted nature of the accumulated waste.

As works to rebuild the collapsed portion neared completion, a blocked passage, possibly used by Hazrat Nizamuddin Auliya, to access the *baoli* from the Mosque, was discovered in mid April, resulting in much cheer amongst the local community.

This article is compiled by Ratish Nanda on behalf of the multi-disciplinary project team involved in conservation works representing both ASI and AKTC and including archaeologists, historian, conservation architects, structural engineers, archaeological engineers, social scientists, designers, architects and master craftsmen.

Session 6

Presentations by Municipal Corporations and Government Agencies

Municipal Initiative in Heritage Conservation: The Case of Ahmedabad

Shri Debashish Nayak - Advisor, Heritage Programme, Ahmedabad Municipal Corporation

Introduction

Communities live and work in towns and cities; as society changes so does urban form, responding to accommodate change and growth. In today's pace of economic development, such historic resources are often perceived as inefficient, unproductive and even inconvenient. They are often replaced with buildings that appear contemporary and more efficient. This neglect has led to decay, depressed economic conditions and dilapidation leading to migration of the population to newer areas.

Familiarity breeds contempt. The citizens get accustomed with their environment and gradually become less aware of it. The city becomes a habit. Herein lies the need to make the citizens aware of the importance of their built environment and to help them develop a harmonious and contemporary relationship with it. In a sense, urban renewal does not just rebuild the city; it rebuilds people's relationship with the city. There lies a need that the old buildings and older areas of the city should be looked upon as assets rather than as liabilities because they represent the history of communities, embodying their tradition, heritage and culture through architecture and the urban form.

This paper explains the importance of an alternative way of connecting conservation and community participation for a sustainable process of revival for historic cities in India.

Role of Municipal Corporations in Heritage Conservation

The local government plays a very important role in the whole implementation process and the achievement of the ultimate goal of an integrated heritage conservation effort.

The Ahmedabad Initiative

Background

The birth of the Old City settlement dates back to a 10th century AD town known as Ashaval. In the later part of the 11th century, another city grew adjacent to Ashaval, known as Karnavati. The present Walled City was created during the Ahmed Shahi period in the 15th century. A new palace and fort were built near Bhadra, which covered a rectangular area of around 500 * 800 metres. During the 17th and 18th centuries, the city expanded outwards. Fortifications were strengthened. The 18th century saw the decline of the city and many suburbs and even parts of the inner city were abandoned and ruined. During the British rule due to political stability and later the introduction of textile mills resulted in economic growth and prosperity. Military and administrative centres, cantonment and railways, churches, administrative and residential buildings were also established during that period. Wholesale markets at Kalupur, mechanized industries and worker's quarters on eastern suburbs, Ellis Bridge, residential buildings and educational institutions were established. Fort walls were mostly pulled down in mid 20th century. The absence of any decentralization policy with regard to economic activities resulted in congestion and decay of Walled City.

Urban Character

Streets and Neighbourhoods: The nucleus of activities at Bhadra and Manek Chowk, and the twelve gates on the wall, created a radial pattern of streets. *Puras* were connected with wider streets and entered through gates. Each micro neighbourhood around residential streets became typical and is called '*pol*' which consists of a street and houses on its both sides. It would have at the most two gates that bar entry at night.

The city of Ahmedabad has been able to display examples worth replicating in the field of heritage conservation. AMC and Ford Foundation, New Delhi prepared a report on 'Urban Conservation of Walled City of Ahmedabad'. The study concentrated on the essential elements required in the city's conservation with a focus on the historical areas. The historical importance of the city, city form, wall, gates, *pols*, house patterns and the problems related to old fabric were analyzed. A list of heritage buildings and precincts was prepared. A conservation policy and a demonstration project were also proposed.

Sharing the Concerns

In the initial phase of intervention an attempt was made to identify the various factors making conservation of heritage difficult in the Walled City area. Some of these issues are listed below:

Problems in Regulations and Policies

Road Line: During the British rule a proposal was mooted for widening the roads in the Walled City. Proposed road boundaries, known as 'Road lines' were demarcated. All new construction was to be done beyond this line. This created a negative attitude among the community members with the result that the front portion of the building, coming under road line, has been neglected. This has resulted in the decay of many a valuable building façades.

Floor Space Index (FSI): The permissible FSI in the Walled City, except for the 'City Centre' area was 3.0. The traditional neighbourhoods normally consume much less. This additional FSI is actually being used for constructing multi-storied buildings by amalgamating three or four plots. This used to destroy the character of the area. Now it has been reduced to 2.0, so the only development possible is restoration and upgrading the existing property.

Tax Structure: Certain aspects of the Tax structure do not favour heritage conservation. For example, *Chabutaras* (bird feeder) are considered as commercial buildings and are taxed on such rates. Similarly, vacant properties are taxed less, leading to buildings of heritage value being locked up and left to ruin.

Changes in the Economy

Closure of Textile Mills: A large part of the residential population in the Walled City consisted tenants working in textile mills. With the mills closing down, they were rendered jobless and stopped maintaining the old buildings that they occupied. This led to a variety of heritage properties getting ruined.

Growth of Gold and Silver Units: The gold and silver industry in the Walled City grew and attracted many skilled persons into the fabric. This influx of people from outside has disturbed the homogeneity of the social fabric in *pols*. This is also suspected to have increased the crime rate in the Walled City.

Commercial Ingress in the old fabric, especially after the addition of Relief Road, created a lot of undesirable changes in the landuse. Warehouses coming up inside the *pols* greatly disturbed the residential character.

Social Problems Leading to Migration: Successive riots and communal problems have forced people to migrate thus weakening the upkeep of the fabric.

Lack of Information

Awareness among the people about conservation is very poor. Also the unavailability of proper building materials for repair works caused decay. Proper maps and drawings of the Walled City were not available. This reduces the access of the police, fire force, ambulances, etc. into the deeper portions of the city.

Strategic Partnerships

The success of any intervention depends on the building of strategic partnerships and in stimulating widespread participation of a variety of stakeholders.

Community Participation

A series of activities were organized to elicit community participation. Some of these are described below:

A Meeting at Khadia: A meeting was held in the Old City 'Khadia' area to discuss the possibilities and strategies of conservation and development of Walled City of Ahmedabad. This was organized by AMC and attended by many citizen groups, renowned personalities and AMC officials.

World Heritage Week Celebration at Desai-ni-Pol: The first public programme entitled 'Preservation of the Past and Glimpses of history' was launched at Desai-ni-Pol in Khadia area on 19th November 1996 on the occasion of World Heritage Week celebrations. This was a unique programme where "Heritage" was the main issue and organized jointly by citizens' groups and Municipal Authorities.

Desai-ni-Pol has a place in history because of its rebellious past during the British rule. The residents of the *pol* released a booklet to mark the Heritage Day, listing the historical houses, personalities who lived there, and a chronicle of important events.

Krantidarshan Padyatra **(Freedom Walk):** On 14th August 1997 a Freedom Walk was organized where several houses, connected with the history of Indian freedom struggle came to light. Twenty-eight important houses were identified and the citizens under the leadership of elected and government officials visited the same. Based on this on 2nd October 1997, many *pol* groups celebrated Gandhiji's birthday and buildings associated were visited.

Netaji's Birthday Celebrated in Bengal Home: A celebration similar to that in Desai-ni-Pol marked the birthday of Netaji Subhash Chandra Bose on 23rd January 1998. Bengal Home in Dhobi-ni-Pol, established in 1905 was the center of actions. This is where revolutionaries from Bengal stayed and trained local people in revolutionary activities during the freedom struggle. During a public meeting on this occasion, the need for preserving cultural heritage was stressed.

Kavi Sammelan **(Poets' meet):** A *Kavi Sammelan* was organized on Kavi Dalpatram's death anniversary on 25th March 1998, in the *pol* where he used to live. Organizations like Gujarat Sahitya Parishad also worked to make it a success.

Revival of Traditional Local Governance System – ***Panch*****:** A street play called *'Pol – Etale molun dahin ne upar katke gor'* was developed with an intention to create awareness at a larger scale amongst people, which was used as a tool to initiate a dialogue with the *pol* people. The play was organized by the collaborative efforts of

CRUTA foundation (Advisor – Heritage Programme, AMC), Theatre Media Centre (TMC) and Ahmedabad Community Foundation (ACF).

The play described the life and culture of the people of the *pols*. It tried to discourage the breaking down of the traditional *pol* house with the *otla, chowk, tanka*, wooden carved facades etc., to be replaced by concrete and brick structures. Thus the play was an effort to encourage people in the *pols* to revive their effective system of local governance. It was an effort to evoke the residents to create their '*panch*' and set strong local governance.

Heritage Walk: A Heritage Walk was initiated through the old neighbourhoods by AMC and the programme was well publicized through brochures and posters. The community itself came forward with whatever help they could do. The residents in the route make efforts to keep the route clean and restored.

Volunteer involvement is very crucial for long-term sustenance of any movement. Official recognition of citizen efforts is also vital. AMC has recognized this role and a proper certification process are also established.

Street Signage Programme: Name of an Area, particularly in historic inner city neighborhoods, is very important for the residents. They closely identify with the name. Unfortunately the street plate recognizing the identity of those areas has never been a priority. AMC took it up as an issue and has started to display name plates with municipal symbols and appropriately inaugurated them in the presence of AMC officials, local political representative and elderly persons of the neighborhood.

Role of Media: In all these activities the role of media is very important to give wide publicity and create awareness among the common people.

Inter-Departmental and Public Private Partnerships

City Gates: The AMC in association with ASI (Archeological Survey of India) set out on a beautification process focusing on the fort wall and city gates. ASI works on the physical restoration and AMC works on the landscape and lighting around the gates. Astodia gate is the first gate ready for first touches.

Façade Grant: AMC with the assistance of state government and Gujarat State Archeological Department is giving 50% grant for façade restoration. This type of inter-departmental partnerships can include citizen groups and NGOs also.

Kavi Dalpatram Memorial: AMC and the citizens of Ahmedabad proposed a memorial at the site of the house of the great poet. In absence of any proper drawings and plans of the poet's actual house, here the memories of the old residents were tapped and adjoining studied to bring authenticity into the creation of the memorial. The memorial comprises the façade of the original house, Tulsi Manch and a larger than life size 120 kg bronze statue of Dalpatram.

Memorial of Poet Akha Bhagat: A project has been initiated by AMC Heritage Cell to install the statue of poet Akha Bhagat at Desai-ni-Pol, based on the painting of him by Late Ravi Sankar Rawal.

Development of the Manek Burj: The Manek Burj, which stands at the southwest tower of the Old City wall, is associated to the ceremony of founding of Ahmedabad. A project was initiated for the restoration of the remains by AMC Heritage Cell. The restoration work was supported by Swaminarayan Temple Trust.

Transformer Design in Old City: Pole-mounted transformers installed by the Ahmedabad Electricity Company (AEC) are usually eyesores in many parts of the walled city. One of these, located next to a *Chabutara* was redesigned by AEC in association with local Architect in such a way as to highlight the importance of *Chabutara*.

Panchkuwa Ward Office: An old building near Panchkuwa Gate was identified by AMC for conservation. This building was restored and used for its ward office.

Heritage Gate of the Collectorate: Inspired by the heritage initiative the Collector of Ahmedabad requested AMC to help them to design a heritage gate for their complex and took up renovation of their buildings.

City Museum: A City Museum has been established with the help of Vastushilpa Foundation.

Involvement of Elected Representatives: This is an important factor in the success of any such activities as they have direct contact with the citizens and influence on them. Their involvement must be assured at all stages.

Establishment of a Heritage Cell: A heritage cell has been established in the AMC to look after heritage activities and policies. A separate budget of Rs. 50 lakhs was allocated, as a start up fund.

Heritage Walk: A Key Tool for Urban Revival

Heritage Walk – as the name suggests, behaves as an effective tool whereby the inner areas of the city shall be explored in terms of the architectural heritage, cultural heritage and the craft heritage. The walk shall in its due course take the people through specific routes penetrating through the inner areas and habitats of the people, exploring the beautiful temples, heritage buildings, *havelis*, *pols*, shops and a lot more.

The exploring and exposing of the inner areas of the Walled City requires an initiative from the Municipal Corporation of the city, which needs to provide some basic infrastructure – in terms of proper paving, cleaning up of the streets, provision of street lights, signage, public amenities. The walk carries with it another kind of advantage – the changes it can bring about in the landuse pattern of the area, by conversion of a part of the heritage building into a cafeteria or into a paying guest accommodation, whereby the tourists can get the actual feel of the cultural heritage by staying within the precincts of it. This can allow a total change in the economy of the area wherein the tourists can stay in and spend at these inner areas.

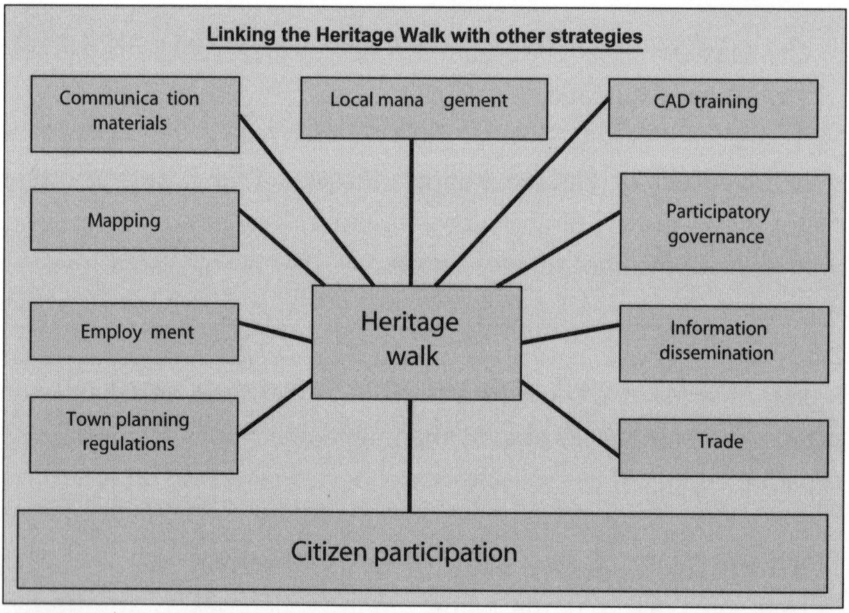

Preliminary Roles of the Municipal Corporations

To summarize, one can list down the following roles of Municipal Corporations for heritage conservation:

1. Intervene strategically. 2. Start with available resources. 3. Elicit support of local architects, professionals and NGOs. 4. Get support of local people. 5. Identify implementable projects 6. Involve elected wing. 7. Coordinate with other government and non-government agencies. 8. Establish a heritage unit in the local government. 9. Sensitize all official agencies towards heritage work. 10. Recognize and cooperate with International bodies and coordinate their actions.

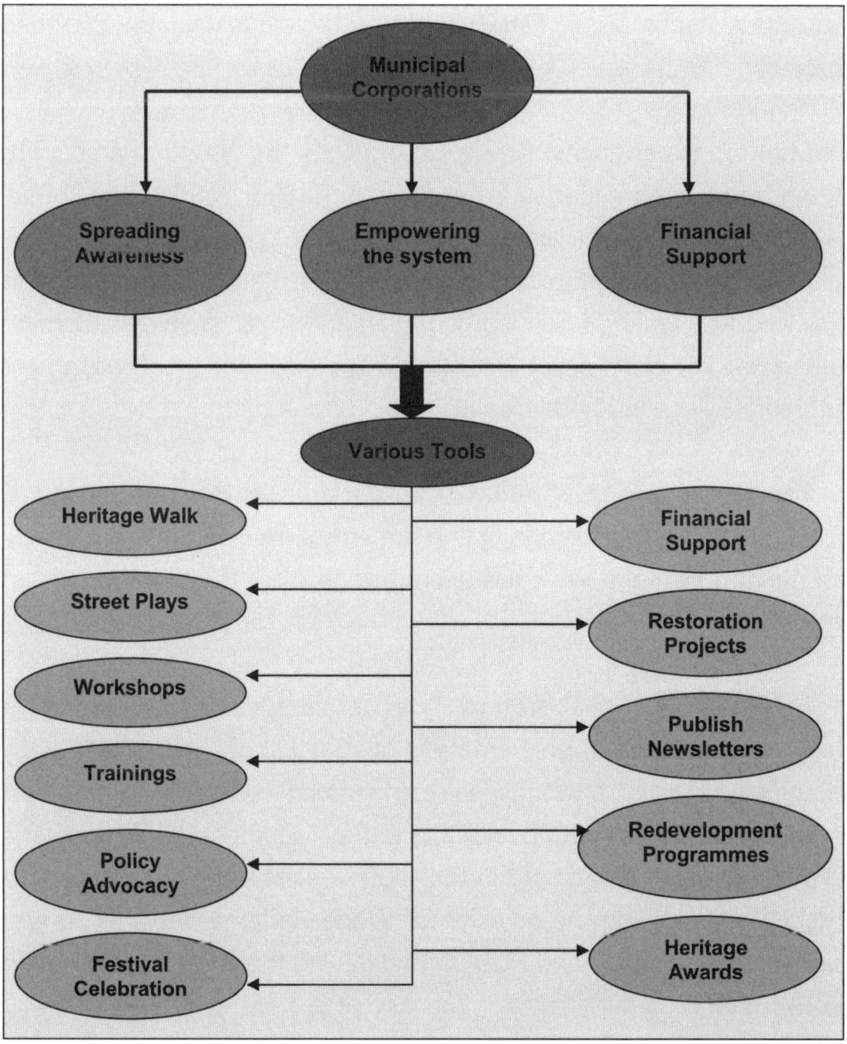

Reaching Out

These experiences and lessons should be used to prepare a comprehensive strategy in a wider level:

Replicating the Model: The model of Heritage Walk and other initiatives of AMC are getting replicated. With certain additions as per local characteristics, has already replicated the idea, and among other cities like Amritsar, Pondicherry, Baroda, Jamnagar, Delhi, Bhuj, Siddhpur, Jaipur, Surat, Patiala, Jodhpur have already launched their projects.

Sharing Experiences: These experiences are being shared with towns around Ahmedabad like in Dholka, Dabhoi, Nadiad and Lothal. AMC Heritage Cell officials are helping them to prepare comprehensive plans for improving physical conditions and heritage conservation. This will lead to a regional development plan and small town development initiatives. The experiences are also being utilized for the development of Vadtal village in Kheda district.

The Tera village in Bhuj has been declared as Heritage Village of Government of Gujarat and establishment of an Interpretation Centre along with Heritage Walk has been proposed for the development of the village.

HUDCO-AMC Collaboration: Finance always plays an important role for successful implementation of renewal projects. Particularly housing finance and building repair loan segment could play an important role. On 31st January 2000, HUDCO board has approved the heritage exploration with investment in the septennial of a Heritage sector. On the 18th of April, on the occasion of World Heritage day a MOU was signed between AMC and HUDCO to detailing the financial implication in this sector.

International Collaborations

AMC-French Govt. Collaboration: International agencies should be contacted to share the experiences of various agencies working in this field. This will give a wider perspective and awareness of the methods and approaches. On 14th of January 2000, empowered with 74th comment of our constitution, AMC signed MOU with French Government for a scientific study of the Walled City. This was initially for one year and was later extended. A French team along with AMC staff worked jointly to achieve these goals. MOU was signed between Government of France, AMC and HUDCO for the implementation of the programme for historic city conservation in Ahmedabad on 19th December 2001. On 18th of February 2003 an agreement between Government of France and Ahmedabad Municipal Corporation was signed for the establishment of the Ahmedabad Heritage Centre. Financial Agreement was signed for Historic City Conservation in Ahmedabad between Government of France and HUDCO for providing subsidy in building repair loan on 16th June 2003.

AMC-Dutch Govt. Collaboration: Dutch had a small presence in Ahmedabad in earlier days in connection with trade & commerce. A Dutch factory and graveyard still reminds their past presence in the city. Restoration and an interpretation booklet exploring the related history in under way.

The Dutch cemetery, on the east side of the Kankaria Lake is a historic site. On the cemetery are four types of tombs: domed tombs, pyramids, 'walled' tombs and plain gravestones. The tombs were badly damaged by the earthquake of 2001. The Archaeological Department with the support of Ahmedabad Municipal Corporation restored them to original shape.

World Monument Fund listing: Walled City of Ahmedabad was included in the list of endangered heritage sites by the World Monument Fund during the year 1998-1999. This was used to intensify the conservation activities in Walled City and generate international attention.

The 300-year-old Dwarkadheesh Temple in Boua-ni-Pol, partially destroyed in the earthquake of 2001 received the attention of the World Monument Watch to be listed in its most endangered 100 sites in the World in the year 2002 and the World Monument Fund has awarded a sum of $32000 for the renovation of Dwarkadheesh Temple through the World Monument Fund-Robert Wilson Challenge Fund for restoration of the temple which is currently in progress.

Urban Renewal: Exploring New Horizons

Mr. D.L Bhakar - Chief Engineer, Jaipur Municipal Corporation

Urban History

Urbanization has the history immemorial and perhaps co-existed with the civilization of the human being. The town planning of ancient civilizations affirms the fact that the civic organizations of the cities were highly developed. The roads, dwelling houses, large buildings and forts were well planned and constructed. The dwelling units were so designed as to protect residents from noise, odours, and thieves. Houses were properly constructed on both sides of the roads, and doors of the houses opened in the lanes and not on the roads. The planning anticipated the inflated movement on roads, so the roads were straight, wide and well organized. The cities from Kotdi Ji, (Mohen-jo-Daro) to Jaipur had defensive outer walls. Most of these walls were built of chiseled stones and burnt bricks. The Harappan cities give a detailed account of a very good drainage and sanitary system. The main drains were connected with every house ensuring the proper disposal of waste. In order to check the maintenance, inspection holes were provided. The drains were covered and connected to the larger sewerage outlets, which ensured the passage of dirt out of the city.

Causes of Urbanization

The urbanization started with advent of permanent settlement of human beings. The concentration and dense population on particular point gave rise to huge cluster of houses, which in due course transformed to the towns and further grew to big cities. All the old cities had the central administration system and the cities had been placed with proper planning. The resources available for economic growth can be termed as the chief cause of urbanization.

Cities: The Gateway to Globalization

In the present phase of fast development, the cities are the gateway to globalization. All the amenities and infrastructure available in the mega cities lead to globalization and become the nerve centre of the economy of the country.

Urbanization: A Complex Process: The urbanization is the complex process and brings enormous day-to-day challenges before the agencies responsible for the development and maintenance of the civic facilities. The tremendous pressure of population over throws the developmental works. Steep escalation in the slum population in the urban areas pose new threats of law and order and the civic amenities are thrown out of gear.

The multiplicity of agencies responsible for development of the city and lack of co-ordination among them also result to inflated expenditures on developmental works without the desired results. The following are the generic tribulations in the urban areas across the country and need to be addressed effectively.

- Weak administration system
- Urban poverty
- Public transport
- Massive financial requirement

- Integrated services for the poor
- Establishment of bench marks (qualitative and quantitative)
- Comprehensive city plan
- Slums eradication
- Encroachments
- Parking
- Effective disposal of municipality waste
- Recycling of sewerage water

Government Planned Development v/s Private Developers

The chief cause for poor civic infrastructures in the urban areas is the townships developed by the private developers near the government developed colonies. These private townships without the basic facilities e.g. road, sewer system and other infrastructure ultimately become part of the urban area and municipality limits. Such unplanned additions to the urban area adversely affect the town planning and the developmental works takes a nosedive. The long term solution to these problems are:

- to make stringent laws on the subject, strict implementation of the enactment and introduce the town development tax levied on the developer
- Establishment of central autonomous body to control all municipal bodies and UITs

Milestones Achieved by Jaipur Municipal Corporation in Urban Renewal

The JNNURM scheme announced by the Government proved prolific for the city as Jaipur has been included as one of the mission city selected by the Government of India. The following major projects have been taken up under the JNNURM scheme to deliver world class facilities to the dwellers of the Jaipur:

- Urban Renewal of Chokdi Sarhad Ward No. 58 in Walled City
- Solid Waste Management of Jaipur City
- Sewerage System Phase-II
- Resettlements of Slums in Sanjay Nagar Bhatta Basti
- Conservation & Propagation of Panna Meena Baori
- Revitalization of Walled City Area Jaipur

Urban Renewal of Chokdi Sarhad Ward No. 58 in Walled City

The Walled city is the centre of attraction for tourists and other heritage lovers. With the aim to provide hassle free movement to tourists and other visitors in the walleed city area, the developmental works were taken up under JNNURM scheme. The photogenic view of the site after the work is placed below-

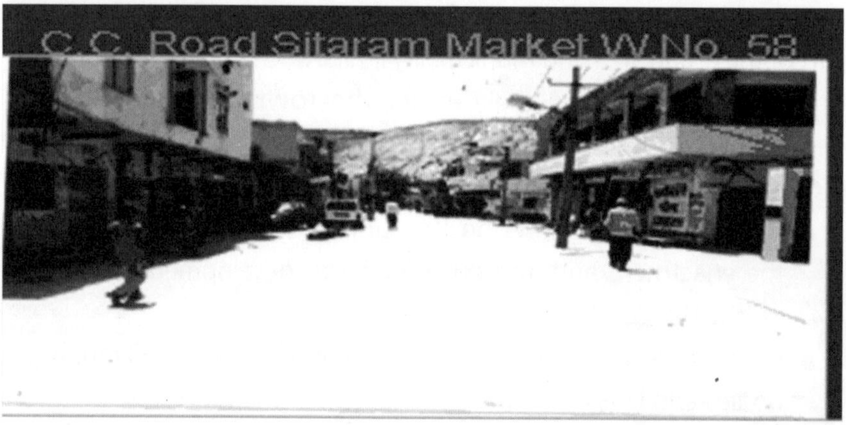

Solid Waste Management of Jaipur City

Municipal solid wastes pose a great threat to human beings as well the environment unless disposed off in a scientific manner. The solid waste of Jaipur city is disposed off at scientifically designed sanitary landfill sites. The feasibility to capture methane from these landfill sites and generate electricity is being explored. Modern solid waste transfer stations have been constructed under the JNNURM and the waste is transferred to landfill sites.

Property Connection under Sewerage System Phase -II

All the streets in the walled city of Jaipur have sewer lines but only toilet waste was connected to sewer system and the sullage from bathrooms and kitchen used to be let out in open drains creating unhygienic conditions. This sullage directly flows to the Jal Mahal area which is an environmental and ecological hazard. Under RUIDP approximately 42,000 households of the walled city have been connected with the sewer lines. Still a large part of population has been left out of property connections. In the Project Sewerage system Phase-II, 90,000 houses have been taken up for the property connections. This would ensure that all the streets, even the narrow lanes and bylanes would be free from liquid waste flowing in

Before & after work

Before & after work

the open drains. This would help in keeping the city clean and provide a better quality of life to the citizens of the Jaipur. The project is aimed to give neat and clean look to the Jaipur city. The illustrative pictures are placed on left hand side

The objective of establishment of sewerage Treatment Plant (STP) is to remove various contaminants present in sewage so as to produce an effluent and sludge, which can be disposed off in the environment without causing health hazards of nuisance. The safe disposal also reduces spread of diseases caused by pathogenic organisms present in sewage. The effluent and stabilized sludge, thus produced, could be gainfully utilized in agriculture, gardens as manure.

The Jaipur Municipal Corporation (JMC) has started work on the sewage treatment plant (ST project at Delawas and Jaisinghpura Khor in Phase II). Delawas plant capacity will be 62.5 MLD and would cost Rs 28 crore. Jaisinghpura Khor STP capacity will be of 50 MLD and the project cost is anticipated to be Rs 25 crore. Project will be completed by December 2009. The JMC also plans to setup a special sewage treatment plant under JNNURM in Pratap Nagar of the city. This project will generate 8,000 units of power per day and purify sewage water for non-kitchen use.

62.5 Mld Unit-II STP At Delawas and 50 MLD treatment plant at Jai Singh Pura Khor (85% Complete)

Power Generation from Bio Gas being Produced at Unit-I Delawas

The proposed power generation unit shall generate power from biogas (being generated at existing 62.5 MLD STP Unit-I at Delawas). At present, this biogas is being flared without any gainful utilization. This plant was constructed by RUIDP without the provision of power generation. The proposed generation of power at the Unit I shall be sufficient to run the unit equipments of existing STP. The plant has anticipated capacity of 8800KWH power generation per day. The present requirement of process equipment is 8596 KWH daily.

Slum Rehabilitation

The step to make Jaipur slum free, Jaipur Municipal Corporation has taken up the project of Sanjay Nagar Bhatta Basti. The Project aims to construct (G+3) 12000 dwelling units. The work has been started and the leveling works has been completed. The project is proposed to be completed by March 2010. The pictorial view of the Surveyed kachi Basti exhibits the living conditions.

Conservation and Propagation of Heritage works

Rajasthan has rich and unique heritage values. To conserve and propagate these heritage monuments of the Jaipur city, the works of conservation and propagation of Panna Meena Bawari, Kunds and other temples have been under taken by the JMC. Various works have been executed to save these monuments from decay. These monuments are hot spots for the tourists.

Panna Meena bawari

Kalyan Ji Temple

Maha Maya Temple

Bihari Ji ka Temple

Depot of irrigation

Sagar

Watch tower

Ambikeshwar temple

Revitalization of Walled City

The integrated Planning has been done to conserve the heritage value of walled city as due to increased commercial activities within the walled city area it became difficult for the tourists to catch the glimpses of architecture of the old city. The following works have been proposed under the project.

1. Construction of information centers for the guidance of foreign tourists to enable their free and independent movements.
2. Heritage walkway to ensure tourists free movements
3. Mapping of important places & tourists hotspots.
4. Display of tourism related information at public places.
5. Conservation and upkeep of monuments.
6. Conservation of important *chopads* and roads.

BRTS

The traffic congestion and effective public transport system are the cause of concern. To ease the Jaipur city from the above problems BRTS has been planned in three phases and is under execution. The company named Jaipur City Transport Services Limited (JCTSL) intends to commission Bus Rapid Transit System (BRTS) in Jaipur city under JNNURM. Under this project, dedicated bus corridors in the North-South and East- West directions of Jaipur city are in the process of development upto a length of 47 kms. The initial investment for the first phase of 47-km will be Rs 469 crore. The first phase will have three packages. All the three packages have been approved by the government.

Parking

The tremendous increase in vehicles pose great challenges in terms of road congestion and parking. To ease the problem the JMC is developing multilevel parking lots at nine identified places in the city. The projects are expected to be completed by Dec 2010.

Parks

Safe and clean environment for the citizens of Jaipur is the thrust area for the Jaipur Municipal Corporation. There are 500 parks within the jurisdiction in the municipal area and JMC proposes to develop 400 more parks and avail carbon credit on them. Besides parks, to ensure greenery in Jaipur the road sides and landscapes have also been developed.

Transforming Jaipur into a World-Class City.

Maharaja Jai Singh II founded the city of Jaipur, also called as Pink City in 1727. Architectural designs based on scientific principles were formulated and implemented by Vidhyadhar Bhattachary, chief architect from Bengal. Jaipur is the capital city of Rajasthan and is known more as a world-class tourist destination. Jaipur is endowed with rich heritage structures in terms of palaces, museums, forts etc. The city is surrounded by the Nahargarh hills in the north and Jhalana in the east. These hills are part of Aravalli hills ranges. The city is the first planned city of India. The city follows the grid system with wide straight roads, streets and lanes. One can find uniform rows of shops on either side of main roads. As per 2001 census, the population of Jaipur city is more than 2.3 million and is spread over an area of 467 sq. km. Government of Rajasthan is proactive in promoting Jaipur as one of the most sought after tourist destination in the world. Around 3000 tourists visit the City everyday. Development of Jaipur as a world class city is the thrust of the State Government. The city has an international airport and is well connected by road and train with all major cities of the country. It is 261 km. from the National capital.

Heritage and Urban Renewal: Facts and Challenges Scenario in Cities of Madhya Pradesh

Shri. Raghav Chandra - Principal Secretary, Urban Administration and Development Department, GoMP

1. Introduction

Historical trends

The historic trunk roads running from the south to the north called Dakshinapatha and crosswise from east to the west called Uttarapatha carried most of the trade consisting of textiles, precious stones etc. for which the Jambudwipa (comprising of what is India today) was so well known. These important routes had to necessary pass through the heavily wooded central lands of what constitute the State of Madhya Pradesh today. This gave rise to early urbanization and mushrooming of well protected cities such as Ujjayini, Tripuri, Besnagar (Vidisha) etc. in the early years of our era some two millennium years ago. These cities consisted of well laid out streets, sewage networks with complete buildings. It was then understood that whoever controlled this central heartland controlled the country, therefore, it also become one of the most contested territory, bringing in marauders and waves of influences in building technology and town planning. Several new urban centres were born in the areas of Gopakshetra, Malwa, Bundelkhand,

Baghelkhand and Chedi Kshetra. With the passage of time new towns of Gwalior, Maheshwar, Bhopal, Indore, Jabalpur etc. took over from old ones. Large water reservoirs, sewage disposal systems, electrical network and other technological advancements came early to these places and added to the urbanization process which over time emerged as powerful urban centres influencing the shaping of Indian political, religious and trade history.

Madhya Pradesh comprises of several territories, which have played a significant role in shaping the India's history. Prominent amongst these are Malwa, Mahakoshal, Gwalior etc. From the time of King Asoka of the Mauryan dynasty to that of the Guptas in the 4th century AD, many dynasties came and went. Principal among them were the Sungas, the Andhras, the Satavahanas, the Ksaptrapas, the Nagas and King Harshavardhana's empire. In the 10th century, a number of dynasties were ruling various corners of the region; the Chandelas at Khajuraho and the Kachhawahas at Gwalior were the more prominent among these.

Dynasties again changed hands in the 13th century. The Khaljis had penetrated as far deep as the Malwa region. The grand Mughal Akbar annexed this area into his empire in the mid-16th century. From then on whatever few upheavals this state had been witness to. Madhya Pradesh became a tranquil oasis in the midst of chaos, great battles, and many other feats that might have gone ringing down in the annals of history but were not very conducive for serenity and hence good living. With the fading of the Mughal power, the Scindia and Holkar dynasties of the Marathas ruled independently at Gwalior and Indore respectively during the 18th century. When the British came to India some of the region's ruling dynasties continued to rule under British protection. However, even then, Central Provinces (as it came to be called) was known to be one of the least troubled and most peaceful states. After independence, the Central Provinces was re-organized and the modern state of Madhya Pradesh was created.

Madhya Pradesh came into existence on November 1, 1956, during the reorganization of states in India on the linguistic basis. It is made up of five regions namely, Madhya Bharat, Vindhya Pradesh, Bhopal, Sironj sub division of Vidisha district and Mahakoshal. Before independence, Madhya Bharat, Vindhya Pradesh and Bhopal were separate states while Sironj sub division of Vidisha district was the part of former Rajasthan. Madhya Pradesh, in its present form, came into existence on November, 2000 following its bifurcation to create a new state of Chhattisgarh. It is the second largest Indian state in size with an area of 308,000 sq. kms. In the decade of the nineties, Madhya Pradesh has shown a high urban growth rate.

Urban Trends

According to the 2001 census, total population of Madhya Pradesh is 6.03 crores, of which 1.61crores (26.67 %) is the total urban population. Presently, Madhya Pradesh has 357 ULBs, out of which there are 14 Municipal Corporations 92 Municipal Councils and 251 Nagar Panchayats.

A significant proportion of the urban population lives in the five major cities of Bhopal (1437354) Indore (1474968), Jabalpur (932484), Gwalior (popn 827026) and Ujjain (430427). Madhya Pradesh has the fifth highest rate of urbanization in India, with a decadal growth rate of 31%. This high growth rate is expected to continue, with the urban population rising by a further 50% to over 25 million people living in the towns having more than 1 lacs population by 2021. Bhopal, Indore, Gwalior and Jabalpur are developing as major urban centres as well as growth centres for the surrounding areas. Indore is emerging as commercial capital of state and is progressing at very fast pace with investments in infrastructure and industrial sectors. Bhopal, Indore, Jabalpur and Ujjain are included in 63 mission cities of India under the recently launched Jawaharlal Nehru National Urban Renewal Mission (JNNURM) by the Government of India.

Problems faced by urban areas

The unprecedented pace of urbanization overtook the planning and governance trends and gave rise to several problems like inadequate supply of water, absence of underground sewerage, coverage problems of primary collection and segregation of waste and inadequate intercity public transport system along with highly congested streets in the core areas. These problems are basically related to infrastructure and major interventions have been made for solving them. At the same time, one major sector which is a part of development—Heritage and Conservation remains neglected. The quest for economic development is resulting in demolition of priceless historic structures, and these structures are replaced by freeways and expressways, housing projects, and shopping malls. Thus a need has been observed to make proper policy decision for conserving our rich heritage and continuing the process of development.

First of all it is important to understand the terms Heritage and Urban Renewal in brief. As defined by UNESCO the term "cultural heritage" encompasses several main categories of heritage: like:

- Tangible cultural heritage: movable cultural heritage (paintings, sculptures, coins, manuscripts, etc.); immovable cultural heritage (monuments, archaeological sites, and so on); underwater cultural heritage (shipwrecks, underwater ruins and cities and so on);
- Intangible cultural heritage (oral traditions, performing arts, rituals, and so on);
- Natural heritage (natural sites with cultural aspects such as cultural landscapes, physical, biological or geological formations, and so on)

The term 'Urban renewal' can be understood as—Whilst suburbanization has been occurring at the peripheries of the city, important processes have been in operation at the city centre. The most important of these have been urban renewal. Urban renewal is a continuing process of remodeling urban areas by means of rehabilitation and conservation as well as redevelopment. In other words "Urban renewal or urban regeneration is a process of land re-development in areas of moderate to high density urban land use". In urban renewal the emphasis is on those parts of the city which have fallen below current standards of public acceptability.

2. Heritage and Urban Renewal Policies of Madhya Pradesh

Policy on Redensification

Urban redensification is critical to the success of local communities and the long-term prosperity of citizens living in urban areas. Urban redensification in cities and towns across the state have shown that it is possible to save relevant parts of the town and make significant improvements to the lives of the people living there, by 'unlocking' land assets that are being exploited at a sub-optimal level. In other words, it can be understood as: redensification is needed to unlock real estate assets that are hitherto being sub-optimally utilized to liberate their true economic potential, generating employment and economic opportunities and new social and physical infrastructure.

The State Govt. recognizes the need for striking balance between development and conservation and has adopted a holistic approach of heritage conservation along with economic development of cities. In many cities of Madhya Pradesh, various areas have been subject to redevelopment and regeneration: eg. in Bhopal, CBD project and Platinum Plaza (in which the old Government quarters covering a large chunk of land have been undone and new and compact housing with commercial provisions has been constructed), Riviera Township project etc.are some of the major redensification initiatives that have been taken up. In case of Gwalior, redensification of Thatipur area is proposed. The project has been conceptualized to decongest the existing CBD, Maharajbada area, of Gwalior by developing a new CBD at another place, 'Thatipur'. The project comprises of development of 70 acres of land where presently Govt. quarters exist in a haphazard manner. The new plan proposes resettlement of all these existing quarters in a well-planned manner in 20 acres (approximately 1010 housing units will be constructed) and the rest of the land would be used for private housing and commercial purpose. Similarly, in another Municipal area, Seoni, redensification of an area of approximately 30 acres has been proposed with a provision of bus stand, housing and commercial complexes.

Policy on Urban Renewal and Heritage

The Urban Administration and Development Department of GoMP is utilizing funds available under various schemes like JNNURM, DFID assisted project 'UTTHAN' and ADB assisted project 'UDAY' for urban renewal and heritage conservation. Ujjain city envisages a total investment of Rs.326 crores in the Heritage and Urban Renewal sector and Bhopal has proposed an investment of Rs. 200 cr for the same. In Ujjain complete restoration of the Mahakal Van and Rudrasagar and temples is envisaged under JNNURM.

Under the DFID assisted project 'Utthan', some initiatives have already been taken in the heritage area. Along with this the Govt. of Madhya Pradesh has also made an agreement with the Archaeology department to fasten its efforts for conservation. In the recent years many organizations have come forward to work for Conservation and preservation of natural and built heritage. Archeological Survey of India and State Archives department has already listed heritage buildings and precincts and taken most of them under control. Indian National Trust for Art and Cultural Heritage (INTACH) has done listing of Heritage Structures in Ujjain and Bhopal and has conducted heritage walks and awareness workshops.

An example of the strategy and approach adopted by the cities and State Govt. for the three Historic cities Ujjain, Gwalior and Bhopal is illustrated below.

The three historic cities of Madhya Pradesh: Bhopal, Ujjain and Gwalior also like other historical towns have distinct social and cultural manifestations in the matter of art, culture, recreation etc. that form the non-tangible and living heritage of the place. These cities have also experienced impacts of booming economy. These cities have undergone a considerable amount of transition in their spatial structures, economic spread, ecological impacts and culture due to the impacts of booming economy. The following section analyses the scenario prevailing in the three main cities with respect to Heritage and Urban Renewal.

Citywide Potential and projects: Ujjain, Gwalior and Bhopal

• Ujjain

Ujjain (also known as Ujjaini, Avanti) is an ancient city situated on the eastern bank of the Kshipra River. Home to one of the twelve Jyotirlinga shrines to the God Shiva, it is one of the seven sacred cities of the Hindus and hosts Kumbh after every twelve years. Great poets like Vedavyasa and Kalidasa have eulogized the city. Vikramaditya, the legendary emperor, ruled the city with his famous *Navratnas* (nine jewels) including Kalidasa.

Mahakaal Temple: Ujjain

The city has got a rich built and natural heritage. While the Mahakaal parisar, temples, *Chhatris*, *Ghats* and wooden architecture buildings becomes a part of built heritage, the Sapta sagars come under natural heritage.

Ujjain is known all over as an ancient city that has its origins as a sacred landscape in the remotest historical past of India. However, much of it is based on the ancient texts such as the Vedic literature, Brahmanas, Upanishads, Dharmasutras and Dharmasastras. Avanti is mentioned in the Kishkandha Kand of the epic, Ramayana. Ujjayani is mentioned in the Mahabharata. The multiplicity of contributions and their accommodation in the spatial structure of the city have played a decisive role in shaping the built heritage of Ujjain. Ujjain has had a multifaith history with Hinduism, Buddhism and Jainism co-existing peacefully for a long time. Islam has made its own contribution and Ujjain is one of the revered pilgrimage centres of the Bohras in the country.

Heritage Issues in Ujjain: Ujjain today is one of the most poorly interpreted and understood city of India. Its antiquity is not apparent immediately, the city having been destroyed completely at some point in history. Independent India has not made much attempt at bringing to the fore this character of the city.

The city has undergone organic development and like many other cities it is presently facing many problems in the Core areas. The Ujjain Core Heritage Zone is in the very initial stages of this change and has tremendous tourist pressure, which ultimately results in the problems of traffic congestion, encroachments and disturbed streetscapes.

The city receives tremendous tourist pressure; everyday 3000 tourists visit the place. Apart from this, on the occasions of Nagpanchami and Mahashivratri nearly 3 to 5 lacs piligrims come to Ujjain. All these factors ultimately demand for proper infrastructure and in the absence of which the city is gradually crumbling.

Conservation and Development plans for the holy city are aimed at respecting the historicity of the tradition and its sanctity in the ancient texts along with reaffirming its spiritual and religious importance. Accordingly a comprehensive restoration project of about Rs 300 crores is being prepared by INTACH (as consultants) for the Department of Urban Administration and Development, MP.

• Gwalior

The similar scenario has been observed in Gwalior. The existing city of Gwalior has a rich history and distinct character of its own. Serving as the seat of the powerful Maratha kingdom - the city wielded its influence in a large region around it. Many of the economic activities in the region (mostly agriculture) have traditionally been traded here. The city continues to be the predominant centre for trade and commerce till date. Additionally, it has also maintained its role as the seat of administration.

Gwalior Fort

The Marathas were powerful and a wealthy dynasty - as a result art, education and cultural flourished in the city. Till date, the city continues to attract a large number of tourists to its magnificent monuments that stand testimony to its glorious past. The standards to education in the institutes established by the earlier monarchy compete with the very best in India.

In terms of physical growth, Gwalior is a tri-nodal city consisting of - Old Gwalior settlement around the fort, Lashkar - area developed by the Marathas and Morar - the British cantonment. These were established at different periods in history.

In recent decades, all three settlements have witnessed increase in size and population resulting in almost contiguous urban growth as well as congestion, dense and haphazard development. Out of the three settlements the Lashkar area comprises of CBD of the town "the Bada". 'Bada' is a beautifully planned area and resembles with the Agora or Forum of Greek and Roman period.

Maharaj Bada Area of Gwalior

Heritage Issues in Gwalior: In the present scenario the city accommodates 10 lac habitants and requires major planning interventions in the core areas. Like all other cities the road network in the Lashkar - Morar area with little or no scope for widening, is quite inefficient and inadequate for the present day traffic. Moreover, there is a very high degree of pedestrian traffic , heavy commercial activities including the informal sector, absence of any organized parking space make the situation worse. Though some traffic management measures in the form of banning of heavy vehicles, one-way operation etc. are in place, but due to lack of strict enforcement measures it fails to give any relief to the core area. There are hundreds of buildings present in the Lashkar, Morar and Fort area that require conservation and heritage management measures. All these factors eventually lead to need of Urban renewal.

The Gwalior Development Plan 2005 (Draft) prepared by the Directorate of Town and Country Planning, Madhya Pradesh has proposed to retain the existing form of the city as a combination of three sub-cities by integrating them physically without letting them loose their individual identities. The Plan proposes to develop a number of relatively self-contained planning units with each unit meant to function as a distinct entity in respect of local level shopping, primary education. But it focusses very less on the urban regeneration initiatives.

As mentioned earlier, one of the major redensification project has been proposed to decongest the 'Bada' area. The proposed interventions for the delineated project area mainly inside the Bada area is based on the concept that the public city squares are breathing areas for the city. The disorganized retail activities, building transformation, insufficient service capacities, visual noises etc have highly contributed to the fragmented image of this public square.

Therefore to sustain and enhance the fundamental characteristic of the public square, the broad proposals for this area are dictated by the project vision to help achieve public space area improvement and heritage management in the overall context of urban renewal of the historic city.

Heavy pedestrian and slow moving traffic in the 'Bada' area

• Bhopal

The story of Bhopal is quite different as it got the Status of State capital in 50s and saw a planned approach in the expansion. It is said that Raja Bhoj, the famous Parmar king of Dhar, founded Bhopal City in the 11th century at its present site. He created the Upper Lake by constructing an earthen dam across the Kolans River. The traces of the original town, however, do not remain. The city was established again and fortified in the 18th century by Dost Mohammed Khan. The Lower Lake was created by Nawab Chhote Khan in 1794. The city remained a capital of a feudal state till it was merged in the Indian union in 1948.

Several dynasties have left their mark on the city. The antediluvian remains of the forts built by the Rajputs, Afghans and the Mugals silently speak of the battles, victories and failures of the past era. These icons are testimony to the grandeur of past and provide a marvellous treat to the eyes. Even by seeing the remains of the city one can have the glimpse of different cultures, which existed in the past. Many kings have ruled here and enriched the character of the city. Bhopal has not grown as a single city but as discreet townships, with sparse outgrowth in between. Today Bhopal has blossomed into a city, which in spite of being modern

Glimpses of Historic Bhopal

upholds the patrician mark of its bygone rulers. The city provides a fascinating blend of scenic beauty with its lakes, parks, temples, mosques, gardens, museums, statues and buildings.

Urban image of the city is a collective visual appearance contributed by natural and man made elements, like Jumerati Gate, Kamala Park, Raj Bhawan, Chowk area, Jama Masjid, Moti Masjid, Sadar Manzil and Gauhar Mahal etc.

Heritage Issues in Bhopal: A 1.5 million-population city, Bhopal, is continuously losing its grace and beauty under the growing pressure of up-gradation and densification of activities. The New Bhopal planned in 1956 can sustain with the present infrastructure for next few years but the Old city area requires planning interventions. Revitalization of inner city as a whole or in parts becomes essential due to the growth pattern, rapid expansion, and economic development, congestion and overcrowding. Presently the population density of the CBD area is much higher than the overall city population density. This also affects the infrastructural services laid at the time of initial development and upgraded from time to time in unplanned manner. Thus this area required a Renewal Plan to develop it in accordance to the total city development.

One of the core city area of Bhopal, 'Pari Bazar' was facing the problems of negligence. Pari Bazar was established by the erstwhile Begum Shahjahan of Bhopal during the expansion of the town in an area called Shahajanabad in 1870's.The idea was to involve women of the town in the active economic and trade affairs of the State. As the time passed on, the area as well as the activities lost identity. In order to revive the image of this area, a committee has been formed by the Principal Secretary, UADD, which will decide the feasible solutions for this. In this regard, suggestions were made to convert Moti Mahal in to a women's shopping corridor where women's self help groups could sell their wares. This may lead to participation of women in the day-to-day affairs of the city in a more active way.

Challenges

When a major event takes place, the 'old order changes giving place to new' but if those in the new order are not sensitive to the sensibilities of the old order and its symbols that constitute heritage, the result is destruction of cultural heritage. What gives identity to these historic cities today are the heritage assets of the city. Based upon the experiences, the key issues which pose a challenge for policy makers today are:

• *Absence of Heritage Focussed Dimension in Master Plans*

Master Plans as prepared in the recent times are delinked from traditions. The analysis shows that in most of the Master Plans that have been prepared in the recent decades, the social, cultural and emotional integration of the new city and the old city is viewed merely in terms of strengthening the physical and social infrastructure rather than in terms of revitalization. Even here, the protection and conservation of cultural heritage takes only a passing mention. The Central and State Governments have laws and guidelines for preserving the monuments. The State Town & Country Planning Department's 'master plans' for these areas are not effective because a consensual approach has not been built up by involving the local community. The multiplicity of governmental agencies and the lack of coordination between them are nullifying the impact of the conservation regulations and the conservation of heritage monuments that are the main tourism resource. Archaeological Survey of India is unable to secure ready cooperation of district administration in removing encroachments from the monuments' peripheral areas. Despite all the drawbacks, the time is ripe for formulating a creative approach to heritage preservation, environmental conservation and people's participation.

• *Value of Land – a challenge*

In most of the cases heritage areas lie in the inner city where the land prices are high. Any interventions that do not take into account the economic incentive part may not only be detrimental to the interest of the owners but may also lead to the deterioration of the properties on account of the value of land in such areas going down. How to solve this conundrum is a real challenge to heritage lovers and policy planners.

• *Ownership of the Assets in Private Hands*

In most of the cases the heritage buildings have private ownership and it becomes difficult to acquire it for conservation. It becomes very difficult to implement heritage initiatives as land values are very high and sensitivity of the private owner towards conservation is very less. For example in case of an old structure *Hammam* of Bhopal the owners don't want any significant change or upkeep. The presence of a living *Hammam* in Bhopal was well recognized. It is a rare asset and can be developed in to a tourism destination in these times of 'Recreational Tourism' where spas play a major draw. The trouble arises due to the disputed nature of its ownership where a clear solution to the development of this asset is illusive to both: owners and the State. State government is planning to intervene in terms of policy to provide solution to such situation.

• *No Promotional Support to the Old and Traditional Handicrafts and Livelihood*

Most of the historic town consists of an interdependent network of crafts and skills that provides livelihoods in multiple ways and is difficult to replicate in any new development. Therefore these areas should be viewed as Economic Opportunities and not a liability. Conservation of inner cities and historic areas has resulted in economic revival. In terms of Ujjain the bullion trade, handicrafts (textile printing, metal work etc.) are centred in city core area. An in-depth survey is required to identify area specific skills and strengths and development/conservation plans need to address their needs and growth.

The Road Ahead

A "people-centered" approach should be used to carry out urban renewal. The purpose of urban renewal is to improve the quality of life of residents in the urban areas. The Government has to balance the interests and needs of all sectors of the community without sacrificing the lawful rights of any particular group. The aim is to reduce the number of inadequately housed people.

A policy framework is needed which is based on community participation, involvement of stakeholders, holistic planning and an enlargement of vision for the city and citizens. The role of Urban Planner is to act as a catalyst for improvement of cities and quality of life without hampering the image of the city. With due understanding of demographics, social structure and economics, and aesthetic appeal of the city, Urban Renewal can be a much needed positive intervention. The protection and revitalization plan of cities must be placed under the responsibility of the ULBs, which, in conjunction with the State Government should fulfill the objectives of JNNURM and GoI's Heritage Guidelines. The State Government is planning to establish a heritage Cell, comprising of conservation architects and related professionals in each ULB (Heritage cell is already formed in Bhopal). The local authority cannot by itself take on the responsibility of implementing the conservation plan, as there are too many players on the scene.

Master Plans must Emphasize on Heritage Regulations

As per CDP Ujjain, the studies conducted by INTACH (studies of conservation in development) in old towns and cities such as Bhopal, and Ujjain came to the conclusion that conservation of built heritage in such conditions was possible only if 'heritage areas' or 'heritage zones' were identified in the Master Plans and conservation plans were prepared for each such area on a location specific basis. Even within the 'heritage zone, a 'core zone' was sought to be identified. Today, everyone recognizes that even a notified monument or heritage precinct has to be taken in its environmental context. That is why restrictions are sought to be placed for any development within 300 meters of the boundary of any notified monument or precinct. However, such a restriction does not necessarily identify or define the environmental context. The limit is obviously arbitrary and therefore, instead of solving the problem, in many cases it aggravates it. One of the objectives of listing should be to identify and delineate 'heritage areas' or 'heritage zones' and 'core zones' within them. In certain cases, the 'heritage areas' could also be networked into an "artpolis" ensuring inter-visibility of such areas and strengthening their inter-relationship. Specific interventions for heritage conservation for such areas could then be suggested in the development (master) plan.

As elsewhere, architectural controls, by way of FAR or FSI, setbacks, façade /front elevation, height of buildings, etc are prescribed in the Master Plans for Ujjain, Gwalior and Bhopal City on the basis whether the particular area is commercial or residential or industrial or whether it abuts a 40 feet wide road or a 60 feet road or a 100 feet wide road. There is no reason why a somewhat similar approach cannot be followed in laying down that the FAR/FSI in areas that are notified as 'heritage areas' or 'heritage zones' or 'core zones' within these. It should be on the ground that heritage needs to be protected and conserved. The guiding principle in working out and prescribing such controls should be:

- Protection and conservation of the built and natural heritage in that area.
- Maintenance of the skyline or the streetscape should be part of these controls.
- No change of the façade or the elevation should be permitted if such is the unique characteristic of that area.

Thus, if the buildings are predominantly two storied then the FAR/FSI must be fixed accordingly. If there are open spaces within such as courtyards then such spaces must be maintained in working out the FAR/FSI. It is true that such restrictions should be in the overall interest of maintenance of the heritage character and ambience of that area and the individual buildings or complexes and precincts that are its constituents, as well as of the owners of these properties. The most important aspect here would be to review the existing Master Plans to ensure that the aspects of heritage preservation, environmental conservation and people's participation are given due weight age.

4 Incentives for the Heritage Assets Ownership

One of the solutions that some of the parts of the world have adopted for provision of incentives to the owners of the buildings and precincts in the 'heritage area' is by notionally giving them the FAR/FSI prevailing in another area, which they could trade in the area contiguous to the 'heritage area'. Owners whose properties are acquired/ resumed for the implementation of redevelopment projects should be offered fair and reasonable compensation. Similarly, tenants affected by redevelopment projects should be provided with proper rehousing.

Pragmatic and enforceable incentives and disincentives have to be thought of and debated for this purpose. We need to examine the feasibility of these solutions before adopting them in our cities.

5 Conservation of Private properties

As far as the cities of Madhya Pradesh are concerned there are no specific policies for the conservation of private properties. The analysis of existing approach to heritage conservation in other parts of the world, which has owners bearing the cost of conserving heritage properties with only minimal or variable assistance, has not been effective in all cases, and particularly where heritage values are under threat. Regulation has been considered successful where it imposes low costs and owners have normal commercial incentives to conserve heritage values. However, regulation has not been effective where it imposes high costs on property owners. The major problem in making owners bear these costs is that it necessitates compulsion.

Along with the above, the State Government plans to formulate policies that support the owners of the heritage properties in following fields:

- Financial Support – Government plans to provide financial help in case the owners cant afford to pay for conservation
- Technical support – If the owners show their interest for the conservation, they must be given technical support to conserve their properties as per the Heritage Regulations.
- Awareness – Awareness programes must be initiated to let the owners know that the ownership of Heritage asset is a matter of pride and not a liability.

The Govt. plans to provide proper incentives so that their owners, instead of leaving them in a state of benign neglect, or worse still, demolishing them, actively conserve historic heritage places. If the conservation of heritage places can be made more compatible with the interests of property owners, then more conservation will occur voluntarily, and in a way that supports the long-term preservation of heritage values.

6 Measures to Promote Support to the Old and Traditional Handicrafts and Livelihood

It should be noted that in most of the cases of renewal and redevelopment the social aspect gets neglected. In most of the heritage cities, the old city areas have skilled craftsmen, artists and these people suffer when the urban development initiatives are taken without any social analysis. One of the major problems is that these people are bound to live in very miserable conditions due to the absence of specific livelihood projects. Initiatives should be taken to lay a great stress on building capacities of local institutions and communities and convergence of resources, schemes and efforts at the local level. The emphasis should be on seeking active partnership of people and their groups, civil society organizations and non- governmental organizations in planning, mobilising, execution and monitoring of different programmes for widening livelihoods of people on a sustainable basis.

Our Commitment

Fortunately in the three cities we analyzed, the built heritage still quite surprisingly remains, against all odds. And it needs to remain.

The in-sensitive construction and thoughtless development is giving a challenge to our efforts for preserving this heritage. But we are committed to meeting this difficult challenge, working with all of our partners, because the cost of losing our rich heritage would be unimaginably immense to our environment, people and culture.

We can conclude with the visions of the two cities as per their City Development plans:

To make Bhopal, a well-maintained historic urban centre and an historic town to attract the tourism activity, by the end of horizon year 2012.

To make Ujjain a knowledge and pilgrim centre – maintaining its great religious and cultural image and providing a better and sustainable environment to all walks of life

Valedictory Session

Recommendations

Recommendations

A. Urban Renewal in the Context of the 73rd / 74th Constitutional Amendments

1. The Conference noted with satisfaction that the 73rd (rural) and 74th (urban) amendments to the Constitution of India (as mandated in 1992) is gradually encouraging statutory spatial canvases for the States of the Union that enable participatory integrated development and which recognizes the rich natural and built heritage of India. This canvas ideally is to be developed through a) State Vision documents, b) Metropolitan Area and District Regional Development Plans, c) Settlement Development Plans (for Municipalities and Panchayats), and, d) Detailed Plans for the Wards (of the Municipalities and Panchayats), each with an accountable elected Councilor (urban) or Panch (rural). The Conference further noted that to make such Development Plans operational the Constitutional Amendments encourage Programme Plans with 5 year time-frames and committed annual budgets as an integral component of 20 years Perspective Plans as comprehensively updated every 5 years.

2. Thus, INTACH's expanding involvement in the Conservation, Protection and Promotion of India's natural and built heritage within Buildings, Plots, Precincts, Trails and Landscapes/ Towscapes as Projects can now be pointedly mapped/listed on Statutory Development Plans for programmed implementation through a process that facilitates

dedicated resources from several sources for Conservation as an integral component of Development.

B. Protection of Built Heritage

1. Within the above framework heritage conservation legislation is an essential prerequisite to achieving the objectives of conserving the built heritage, and must be viewed as an important tool for mediating change. Therefore, heritage regulations should be part of Development Controls in Development Plans.

2. Accordingly, permission to approve development around protected sites or within heritage precincts should not be subject to routine Building Permits and Development Control regulation administered by local bodies, but must be considered by a Heritage Conservation Committee (H.C.C.) comprising of the local authorities, NGO's/ CBO's and experts.

3. Heritage Legislation must bridge the gap between planning and implementation by identifying new types of partnership for planning, implementing, monitoring and enforcing, including the compilation and maintenance of authentic statistical and spatial data of heritage areas.

4. All Urban Renewal schemes must obtain the approval of H.C.C. and all Tourism Development proposals must be whetted by the H.C.C.

5. The process of achieving the objectives of conserving built mandate heritage and natural heritage must invariably include:
   i. Listing of all heritage structures and elements and mapping them clearly in statutory Local Area Plans or Ward plans of settlements;

ii. Grading of listed elements into categories of significance;

iii. Defining the scope of interventions permissible, that is, architectural control for various categories of significance including para legal tools like, standard operating procedures (SOP's) and guidelines.

iv. Notifying the heritage list under the Urban and Regional Development Planning Acts or a separate Heritage Conservation Act.

6. Focus on pilot demonstration projects is an effective strategy to catalyse the process of heritage conservation.

7. Objectives of heritage conservation can often be met by utilizing the maintenance budgets of owners and empowering them to undertake the works themselves. The objective should to be create a variety of financial incentives to promote heritage conservation projects instead of only depending on grants from government sources.

8. Publishing an annual state of Heritage Report for the H.C.C. This should be put on a website for wider dissemination. Suitable benchmarks must be created to monitor how heritage conservation is benefitting the local population.

C. Jawaharlal Nehru National Urban Renewal Mission (JNNURM)

1. The JNNURM should be realigned in consonance with similar missions for rural development. The Conference noted that it has the propensities to attract migration in to cities, which could be mitigated through enhanced investments to projects in rural areas.

2. All major projects involving developments and interventions in Heritage Precincts being considered for JNNURM funding should be evaluated by the H.C.C.

3. The Conference noted that certain reform conditionalities like scraping rent control legislation could be harmful to heritage conservation and therefore recommends that it should be modified to ensure the larger good of society.

4. Before funds are dispersed under the JNNURM, the following conditionalities need to be imposed:
   i. Heritage regulations must be in place;

   ii. Heritage listing to be notified;

   iii. Suitable legal regime to implement heritage conservation objectives, which are simple, direct and easy to understand by both civil society and regulating authorities should be in place;

   iv. There must be no regularization of illegal structures;

   v. Permissible FSI/FAR should under no circumstances be increased in heritage conservation areas;

   vi. Widening of road right-of-ways in historic areas should be discouraged and instead public transport should be encouraged to cater to the increased demands of travel;

   vii. Mixed land use, where existing, must not be discouraged with the caveat that incompatible functions should be removed;

   viii. Civic authorities should be encouraged to route power supply through ducts;

ix. Adequate attention must be paid to the informal sector of the economy in Heritage Precincts;

x. In Heritage Precincts, multiple projects must be attempted so that some initiative is always visible and achieved in a step-by-step time frame.

D. Role of INTACH

1. Support local initiatives through partnerships and networking, including seeking support to access funding for conservation projects.

2. Build capacity in government agencies to access JNNURM funding.

3. Undertake comprehensive listing throughout the country and publish it as an authentic record of buildings, precincts and landscapes to be protected/conserved. In particular, ensure that the ASI and State Archaeology lists are incorporated in Spatial Development Plans along with environmental lists and their regulatory prescriptions.

4. The unfinished agenda defined in the 2005 Hyderabad Conference on Heritage and Conservation needs to be pursued.

5. INTACH should generate awareness among civil society and government agencies about the strengths and weaknesses of JNNURM. The broad objective of this initiative should be to create a 'vested interest' to gain political and public support for Heritage Conservation.

6. INTACH should identify and publicize best implementable practices in conservation including the awareness about the value of cultural heritage to society and issues of sustainability.

7. The best practices should particularly focus on 'Indian solutions'. This must include undertaking research studies and structured consultations with specialists.

8. Use the media to promote awareness of heritage issues.

9. Build international partnerships.

E. Issues about Jodhpur

1. Jodhpur which already has over 8.00 lakh people, should be included as a JNNURM city.

2. The development of Jodhpur is intrinsically linked with water management, and so the Development Plan of the city must be linked to the water management regime, especially traditional practices.

3. Vision statement for Jodhpur should be formulated with the participation of all stake holders before the City Development Plan (C.D.P.) is formulated.

4. Focus should be on the provision of basic infrastructure, inclusive housing, promotion of Heritage Conservation and improving the process of participatory development through the Wards of the Municipal Corporation.

The above recommendations emerged from the International Conference on Heritage and Urban Renewal conducted by INTACH in Jodhpur from September 2 – 5, 2009. They were adopted during the Valedictory Session on September 5, 2009, and subsequently refined through email dialogue with all participates.

Maharani Preneet Kaur- Hon'ble Minister of State for External Affairs, Government of India

First of all, I would like to begin by congratulating INTACH for organizing this important and timely international conference on urban renewal and heritage and that too not as it is routinely held in Delhi, but in this historic city of Jodhpur. I have heard the summary and recommendation with great interest. It has covered a wide range of subject from policy and practice to a variety of case studies. I am particularly struck by the inclusion of respresentatives from Municipal Government because their voices are often not heard in the debate and policy formulation process by the bureaucracy and the policy makers. I am also very happy to note the presence of foreign participants – if only because I am the Minister of State in the Ministry of External Affairs.

Our great poet Rabindranath Tagore once said that India should have open windows to allow the breeze from other countries flow through but we should not be blown away. I am glad that INTACH in a similar vein is looking beyond our shores to seek ideas and advice to refresh our practices to develop new strategies to solve the problems of our cities.

Over the year, I have noted with great interest the growth and development of INTACH. I got to know about the Institution through my husband, who for a few years served as its Chairman. Now under

Shri S.K. Misra, I am happy to know how it has greatly expanded its activities and is now a renowned advocate for conserving the diverse heritage of our country. This heritage is a living heritage that is inextricably linked to all the manifestations of the built and the natural heritage, the tangible and intangible ones. This living heritage is under great stress on account of economic development and cultural globalization. Of course, I realize that the characteristics of this heritage cannot be preserved as museums or as tourist attractions, but must be allowed to grow and develop in response to contemporary forces of change. But I do believe that such evolution can be sensitively mediated so that our society is not left rootless and without identity. I am sure that much of the concerns of this conference would have covered these grounds and examined these issues. It is one of the greatest challenges of our times that even as we strive to develop and change; we have to decide on what legacy we leave behind for our children. Much of this legacy has been lost in developed counties through wars and industrialization, but in our country, it is largely intact. As we engage with the future we have to decide whether this heritage, is a burden or an asset. It is the same dilemma we face when we plan to renew our failing cities. We will have to decide what we must save and what we need to change and rebuild. I am glad that INTACH has highlighted this problem of conserving out heritage while simultaneously developing our cities. These two must be seen as two sides of the same coin.

India is a rapidly developing country and today it is an important player in global economy and its politics. In my present assignment, I deal with India's growing stature in the global arena. This makes me proud. But I am acutely aware that the state of our cities and villages reflect our international stature. A heavy down pour brings Mumbai and Delhi to its knees. The streets are often clogged with traffic. The infrastructure is collapsing. The quality of life for a majority in our cities is pathetic. The problem is not the lack of resources, but one of lack of ideas and will. Our town planning laws more often prove to be impediments to citizens who could with little assistance have created a better environment for themselves, even if the Government cannot provide for them. We will have to rethink our city planning strategies to make our cities meet the international standards, we once had great cities from the time of Indus Valley Civilization, and our medieval cities were the envy of other societies. Such cities are not the products of the people but produced in partnership between the citizens and authorities. Somewhere along the way we have lost our ability to nurture that kind of partnership to create better cities. Perhaps it was on account of colonialism, but for several decades there has been no attempt to revive that tradition of partnership and our cities are in their sorry plight as a consequence. Such public-Private-Partnership (PPP) initiatives are the order of the day. It will make investments economically sustainable while simultaneously providing a sense of ownership among citizen and civic authorities which will make projects socially sustainable as well.

I am glad that our Government has now taken initiatives to remove the anomaly of our growing world stature and failing cities. It has initiated the bold and innovative Jawaharlal Nehru National Urban Renewal Mission and backed it with credible funding mechanism. Urban renewal has to be at the heart of any strategy we devise to upgrade our cities and I am glad that this conference has focused on this issue. In our eagerness to accomplish our task to upgrade our cities, we should be careful not to wipe out the heritage that is deeply embedded in them.

I belong to Patiala which is well known for its magnificent architecture and its various forms of cultural expressions. INTACH has been deeply involved in protecting both of these at Patiala. The conservation of the massive Mubarak Mandi Palace in the heart of the historic centre of Patiala is going to be an important urban renewal initiative. But like all other urban renewal projects in our country, it is taking time to be implemented. Along with heritage interests there are other vested interests also, both private and public, which have to be painstakingly negotiated in order to arrive at a consensus before substantial works could be undertaken.

I am aware that urban renewal, particularly in sensitive heritage areas, require leadership, dedication and passionate advocacy to overcome bureaucratic lethargy and the practice of business-as-usual. INTACH has these qualities in full measure and I hope that it will continue to partner with the Government to conserve our heritage in the process of conserving our cities. I hope your recommendations will be taken into consideration by our Government while they formulate urban policies.

Annexure-I

Some Features of the Heritage Regulation And Heritage List As of April 1995

1. Power of Heritage Conservation Committee

(a) The advice of the Heritage Conservation Committee is virtually **binding** on the Municipal Commissioner. He is allowed toover-rule the Heritage Conservation Committee, but this power has been severely restricted; it is confined.

  (i) to exceptional cases only

  (ii) for reasons to be recorded in writing

  (i) the power to over-rule the Heritage Conservation Committee cannot be delegated by the Municipal Commissioner to another junior officer.

(b) for religious buildings, the Municipal Commissioner has to take into account the views of the Heritage Conservation Committee.

2. Heritage List

The heritage list is not part of the regulation.

The reason for *this is that,* that to change a Development Control **regulation**, very correctly, a specific and relatively time consuming procedure is required to be followed ie.

(a) The State Government will have to issue a directive under Section 37 of the MRTP Act to the Bombay Municipal Corporation

(b) The Bombay Municipal Corporation will have to invite objections and suggestions from the public

(c) objections and suggestions will have to heard by the Planning Committee of the Bombay Municipal Corporation

(d) Bombay Municipal Corporation will have to submit its report to Government

(e) Government will have to consult the Director of Town Planning.

Only after all the above steps have been completed can the regulation be changed.

Since listing is a continuous process and since the Bombay list was (and still is) woefully inadequate, it is necessary that the process of addition to the heritage list be less timeconsuming.

3. Modification/Relaxation of Other Regulations If Needed For Conservation of Heritage Buildings/Precincts

This is a very powerful regulation

The Municipal Commissioner can modify or relax any other regulation or give relaxations (eg. Regarding setback rules etc) (if that is needed for preservation of heritage).

4. Skyline

The skyline is to be maintained in heritage precincts.

5. Criteria For Listing of Heritage Buildings/Heritage Precincts

It is perhaps best to reproduce page 58 of the booklet entitled 'Bombay Heritage Regulations, 1995'. It reads as follows:

"**Abbreviations of Criteria (Classification) For Listing of Building and Conservation Areas:**

		Abbreviation
(a)	Value for architectural, historical or cultural reasons ...	A
	- architectural	A(Arc)
	- historical	A(his)
	- cultural	A(cul)
(b)	The date and/or period and/or design and/or unique use of the building or artefact ...	B
	- period	B(per)
	- design	B(des)
	- use	B(uu)
(c)	Relevance to social or economic history ...	C(seh)
(d)	Association with well-known persons or events ...	D(bio)
(e)	A building or groups of buildings and/or areas of a distinct architectural design and/or style, historic period or way of life having sociological interest and/or community value ...	E
	- style	
	- historical	
(f)	The unique value of a building or architectural features or artefact and/or being part of a chain of architectural development that would be broken if it were lost ...	F
(g)	Its value as a part of a group of buildings ...	G (grp)
(h)	Representing forms of technological development ...	H (tec)
(i)	Vistas of natural/scenic beauty or interest, including water-front areas, distinctive and/or planned lines of sight, street line, skyline or topographical ...	I (sce)
(j)	Open spaces sometimes integrally planned with their associated areas having a distinctive way of life and for which are and have the potential to be areas of recreation" ...	J

6. Scope of Changes Permitted in Different Grades of Buildings

"Grade-1 Essential and minimal changes allowed only when necessary in the interest of strengthening and prolonging life of the building or any of its features.

Grade-IIA Internal changes and adaptive reuse to be generally allowed, but will be subject to strict scrutiny.

Grade-IIB As in Grade IIA but in addition, extensions or additional buildings in the same compound are also allowed provided that these are in harmony with the existing heritage buildings and precincts especially in terms of height and facade.

Grade-III As in Grade II. In addition, in some cases reconstruction (ie. demolition) is also allowed".

"Grade-1

No interventions would be permitted either on the exterior or interior unless it is necessary in the interest of strengthening, and prolonging, the life of the buildings or precincts or any part or features thereof. For this purpose, absolutely essential and minimal changes would be allowed and they must be in accordance with the original.

Grade-II

Grade-II (A)

Internal changes, adaptive reuse and external changes will be generally allowed, but will be subject to strict scrutiny. Care would be taken to ensure the conservation of all special aspects for which it is included in Heritage Grade-II.

Grade-II-B

In addition to above extension or additional buildings in the same plot or compound could, in certain circumstances, be allowed provided that the extension/additional building is in harmony with (and does not detract from) existing heritage building(s) or precincts especially in terms of height and facade

Grade-III

External and internal changes and adaptive reuse would generally be allowed. Changes can includes extensions, additional buildings in the same plot or compound provided that extension/additional building is in harmony with and does not detract from the existing heritage building/precinct especially in terms of height and/or facade. Reconstruction may be allowed when the building is structurally weak or unsafe or when it has been affected by accidental fire or any other calamity or if reconstruction is required to consume the permissible FSI and no option other than reconstruction is available.

Reconstruction may also be allowed in case of those buildings which attract the provisions of Regulations 33(6), 33(7), 33(9) and Appendix II and Appendix III of Development Control Regulations, 1991.

Reconstruction may be allowed in those buildings being repaired/ reconstructed by MHADA.

However, unless absolutely essential, nothing should spoil or destroy any special features or attributes for which it is placed in the Heritage List."

7. Incentives

Several powerful **incentives** are given to heritage owners as spelt out below:

(a) Transferable Development Rights (TDR)
TDR will also be granted in case of loss of development rights due to heritage provisions.

Normal TDR is allowed to be consumed only in the suburbs; however, TDR from heritage buildings can also be consumed in the same ward as the heritage building even in the island city. This is the only type of TDR allowed to be consumed in the island city. This is a tremendous incentive.

Most buildings in the island city have exhausted their permissible FSI. If a family wants more accommodation close by, say for their children - then the only way out for them is to get heritage TDR.

A word regarding TDR

What exactly is TDR?

If you have 1000 sq. ft. of FSI and lose 400 sq.ft. because of heritage restrictions, the owner will get a certificate of 400 sq.ft. of FSI - which he can sell to builders in specified receiving zones.

(b). A bigger incentive is that heritage buildings can have office user in those areas where these users are not allowed .

In case the owner agrees to maintain the heritage building in its existing state and to preserve it with due repairs and gives a writtenu ndertaking to that effect, he will be allowed, with the approval of the Heritage Conservation Committee, to convert part of or the entire non-commercial area for commercial/office uses.

In a city like Bombay this is a tremendous incentive.

(c) In a heritage precinct if there is any sanctioned Development Plan reservation shown on the site of a listed heritage building, the same shall not be implemented unless it is absolutely necessary; it can even be deleted/modified.

This also is a powerful incentive since it prevents a heritage building from being taken over/demolished.

(d) No road widening would be allowed in such a manner so as to adversely affect an existing heritage building.

(e) In heritage precincts, road widening line shall be prescribed only so as to preserve and not detract from the heritage precinct.

(f) Though not mentioned in the regulation, a big incentive for residents in a heritage precinct is that the precinct cannot be ruined by a maverick builder, i.e. in a lowrise precinct, no high rise building can come up.

8. Heritage Conservation Committee

As mentioned earlier, this is the lynchpin of the heritage regulation. Its composition and terms of reference are therefore crucial. For some reason these were not included in the main heritage regulation but were spelt out in a separate Government Gazette of 25th April 1995. It was specified that the qualifications for membership would be as under:

(i) Chairman to be Retired Municipal Commissioner of Bombay Municipal Corporation or Retired Secretary to Government of Maharashtra with relevant experience

(ii) Two Structural Engineers of 10 years field experience

(iii) Two Architects having 10 years experience in the field of urban design and/or conservation architecture

(iv) Director, Prince of Wales Museum

(v) Environmentalist having 10 years experience

(vi) City Historian having 10 years experience

(vii) Director of Municipal Engineering & Services as Member Secretary

(viii) Five additional members to be co-opted by the Committee.

The Terms of Reference of the Heritage Conservation Committee were also spelt out as being, inter alia, :

4.1. To recommend to the Municipal Commissioner whether development permission should be granted under regulation no.67 and the conditions thereof.

4.2. to prepare a supplementary list of buildings, precincts, areas, artefacts structures, of historical, aesthetical architectural, or cultural value to which this Regulation No.67 would apply.

4.3. To advise whether any relaxation, modification, alteration, or variance of any of the Development Control Regulations of Greater Bombay, 1991, is called for under Regulation No.67(4).

4.4 To advise the Municipal Commissioner in the operation of Regulation No.48 to regulate or eliminate/erection of outside advertisement/billboard on the facade and to recommend to the Municipal Commissioner guidelines to be adopted by the private parties who sponsor beautification schemes at public intersections.

4.5. To advise whether to allow office user in the island city and when to terminate the same.

4.6. To advise whether Development Right Certificate may be allowed to be consumed in a heritage precinct.

4.7. To advise the Municipal Commissioner to evaluate the cost of repairs required to be given to the owners to bring the existing buildings in the original shape. For this purpose the committee may also try to help the Municipal Commissioner to raise funds through private resources.

4.8. To prepare special designs and guidelines for listed/cessed buildings and non-cessed buildings, control of height and essential facade characteristics such as maintenance of special type of balconies and other heritage items of the buildings and suggest suitable designs adopting new materials for replacements keeping the old form intact to the extent possible.

4.9. To prepare guidelines relating to design elements and conservation principles to be adhered to and to prepare other guidelines for the purposes of Regulation 67

4.10.To frame special Regulations for Heritage precincts and to advise the Municipal Commissioner regarding the same.

4.11.To advice Municipal Commissioner on any other issues as may be required fromtime to time during course of scrutiny and in overall interest of heritage conservation.

To appear before Government either independently or through or on behalf of the Municipal Commissioner in cases of appeals u/s 47 of MR & TP Act, 1966 in cases of listed buildings/heritage buildings and listed precincts/heritage precincts"

Annexure-II

January 12, 2009

Model Regulation for Conservation of Heritage Sites (Both Natural and Man Made)

Regulation No.

Conservation of heritage sites which shall include buildings, artefacts, structures, streets, areas and precincts of historic or aesthetic or architectural or cultural or environmental significance (heritage buildings and heritage precincts) and natural features of environmental significance and sites of scenic beauty.

1. Applicability

This regulation will apply to heritage sites which means those buildings, artefacts, structures, streets, areas and precincts of historic or aesthetic or architectural or cultural or environmental significance (hereinafter referred as Listed Buildings/ Heritage Buildings and Listed Precincts/Heritage Precincts) and those natural features of environmental significance and sites of scenic beauty including, but not restricted to, sacred groves, hills, hillocks, waterbodies (and the areas adjoining the same), open areas, wooded areas, points, walks, rides, bridle paths (hereinafter referred to as 'listed natural features') which are listed in a notification to be issued by Government. The list issued in the notification shall be hereinafter referred to as the said list.

2. Restriction on Development/Re-Development/ Repairs Etc

i) No development or re-development or engineering operation or additions, alterations, repairs, renovations including the painting of buildings, replacement of special features or plastering or demolition of any part thereof of the said listed buildings or listed precincts or listed natural features shall be allowed except with the prior written permission of the Municipal Commissioner.

Before granting any such permission, the Municipal Commissioner, shall consult the Heritage Conservation Committee to be appointed by Government (hereinafter referred to as the said Heritage Conservation Committee) and shall act on the advice of the Heritage Conservation Committee.

ii) Provided that before granting any permission for demolition or major alterations/additions to listed buildings (or buildings within listed streets or precincts), or construction at any listed natural features, or alteration of boundaries of any listed natural features, objections and suggestions from the public shall be invited and duly considered by the Heritage Conservation Committee.

iii) Provided that only in exceptional cases, for reasons to be recorded in writing, the Municipal Commissioner may refer the matter back to the Heritage Conservation Committee for reconsideration.

However, the decision of the Heritage Conservation Committee after such reconsideration shall be final.

3. Responsibility of the Owners of Heritage Buildings

It shall be the duty of the owners of heritage buildings and buildings in heritage precincts to carry out regular repairs and maintenance of the buildings at their own cost. The Government, the Municipality / Panchayat or the local bodies and authorities shall not be responsible for such repair and maintenance except for the building owned by the Government, the Municipality / Panchayat or the local bodies.

4. Preparation of List of Heritage Sites Including Heritage Buildings, Heritage Precincts and Listed Natural Features

The said list of heritage sites to which this regulation applies shall not form part of this Regulation for the purpose of section.................of the....................Regional Town & Planning Act. This list shall be supplemented from time to time by Government and/ or the Municipal Commissioner on the advice of the said Heritage Conservation Committee, or by Government suo moto or by the Municipal Commissioner suo moto, or by the Heritage Conservation Committee suo moto, provided that before the list is supplemented, objections and suggestions from the public shall be invited and duly considered by Government and/or the Municipal Commissioner and/or the Heritage Conservation Committee respectively.

Provided that any list which is in draft form and pending for approval will, in the interim period, also be deemed to be part of the heritage list for purposes of development permission.

When a building or group of buildings or natural features are listed it would automatically mean (unless otherwise indicated) that the entire property including its entire compound/plot boundary along with all the subsidiary structures and artefacts, etc. within the compound/plot boundary, etc. form part of list.

5. Criteria for Listing of Heritage Sites

		Abbreviations
(a) Value for architectural, historical or cultural reasons	....	A

- Architectural ... ... A(arc)
- historical ... ... A(his)
- cultural ... ... A(cul)

(b) The date and/or period and/or design and/or unique use of the building or artefact B
- period ... ... B(per)
- design ... ... B(des)
- use ... ... B(uu)

(c) Relevance to social or economic history ... ... C (seh)

(d) Association with well-known persons or events ... . D (bio)

(e) A building or groups of buildings and/or areas of a distinct architectural design and/or style, historic period or way of life having sociological interest and/or community value E
- style ... ...
- historical ... ...

(f) The unique value of a building or architectural features or artefact and/or being part of a chain of architectural development that would be broken if it were lost F

(g) Its value as a part of a group of buildings ... ... G (grp)

(h) Representing forms of technological development ... . H (tec)

(i) Vistas of natural/scenic beauty or interest, including water-front areas, distinctive and/or planned lines of sight, street line, skyline or topographical ... . I (sec)

(j) Open spaces sometimes integrally planned with their associated areas having a distinctive way of life and for which are have the potential to be areas of recreation J.

(k) Natural heritage sites NH

(l) Sites of scenic beauty (sec)

6. Penalties

Violation of the regulations shall be punishable under the provisions regarding unauthorised development.

In case of proven deliberate neglect of and / or damage to heritage buildings and heritage precincts, or if the building is allowed to be damaged or destroyed due to neglect or any other reason, in addition to penal action provided under the Act, no development permission to construct any new building shall be granted on the site if a heritage building or building in a heritage precinct is damaged or pulled down without appropriate permission from Municipal Commissioner.

It shall be open to the Heritage Conservation Committee to consider a request for re-building / reconstruction of a heritage building that was unauthorisedly demolished or damaged, provided that the total built up area in all floors put together in such new construction is not in excess of the total built up area in all floors put together in the original heritage building in addition to other controls that may be specified.

7. Power to alter, modify or relax other development control rergulations

On the advice of the said Heritage Conservation Committee and for reasons to be recorded in writing, the Municipal Commissioner may/shall alter, modify or relax the provisions of other Development Control Regulations/Buildings Byelaws and of the Master Plan (hereinafter referred to as 'the said Regulations') if it is needed for the conservation, preservation or retention of historic or aesthetic or cultural or architectural or environmental quality of any heritage site.

8. Heritage Precincts/ Natural Features

In cases of streets, heritage precincts, areas and, (where deemed necessary by the Heritage Conservation Committee) of natural features notified as per the provisions of this Heritage Conservation Regulation No.4 above, development permissions shall be granted in accordance with the special separate regulations prescribed for respective streets, precincts/natural features, areas which shall be framed by the Municipal Commissioner on the advice of the Heritage Conservation Committee.

Before finalising the special separate regulations for precincts, streets, natural features, areas, the draft of the same shall be published in the official gazette or in leading newspapers for the purpose of inviting suggestions and objections from the public. All suggestions and objections received within a period of 30 days from the date of publication in the official gazette shall be considered by the Municipal Commissioner/Heritage Conservation Committee.

After consideration of the above suggestions and objections, the Municipal Commissioner acting on the advice of the Heritage Conservation Committee shall modify (if necessary) the aforesaid draft separate regulations for streets, precincts, areas and natural features and forward the same to Government for sanction.

Provided that pending consideration of suggestions and objections and pending final sanction from Government to the above draft special regulations for precincts and natural features, the Municipal Commissioner/Heritage Conservation Committee shall have due regard to the above draft special regulations while considering applications for development/re-development etc. of heritage buildings, streets, heritage precincts, areas, listed natural features.

9. Road Widening

(i) If road widening lines under the .... Municipalities Act (date) are prescribed they shall be such so that they will protect and not detract from the said heritage sites.

(ii) If there are any new road widening lines proposed in the Revised draft or sanctioned Development Plans/Master Plans the Municipal Commissioner shall consider the heritage provisions and environmental aspects while considering applications for development permissions in these precincts. Necessary steps may be taken to modify the Development Plan/Regional Plan accordingly. Pending this action, the road widening/development of new roads shall not be carried out.

(iii) No widening of the existing roads under the ....Municipalities Act or in the Master Plan/Development Plan for................................or in the Regional Plan shall be carried out in a manner which may affect the existing heritage buildings (even if they are not included in a Heritage Precinct) or which may affect listed natural features.

10. Master Plan Reservations

If there are any Development Plan/Master Plan reservations shown on heritage sites the same shall not be implemented. If required, the Municipal Commissioner, on the advice of the Heritage Conservation Committee, shall move government to get these reservations deleted/modified as need be.

11. Grant Of Transferable Development Rights (TDR) In Cases of Loss of Development Rights

If any application for development is refused under this Regulation or conditions are imposed while permitting such development which deprive the owner of any unconsumed FSI, the said owner/lessee shall be compensated by grant of Development Rights Certificate of the nature set out in Appendix I and as may be prescribed by Government from time to time. The extent of Development Rights Certificates to be granted may be determined by the Municipal Commissioner, on the advice of the Heritage Conservation Committee.

12. Incentive Uses For Heritage Buildings (Check)

The Development Control Regulation No. bans office/commercial user/hotel user in (LIST OUT AREAS WHICH THESE USES ARE BANNED.) However, in cases of buildings included in the Heritage Conservation List, if the owner/owners agree to maintain the listed heritage building as it is in the existing state and to preserve its heritage stage with due repairs and the owner/owners/lessees give a written undertaking to that effect, the owner/owners/lessees may be allowed with the approval of the Heritage Conservation Committee to convert part or the whole thereof of the non-commercial area within such a heritage building to commercial/office user/hotel. Provided that if the heritage building is not maintained suitably or if the heritage value of the building is allowed to be spoiled in any manner, the commercial/office/hotel user shall be disallowed.

13. Maintaining Skyline And Architectural Harmony

Buildings within heritage precincts or in the vicinity of heritage sites shall maintain the skyline and follow the architectural style (without any high-rise or multi-storeyed development) as may be existing in the surrounding area, so as not to diminish or destroy the value and beauty of or the view from the said heritage sites. The development within the precinct or in the vicinity of heritage sites shall be in accordance with the guidelines framed by the Municipality/Panchayat on the advice of the Heritage Conservation Committee.

14. Restrictive Covenants

Restrictions existing as on date of this Notification imposed under covenants, terms and conditions on the leasehold plots either by Government or by Municipality/ Panchayat shall continue to be imposed in addition to Development Control Regulations. However, in case of any conflict with the heritage preservation interest/ environmental conservation, this Heritage Regulation shall prevail.

15. Repair Fund

With a view to give monetary help for such repairs of Heritage buildings a separate fund may be created, which would be kept at the disposal of Municipal Commissioner, who will make disbursement from the funds on the advice of the Heritage Conservation Committee. The fund shall be mainly used to support the cost of listing of heritage sites and expert guidance and fees for architects, engineers and other experts while the actual conservation works must be supported by the owners or from sources other than the Repair Fund.

16. Grading Of The Listed Buildings/Listed Precincts

In the last column of the said list of Heritage buildings, Heritage precincts, "Grades" such as I, II, or III have been indicated. The meaning of these Grades and basic guidelines for development permissions are as follows:

Listing does not prevent change of ownership or usage. However, such usage should be in harmony with the said listed precinct/building. Care will be taken to ensure that the development permission relating to these buildings is given without delay.

Grade I

A) Definition:-

Heritage Grade I comprisesBuildings and precincts of National or historic importance, embodying excellence in architectural style, design, technology and material usage and/or aesthetics; they may be associated with a great historic event, personality, movement or institution. They have been and are the prime landmarks of the region.

All natural sites shall fall Within Grade-I.

B) OBJECTIVE:-Heritage Grade I richly deserves areful preservation.C) SCOPE FOR CHANGES:No interventions be permitted either on exterior or interior of the heritage building or natural feature unless it is necessary in the interest of strengthening and prolonging, the life of the building/s or precincts or any part or features thereof. For this purpose, absolutely essential and minimal changes would be allowed and they must

Grade II

Heritage Grade II (A & B) Comprises of buildings, and precincts of regional or local importance possessing special architectural or aesthetic merit, or cultural or historical significance though of a lower scale in Heritage Grade I. They are local landmarks, which contribute to the image and identity of the region. They may be the work of master craftsmen or may be models of proportion and ornamentation, or designed to suit a particular climate. Heritage Grade II deserves intelligent conservation.

GRADE II (A)
Internal changes and adaptive re-use may by and large be allowed but subject to strict scrutiny. Care would be taken to ensure the conservation of all special aspects for which it is included in Heritage Grade-II.

GRADE II (B)
In addition to the above, extension or additional building in the same plot

Grade III

Heritage Grade III comprises buildings and precincts of importance for townscape; they evoke architectural, aesthetic, or sociological interest though not as much as in Heritage Grade II.

These contribute to determine the character of the locality and can be representative of lifestyle of a particular community or region and, may also be distinguished by setting on a streetline, or special character of the façade and uniformity of height, width and scale

Heritage Grade III deserves intelligent conservation (though on a lesser scale than Grade II and special protection to unique features and attributes.Internal changes and adaptive re-use may by and large be allowed. Changes can include extensions, and additional buildings in the same plot or compound. However, any changes should be such that they are in harmony with and should be such that they do not detract from the

Grade I	Grade II	Grade III
be in accordance with the original. D) PROCEDURE:- Development permission for the changes would be given by the Municipal Commissioner on the advice of the Heritage Conservation Committee to be appointed by the State Govt. E) VISTAS/ SURROUNDING DEVELOPMENT:- *All development in areas surrounding Heritage Grade I shall be regulated and controlled, ensuring that it does not mar the grandeur of, or view from Heritage Grade I.*	or compound could, in certain circumstances, be allowed provided that the extension/additional building is in harmony with (and does not detract from) the existing heritage building (s) or precincts especially in terms of height and facade. Development permission for the changes would be given by the Municipal Commissioner on the advice of the Heritage Conservation Committee to be appointed by the State Government. *All development in areas surrounding Heritage Grade II shall be regulated and controlled, ensuring that it does not mar the grandeur of, or view from Heritage Grade II.*	existing heritage building/precinct. Development permission for the changes would be given by the Municipal Commissioner on the advice of the Heritage Conservation Committee to be appointed by the State Government. *All development in areas surrounding Heritage Grade III shall be regulated and controlled, ensuring that it does not mar the grandeur of, or view from Heritage Grade III.*

17. Nothing mentioned above should be deemed to confer a right on the owner/ occupier of the plot to demolish or reconstruct or make alterations to his heritage building/buildings in a heritage precinct or on a natural heritage site if in the opinion of the Heritage Conservation Committee, such demolition/ reconstruction/alteration is undesirable.

18. So as to preserve the beauty of the region, the Heritage Conservation Committee shall have the power to direct, especially in areas designated by them, that the exterior design and height of buildings should have their prior approval.

19. Signs and Outdoor Display Structures/Including Street Furniture

Municipal Commissioner on the advice of the Heritage Conservation Committee shall frame regulations or guidelines to regulate signs, outdoor display structures and street furniture. Till such regulations and guidelines are framed, the following guidelines may be followed:

A) **National Building code to apply** – The display or advertising sings and outdoor display structures on buildings and land shall be in accordance with : Part X – Signs and Outdoor Display Structures, National Building Code of India.

B) **Additional conditions**_– In addition to sub-regulation A, above, the following provisions shall apply to advertising signs in different land use zones:

i) **Residential Zone (R-1)**: The following non-flashing neon signs with illumination not exceeding 40 watt light.

(a) one name plate with an area not exceeding 0.1 sq. m. for each dwelling unit;

(b) for other users permissible in the zone, one identification sign or bulletin board with an area not exceeding 10 sq. m. provided the height does not exceed 1.5 m.

(c) "For sale" or "For rent" signs for real estate, not exceeding 2 sq. m. in area provided they are located on the premises offered for sale or rent.

ii) **Residential Zones with shop lines (R-2)**: Not flashing business signs placed parallel to the wall and not exceeding 1 m in height per establishment.

iii) **Commercial Zones (C-1) and (C-2)**: Flashing or non-flashing business signs parallel to the wall not exceeding 1 m in height provided such signs do not face residential buildings.

C) Prohibition of advertising signs and outdoor display structures in certain cases:

Not withstanding the provisions of sub-regulations of A & B, no advertising sign or outdoor display structures shall be permitted on buildings of architectural, aesthetic, historical or heritage importance as may be decided by the Municipal Commissioner, on the advice of the Heritage Conservation Committee or on Government buildings, save that in the case of Government buildings only advertising signs or outdoor display structures may be permitted if they relate to the activities for the said buildings own purposes or related programmes.

D) Provided that if the Heritage Conservation Committee so advises, the Municipal Commissioner shall refuse permission for any sign or outdoor display structure.

E) The Municipal Commissioner may on the advice of the Heritage Conservation

Committee add to, alter or amend the provisions of sub-regulations A, B and C above.

F) Signs, outdoor display structures (including street furniture) will require the approval of the Heritage Conservation Committee, which may prescribe additional guidelines for the same.

20. Composition Of Heritage Conservation Committee

A. The Heritage Conservation Committee shall be appointed by Government.

B. The qualifications for membership of the Heritage Conservation Committee shall be as follows:

i) Expert with 15 years experience in the field of heritage conservation ... Chairman

ii) Structural Engineers having experience of ten years in the field and membership of the Institute of Engineers ... 2 members

iii) Architects having 10 years experience and membership of the Council of Architecture: Architects shall be those having experience in conservation architecture ... 2 members

iv) Environmentalists having in-depth knowledge and experience of 10 years of subject matter ... 2 members

v) Historians having knowledge of the region having 10 years experience in the field ... 2 members

vi) Natural heritage experts having 10 years experience in the field ... 2 members

vii) Nominee of Government ... 1 member

viii) Representative of Municipal Commissioner ... 1 member

(a) The Committee shall have the powers to co-opt upto five additional members who may have lesser experience, but who have special knowledge of the subject matter. Provided that the additional members may be co-opted for special purposes or on sub-committees of the Heritage Conservation Committee.

(b) The tenure of the Members of category (i), (ii), (iii), (v) and (vi) above shall change after every three years provided however that the same person shall be eligible for re-appointment as Member.

C. The terms of reference of the Committee shall be, inter-alia,

(i) to advice the Municipal Commissioner whether Development permission should be granted under this Regulation No.............. and the conditions oission (vide sub-regulation 2.)

(ii) to prepare a supplementary list of heritage sites, which include buildings, artefacts, structures, streets, areas, precincts of historic, aesthetic, architectural, cultural, or environmental significance and a supplementary list of natural features of environmental significance of scenic beauty including but not restricted to sacred groves, hills, hillocks, water bodies (and the areas adjoining the same), open areas, wooded areas, points, walks, rides, bridle paths etc. to which this Regulation would apply (vide sub-regulation 4.)

(iii) to advise whether any relaxation, modification, alteration, or variance of any of the Development Control Regulations/Building Byelaws, is called for under sub-regulation 6.

(iv) to frame special regulations for precincts and if necessary for natural features to advise the Municipal Commissioner regarding the same (vide sub-regulation 7.)

(v) to advise on the extent of Development Rights Certificates to be granted, in terms of sub-regulation 10.

(vi) to advise whether Development Rights Certificates may be allowed to be consumed in a heritage precinct (in terms of sub- regulation 10,

Appendix I)

(vii) to advise in terms of Sub-regulation (11) whether to allow commercial/office hotel user in the (name the areas) and when to terminate the same.

(viii) to advise the Municipal Commissioner in the operation of sub-regulation 18 to regulate or eliminate/erection of outside advertisements/bill boards/street furniture.

(ix) to recommend to the Municipal Commissioner guidelines to be' adopted by those private parties or public/Government agencies who sponsor beautification schemes at public intersections and elsewhere.

(x) to advise the Municipal Commissioner to evaluate the cost of repairs to be give to owners to bring the existing buildings back to the original condition. For this purpose the Committee may also try to help the Municipality/Panchayat to raise funds through private resources.

(xi) to prepare special designs and guidelines/publications for listed buildings, control of height and essential façade characteristicssuch as maintenance of special types of balconies and otherheritage items of the buildings and to suggest suitable designs adopting appropriate materials for replacements keeping the old form in tact to the extent possible.

(xii) to prepare guidelines relating to design elements and conservation principles to be adhered to and to prepare other guidelines for the purposes of this Regulation.

(xiii) To advise the Municipal Commissioner on any other issues as may be required from time to time during course of scrutiny of development permissions and in overall interest of heritage/environmental conservation.

(xiv) To appear before the Government either independently or through or on behalf of the Municipal Commissioner in cases of Appeals under Section 47 of the Regional & Town Planning Act in cases of listed buildings/heritage buildings and listed precincts/heritage precincts and listed natural features.

21. Implications Of Listing As Heritage Buildings

The Regulations do not amount to any blanket prevention of demolition or of changes to heritage buildings / buildings within heritage precincts. The only requirement is to obtain special clearance from Municipal Commissioner & Heritage Conservation Committee from heritage point of view.

22. Ownership And Usage

Sale and purchase of heritage buildings does not require any permission from Municipal Commissioner or Heritage Conservation Committee. The Regulations do not affect the ownership or usage, unless such usage is in harmony with the said listed precinct / building. Care will be taken to ensure that the development permission relating to these buildings is given without delay.

This Needs To Be Made Location Specific

Appendix – I

***Regulation No*..........**

Regulations For The Grant Of Transferable Development Rights To Owners/Lessees Of Heritage Buildings/Heritage Precincts And Conditions For Grant Of Such Rights.

As provided in Regulation the development potential of a plot of land may be separated from the land itself and may be made available to the owner of the land in the form of Transferable Development Rights (TDR). These rights may be made available and be subject to the conditions prescribed below:

1 As proposed in Regulation, Development Rights of the owner/lessee of any Heritage Buildings who suffers loss of Development Rights due to any restrictions imposed by the MunicipalCommissioner or Government under Regulation shall be eligible for award of Transferable Development Rights (TDR) in the form of Floor Space Index (FSI) to the extent and on the conditions set out below. Such award will entitle the owner of the Heritage Building to FSI in the form of a Development Rights Certificate (DRC) which he may use himself or transfer to any other person.

2 A DRC will be issued only on the satisfactory compliance with the conditions prescribed in this Appendix.

3 If a holder of a DRC intends to transfer it to any other person, he will submit the DRC to the Municipal Commissioner with an appropriate application for an endorsement of the new holder'sname, i.e. transferee on the said Certificate. Without such an endorsement by the Municipal/Panchayat itself, the transfer shall not be valid and the Certificate will be made available for use only by the earlier original holder.

4 A holder of a DRC who desires to use the FSI credit certified therein on a particular plot of land shall attach to his application for development permission valid DRCs to the extent required

5 DRCs may be used in the following zones:

6 A DRC shall not be valid for use on receivable plots in the areas listed below:-
(a) (List out congested areas where extra FSI should not be allowed.)
(b) On plots falling within 50 m. on roads on which no new shops are permitted as specified in sub-regulation.............of Regulation.....................
(c) Any heritage building.
(d) Any heritage Precinct except with the prior approval of the Heritage Conservation Committee and subject to compliance with the Regulations of the particular precinct.

7 The user that will be permitted for utilisation of the DRCs on account of transfer of Development Rights will be as under:-

Zone in which designated/reserved plot is situated			*User to be permitted in receiving areas*
1. Residential	..	..	Only residential users and in Residential zones only.
2. Commercial (C-2)	..	..	Commercial (C-2) users if the plot where FSI is to be utilised is situated in C-2 Zone. Commercial (C-1) if the plot where the FSI is to be utilised is situated in C-1 zone. Residential only in Residential Zones.

3. Commercial (C-1)	.. ..	Commercial (C-1) if the plot where the FSI is to be utilised is situated in C-1 zone. Residential in residential Zones.
4. Industrial (I-1),(I-2),(I-3)	..	Residential only in residential Zones.

8 DRCs may be used on one or more plots of lands, whether vacant or already developed or by the erection of additional storeys, or in any other manner consistent with these Regulations, but not so as to exceed in any plot a total built-up FSI higher than that prescribed in clause 9 below in this Appendix.

9 The FSI of a receiving plot shall be allowed to be exceeded by not more than 0.4 in respect of a Development Right transferred to it. (whether in respect of a heritage building or by any other means.)

10 With an application for development permission, where an owner/lessee seeks utilisation of DRs, he shall submit the DRC to theMunicipal/Panchayat who shall endorse thereon in writing in figures and words, the quantum of the DRC proposed to be utilised, before granting development permission, and when the development is complete, the Municipality/Panchayat shall endorse on the DRC in writing, in figures and words, the quantum of DRs actuallt utilised and the balance remainingthereafter, if any, before issue of occupation certificate.

11 A DRC shall be issued by the Municipality/Panchayat himself as a certificate printed on bond paper in an appropriate form prescribed by Government. Such a certificate will be a transferable "negotiable instrument" after due authentication by the Municipal/Panchayat. The Municipal Commissioner shall maintain a register in a form considered appropriate by him of all transactions, etc. relating to grant of utilisation of DRs.

Heritage & Urban Renewal

Profiles of Participants

Abha Narain Lambah

Abha Narain Lambah is a conservation architect practicing in Mumbai. A recipient of the Eisenhower Fellowship (USA) 2002, Sanskriti Award 2003 and the Charles Wallace Fellowship (U.K.) 1998, her projects have won 5 UNESCO Asia Pacific Awards for Heritage Conservation. Her architectural practice based in Mumbai also deals with a range of conservation projects from the restoration of 15th Century monuments in Ladakh and Hampi, to the formulation of the Management Plan for Ajanta World Heritage Site and the restoration of colonial buildings such as Gole Market in New Delhi and the Viceregal Lodge, Shimla.

Abha has authored "*Through the Looking Glass: The Grade I Heritage of Mumbai*" and co-authored " The Architecture of the Indian Sultanates"; " A City's Legacy" and " *A Conservation Manual for Owners & Occupiers: Heritage Buildings & Precincts, Mumbai*".

Prof. A.G.K Menon

Prof. A.G.K Menon is a well-known architect, urban planner and conservation consultant. He has undertaken many pioneering projects on behalf of INTACH and has held various important positions. He has lectured at many Indian, European, Japanese, Thai and US Universities. A Master's in Architecture from Illinois Institute of Technology, Chicago, he has authored several documents setting guidelines for conservation practice in India. He regularly contributes to professional journals including several critical articles and key note presentations on architecture and urbanism.

Prof. A.G.K Menon is, currently Convenor for INTACH's Delhi Chapter.

A.K.Jain

A.K. Jain, an architect – town planner, is a a member of the UN Habitat Research Advisory Committee. He is a fellow of INTACH and several other national and international planning organizations. He studied at Delhi School of Planning and Architecture, Institute of Housing and Urban Development Studies, Rotterdam and University of Birmingham. He is on Editorial Board of the International Journal of Environment Studies (UK). As Commissioner (Planning), he worked on the Master Plan for Delhi-2021, National Urban Housing Policy (2007), National Urban Transport Policy (2006) and Delhi Urban Heritage Foundation. Mr. Jain is a visiting faculty at Delhi School of Planning and Architecture and is author of several books, which include Cities of Delhi (1994), Lutyens' Delhi (2010) and Dillinama (in print) .

Dr. Anita Smith

Dr. Anita Smith is a Charles La Trobe Research Fellow, after competing her PhD in Archaeology from the La Trobe University she has been associated with the research projects like the taputapuatea Marae and the Opoa Valley (Tahiti) in the histiry of Polynesian Voyaging. ahe has several publications to her credit on archaeology, eco-tourism, aboriginal and historic envirnments, etc related to Australia and the Pacific Islands. Her area of special interests is the cultural heritage management in the Australia Pacific Region, UNESCO and World Heritage Sites.

Aurea Gallen

Aurea Gallen is currently the Director of the Department of Urban Planning Studies City Council of Barcelona, Spain since 2006. Educated at the School of Architecture of Barcelona, she has been working with in the City Council of Barcelona, since 1984 where she has occupied different posts of responsibility. She has also been a member of the design teams for several of the city's most notableplanning projects such as the extension of Avinguda Diagonal or the renovation of thePoblenou 22@ District

Debashish Nayak

Debashish Nayak is an architect who has nearly two decades of experience in managing urban conservation issues of Historic Cites in India and abroad. Based in Ahmedabad, he works as advisor to the City Municipality Heritage Programme for the revitalisation of the historic walled city. Recently AMA (Ahmedabad Management Association) awarded him Anubhai Chimanlal–AMA Nagrikta Puraskar 2006 – citizenship award for his contribution in Ahmedabad.

Currently he is also advising other City Municipalities such as Jaipur, Amritsar, Old Delhi, Pondicherry etc. He is Advisor to the Indian Living Heritage Cities Network launched by UNESCO, India. Among the many awards he has received are the Ashoka Fellowship (1990 - 1993), Salzburg Fellow (1990), Ten Outstanding Young Indian Award (1994) and in 1995, Friends of the United Nations Citizen's Award at New York.

Devi Lal Bhakar

Devi Lal Bhakar is presently posted a Chief Engineer, Jaipur Municipal Corporation. During his service in the Rajasthan State Government, he has worked on various projects and development works in the feild of housing for economically weaker section of society. his work experience includes slum rehabilitation, rain water harvesting, recycling waste water, soild waste management, development of city parking lots, sports complexes, construction of roads and bridges.

Devi Lal Bhakar is appointed as the Chief technical Nodal Officer of the Jawaharlal Nehru National Urban Renewal Mission for Jaipur city.

Prof E. F. N. Ribeiro

Prof. E. F. N. Ribeiro studied architecture at Mumbai and Urban Planning at Manchester, U.K. On retirement he developed the Architecture Heritage Wing of the Indian National Trust for Art and Cultural Heritage (INTACH). Currently he is Director of the Association of Urban Management and Development Authorities (AMDA).

Professor Ribeiro was twice President, Institute of Town Planners, India and for seven years, the Vice-President of the International Society of City and Regional Planners. He has contributed several articles in National and International journals and various forums and has served on several Government committees on spatial Planning and education of urban and regional planners. He currently freelances as an advisor in the context of participatory goverance.

Faith Singh

Ms. Faith was born in India, where her Irish father was Bishop of Nagpur and her English mother served as a surgeon. Faith was educated in UK and returned to India as a visitor in 1967, married John Singh, a resident of Jaipur, where she now lives.

Faith is best known for her work with Anokhi, a world known brand of hand made textiles that pioneered the repositioning of traditional skills and crafts in India to provide steady livelihood in the global marketplace of the 21st century. In 2002, Faith founded the Jaipur Virasat Foundation to apply lessons learnt from her years with Anokhi to a wider constituency. Jaipur Virasat Foundation (JVF) is a charitable trust, committed to generate a citizens' movement for heritage-based social and economic development in Rajasthan. In 2007, Faith was awarded an MBE in the New Years' Honours List in the UK for her contribution to the conservation of India's cultural heritage. She has served as a member of the India CII Tourism Panel 2007- 08 – 09 and continues to guide JVF as its Founder Patron.

Francisco Azconegui

Mr. Francisco Azconegui, expert in heritage restoration and urban renewal, is Director of the Centre for Artisan Trades in Vitoria-Basque Country, Spain.

Ler Seng Ann

Mr Ler Seng Ann is the Group Director in charge of the Conservation and Development Services Group of Urban Redevelopment Authority (URA) in Singapore. He holds a Master of Science degree in Civil Engineering from the National University of Singapore (NUS). He has more than 25 years of experiences in both planning and engineering work, and is a registered Professional Engineer (PE) in Singapore and Chartered Engineer in UK.

As the Group Director of the Conservation and Development Services group, Mr Ler leads his team of Planners, Architects, Engineers and Planners to deliver several major successful conservation and infrastructure planning projects in Singapore such as conservation master plan, infrastructure planning for Singapore River, Changi Point, Southern Ridges and Marina Bay.

Maharaja Gaj singh

Shri Gaj Singh of Jodhpur, former Member of Parliament and a stint in the diplomatuc service as High Commissioner of India to

Trinidad and Tobago, now lives in Jodhpur as the head of the Rathore clan.

In 1972 he set up the Mehrangarh Trust, in one of the largest forts of the country. A vast range of historic objects belonging to the erstwhile Jodhpur Maharajas are on display at the Mehrangarh Fort. A full fledged Mehrangarh Art Conservation Centre has also been set up on the premises. It has become a major tourist destination and venue for cultural events. Following its success, he accepted the responsibility of managing the Ahhichatragarh Fort in Nagaur.

The Water Resource Centre has been set up on another of his family premises in Jodhpur, from where a multi-dimensional project is executed by a strategic partnership of the Jal Bhagirath Foundation, the UNDP and Italian Development Cooperation.

Dr. Neeta Das

Currently a professor of architecture at BBDNITM, Lucknow, Neeta Das is a graduate from CEPT, Ahmedabad, with a Master's from the University of Cincinnati, USA, and a PhD from The Society for the Protection of Ancient Monuments, (SPAB), London. She is an author and co-author of several books and articles on architectural history and conservation and has presented many papers in national and international forums.

She is the proprietor of a design office Neeta Shubhrajit Das Associates in partnership with her husband; and is the Chairperson of Mansara, a non-government organization that aims at the conservation of un-protected heritage properties.

Nicole Bolomey

Ms. Nicole Bolomey of ICOMOS is Programme Specialist Culture

Division, UNESCO since March 2006. She has a Masters Degree in Conservation Studies and Landscape Architecture. She has worked on many projects as independent consultant for landscape architecture and historic conservation.

Prasanna Senaka Rupasinghe Gunawardena

He holds a Masters Degree in Urban and Spatial Plnning, Zagreb. He is currently Presidential Advisor, Hambantota District Infrastructure development; and the Chairman, Urban development Authority of Sri Lanka.

Earlier he served as Mayor of Colombo, and Chairman of the Urban Development Authority of Sri lanka.

Maharani Praneet Kaur

Maharani Preneet Kaur, a Member of Parliament from Patiala to be elected to the Lok Sabha for three consecutive terms, is currently Minister of State, External Affairs, Government of India. She was conferred the Sikh of the Year award in 2009, and is highly regarded for her political and cultural involvement in Punjab.

Earlier she has served as President of the Citizen Welfare Council Patiala, and was a Member of several Standing and Consultative Committees connected with Public Undertakings, Women's Empowerment, Consumer Affairs, etc. As Chairperson of the Patiala Heritage Society she steered the highly popular Patiala Festivals in coordination with INTACH during her husband Shri Amarinder Singh's tenure as Chief Minister of Punjab.

Raghav Chandra

He is currently is currently Principal Secretary, Urban Deveploment Department, Government of Madhya Pradesh. Earlier he held various posts in the Madhya Pradesh State Industrial Development, Road

Development, Civil Supllies Corporations; the Housing Board; and at the Ministry of commerce in Delhi.

After his professional training in Economics, Law and Management in India, he did his masters in public Administration at the John Kennedy School of Government, harvard university, Cambridge, USA. he was awarded the global Scholarship by World Bank/japan. He is creator of the concept and methodology for www.scratchmysoul.com. he wrotes extensively for various economic journals.

Ranjith Alahakoon

Ranjith Alahakoon is a Chartered Architect, having his own practice since 1982. A graduate from the Danish State School of Architecture, Aarhus, he was a Member-Academic Architects of Denmark (MAA) 1974. He is Associate of Sri lanka Institute of Architects (AIA-SL)

Currently, Ranjith Alahakoon is senior lecturer, faculty of Architecture, University of Moratuwa, Sri lanka.

Ratish Nanda

Mr. Ratish Nanda, Conservation Architect, works for Aga Khan Trust for Culture. Following his architectural studies in Delhi he completed Masters in Conservation Studies from the University of York, UK.

He has recently returned to Delhi after completing a project to restore Baghe Babur, a 16th century enclosed garden in Kabul, Afghanistan. His other completed projects include the Garden Restoration of Humayun's Tomb and several projects for INTACH, including, conservation of St James Church, the ruins adjacent Sultan Garhi, the unprotected monuments in the Mehrauli Archaeological Park; Delhi Listing published as Delhi, the Built Heritage and released by the Prime Minister of India.

He has received several prestigious awards: Eisenhower Fellowship 2007, Sanskriti Award for Social and Cultural Achievement, Prince Claus Fund Urbanhero title, Aga Khan Foundation International Scholarship and the Charles Wallace Conservation Fellowship.

Robert Toscano

HE Roberto Toscano, as a career diplomat has served in a number of posts in Chile, USSR, Spain, United States; and at Italy's Permanent Mission to the United Nations in New York. Earlier he was head of Policy Planning at the Ministry of Foreign Affairst till 2003. He chaired the Organisation for Economic Cooperation and Development Assistance Committee network on conflict, peace and development cooperation.

Currently HE Roberto Toscano is Italy's Ambassador to India. He is the author of books and articles on human rights, peacekeeping, conflict prevention, ethics and international relations published in Italy and some countries overseas.

Shalini Mahajan

Ms. Shalini Mahajan is professionally trained as an architect from Sushant School of Art and Architecture, Gurgaon, Haryana (1995-2000) with almost nine years of professional experience behind her. Her interest in conservation further led on to pursue a Master's degree in Economics and Techniques of Conservation of Architectural and Environmental Heritage from the Istituto Universita Architettura di Venezia (IUAV), Venice, Italy (2007-08), and for this she was also the recipient of the Ministry of HRD's Indo-Italian Government Scholarship in the field of "Cultural Heritage and Restoration". Since November 2008, she has been associated with the Culture Sector of the UNESCO New Delhi office and is currently serving as the Project Manager of the UNESCO led Indian Heritage Cities Network.

Ms. Mahajan's professional career reflects her strong interest in the field of heritage conservation. She has had the opportunity of working with some well known private conservation architects and has also been part of the Architectural Heritage Division of INTACH Delhi office. She was also awarded the US/ICOMOS India Internship for the year 2003, wherein she had the opportunity to work with Historic American Buildings Survey (HABS), US National Park Service, upon a historic preservation project in Philadelphia.

Shyam Chainani

Shri Shyam Chainani is the founder-member and Honorary Secretary of Bombay Environmental Action Group since 1977. Along with other members of the group, he spearheaded the heritage movement in Mumbai specially regarding heritage regulations. He is a member of the INTACH Governing Council and also a legal consultant to INTACH on all matters concerning heritage regulation.

He is also Member of many official committees including the Ministry of environment & Forest Heritage Consultative Group which framed the Draft model Regulations, a prototype for all States. He was instrumental in getting the government of India to declare mahableshwar, Panchgani and Matheran as ecologically senstitive zone under the Environment Protection Act.

S. K. Misra

Mr. S.K. Misra is a Founder Member of INTACH and currently it's Chairman. He has strengthened INTACH's administrative structure and professional capabilities. His current focus is on fostering partnerships with civic bodies, professional groups and international organizations. After holding numerous administrative positions both in the State and Central Government, he retired in 1991 as Principal Secretary to the Prime Minister. Since then he has served as Member of the Union Public

Service Commission, and has been nominated to the planning and tourism boards of a number of States.

Mr. Misra has been the recipient of several awards from professional and trade organizations including Shiromani Award for Excellence; Nehru Award for International Understandng (London); Agastya Awards for contribution to the Tourism Industry (by TAAI); IATO Award-Hall of Fame for contribution to Tourism Industry.

He served as Principal Secretary to the Prime Minister. Subsequently he was Member of the Union Public Service Commission. He is the recipient of several awards from various professional and trade organizations; and honoured with the 'Padma Bhusan' by the President of India. Most recently, he was appointed Vice President of International National Trusts Organisations (INTO) that was established during the International conference of National Trusts (ICNT) organized by INTACH at New Delhi in 2007.

S.K.Verma

Shri S.K.Verma is currently Convenor of INTACH Chapter, Udaipur and is actively involved in the urban renewal plans of the city undertaken by the State Government.

Formely a civil servant, he was Principal cheif Conservator of forest, Rajasthan. Post retirement he was President Green Arc society, Udaipur, National Vice President of Bharat Vikas Parishad, Delhi; Chairman, World Wild Fund of Udaipur Division; and also served as Vice President of senior Citizen Forum at Udaipur. He has provided technical support service as Advisor/Consultant to the Union Ministry of Environment & Forest and to researchers in the feild of ecology, forestry and wildlife conservation. He has been a Guest Faculty at several academic institutions of Rajasthan, Madhya pradesh, Haryana and Uttarakhand on subjects like bio-diversity, ecology, rural development and forestry.

S. P. Shorey

S.P. Shorey is currently Director, Urban Management Resource Group at the Centre for Good Governance, Government of Andhra Pradesh, Hyderabad.

He studied Town Planning at the Indian Institute of Technology, Kharagpur and Architectural Conservation at the International Centre for Conservation, ICCROM, Rome. Till 2008 he was Special Officer (Planning) of Hyderabad Urban Development Authority, responsible for Master Plans, Town Planning law, plan-administration, township design, housing and development control. He was associated with Development Strategy, Hyderabad Mega City Project, Urban Development component Vision 2020; and various reports related to 74th Amendment to Constitution and the Jawaharlal Nehru National Urban Renewal Mission.

Shri Shorey has been short term consultant to World Bank and ICCROM in urban development and heritage conservation issues and a visiting faculty at the Indian Institute of Management, (IIM) Ahmedabad, IIT Kharagpur, Centre for Environmental Planning and Technology (CEPT), Ahmedabad, School of Planning and Architecture, New Delhi & other institutions. He has a large number of national and international papers and publications.

INTACH STATE CHAPTERS

(There are several branches in each State)

Andaman and Nicobar

Andhra Pradesh

Delhi

Goa

Gujarat

Haryana

Himachal Pradesh

Karnataka

Kerala

Madhya Pradesh

Maharashtra

Manipur

Orissa

Punjab

Rajasthan

Tamil Nadu

Uttar Pradesh

West Bengal